W9-AVH-213

LADY Q

LADY Q

THE RISE AND FALL
OF A LATIN QUEEN

REYMUNDO SANCHEZ
and SONIA RODRIGUEZ

CHICAGO
REVIEW
PRESS

Library of Congress Cataloging-in-Publication Data
Sanchez, Reymundo, 1963-
Lady Q: the rise and fall of a Latin queen / Reymundo Sanchez and Sonia
Rodriguez. — 1st ed.
    p. cm.
 ISBN-13: 978-1-55652-722-7
 ISBN-10: 1-55652-722-5
 1. Gangs—Illinois—Chicago. 2. Rodriguez, Sonia, 1967- 3. Gang
members—Illinois—Chicago—Biography. 4. Sexual abuse victims—Illi-
nois—Chicago—Biography. 5. Violence in adolescence—Illinois—
Chicago. I. Rodriguez, Sonia, 1967- II. Title.

HV6439.U7C383 2008
364.106'6092—dc22
[B]

                                                    2007041642

The author will respond to questions e-mailed to him at
mybloodylife@hotmail.com.

Interior design: Jonathan Hahn

©2008 Reymundo Sanchez and Sonia Rodriguez
All rights reserved
First edition
Published by Chicago Review Press, Incorporated
814 North Franklin Street
Chicago, Illinois 60610
ISBN 978-1-55652-722-7
Printed in the United States of America
5 4 3 2 1

For my princess

I love you and I'm sorry that I put you through so much.

If my story saves one kid's life, it was all worth it.

What you're about to read is a true story based on the life of former Latin Queen Sonia Rodriguez, who at one time was the Queen of all Kings, as told to Reymundo Sanchez. All these accounts are true; however, names are changed.

CONTENTS

PROLOGUE

by Reymundo Sanchez

DURING MY TIME as a gang member on the streets of the Humboldt Park neighborhood in Chicago, I always wondered what made girls get involved in drugs, sex, and violence. Many girls I knew hung out with gangs just to get high, others were connected to a man in the gang, and then there were those who were considered one of the guys. The girls who earned their place within a gang on their own, without the benefit of a relationship to a man, were by far the most respected and trusted by other gang members. These female gang members sometimes outranked male gang members and usually kept company with the leaders. They were usually attractive, intelligent, nicely dressed, didn't drink, and didn't allow guys to disrespect them. They were also often quick-tempered and had no qualms about fistfighting a guy or pulling the trigger to kill a rival gang member.

Because of my many years on the streets as a member of the Latin Kings, I knew several girls like this. Why did these girls choose to join a gang? I set out to locate at least one to find answers to my questions—to find one woman who was just as disgusted as I was by the loss of young lives to gang violence. I was able to locate a former Latin Queen named Sonia, better known by her nickname, Lady Q.

By pure coincidence I ran into a mutual acquaintance while buying Puerto Rican food from one of Humboldt Park's portable food shacks. The acquaintance, a former Latin King now in his fifties, was in the park selling drugs when he saw me and came over to talk. We started reminiscing about the old days on the streets and the people we'd hung out with. When I mentioned Lady Q, he said that he had recently run into her on the bus and got her phone number. He pulled out his cell phone and located Lady Q's number from his contacts list. Minutes later I was on my way with a mouthful of Puerto Rican food, think-ing about what I would say to Lady Q if and when I was able to speak to her.

I drove to the library on the corner of Troy and North Avenue, across the street from the park. The Humboldt Park branch of the Chicago Public Library didn't exist when I lived in the area. I was pleased to see an educational structure built in the 'hood. I was going into the library to check my e-mail but decided to dial Lady Q's number from my car. I didn't expect her to answer the phone and had no clue what I'd say if I reached her. I can't remember another time in my life when I would have preferred an annoying voice mail greeting at the other end of a phone call. But Lady Q answered.

"Hello? . . . Hello, who is this?" she said as I searched for words to reply.

"Is this Lady Q—Sonia?" I asked.

"Yes, who is this?" she demanded.

I paused for a moment and decided to lay it all on the line, to just come right out and tell her who I was and why I was calling.

"Have you heard of the books *My Bloody Life: The Making of a Latin King* or *Once a King Always a King*?"

"Everyone has," she said. "Those books tell it like it is to kids. Now who is this?"

"My name is Reymundo Sanchez, and I wrote those books. I'm calling because I want to write a book that tells about gang life from a female perspective. I know that your story will help save some little girls from the gang bullshit. Would you be interested in telling me your story?"

The line went silent. I thought she had hung up on me so I said, "Hello, are you there?"

"Yeah, I'm here. You're just freaking me out. Who are you?"

"Are you still involved with the Nation?" I asked Lady Q.

"Fuck, no! And yeah, the female side of gangs needs to be told."

"OK, well then, let's do this. You tell me a place where I can meet you. Then you can decide if you want to tell me your story or not. I get so many e-mails from young ladies involved in gang bullshit, and your story will be one they can relate to and learn from. You can help prevent some of these girls from going through the shit we went through, so please think about it."

"Let's meet tomorrow around noon, OK?" she said.

"Absolutely."

It never occurred to me that maybe Lady Q didn't give a damn about the young women who mess up their lives by joining gangs. For all I knew she might have become one of the many older gang members who use kids for their personal gain, like the guy who'd supplied me with her number. After all, Lady Q became much more than a Latin Queen street soldier. She climbed the hierarchical ladder of the gang to become the Queen of all Kings.

I wouldn't be in Chicago long. I had to act fast without worrying about it or I might miss this opportunity. I knew very well that Lady Q epitomized the female gang member.

Sonia knew gang life very well and had been the leader of many young women. She was their role model and in many ways the only one they felt cared for them. Indeed, Sonia managed to earn a larger-than-life reputation for all the wrong reasons. I knew this and it made me nervous.

I arranged to meet with Sonia on a very chilly Chicago day in April 2005. We agreed to meet in a way that we both felt safe; it was imperative for both of us to feel certain that the meeting wasn't part of a setup. In my mind the only way I could guarantee my safety was to show up in the company of the police at our agreed-upon meeting place. But, knowing Sonia's background, I realized this wasn't an option. The Sonia I remembered could handle the presence of dangerous gang members, but she considered the police a threat to her safety. People from the 'hood grow up with the mentality that the police are a threat. I allowed Sonia to select the meeting place. She surprised me by giving me the address of a Boys and Girls Club near Humboldt Park—my old stomping grounds. I came alone. We remembered each other from our days on the streets so we didn't need a description to recognize one another.

The Lady Q I remembered was a glamour girl with a bad attitude, a quick temper, and a fearlessness that gave her a reputation as a ruthless Latin Queen. She liked to wear designer clothes, always had her face made up, and her hands were adorned with decorated fingernails that went well with all the gold rings she wore. The Sonia I knew was outspoken and never alone, constantly flanked by hangers-on who masqueraded as friends, always with a Latin King nearby protecting her. The Lady Q I knew was loyal to a fault to her colors—the black and gold of the Latin King/Queen Nation—to the five-point crown, and to all who represented them. I wondered if these people were still around her, if her loyalty was still intact, and I worried what would happen to me if this were the case. Sonia was a lost child from the streets who grew up to become one of the most powerful female gang members in the city of Chicago. I could certainly relate to her cautiousness about meeting me and telling me her life story.

As I approached the Boys and Girls Club, my mind raced with all the ways I could be murdered in broad daylight. So intense were the images running through my mind that I drove right past the building where I was to meet Sonia. I drove slowly and grabbed a piece of paper from the book bag sitting on the passenger seat of my car and began looking at it, and then out at the buildings, as if I were lost and looking for an address. The whole production felt very childish and cowardly until I realized that these were my survival instincts taking control. Looking lost and disoriented allowed me to drive around the neighborhood several times, looking for parked cars with possible soon-to-be murderers inside them or any other sign of foul play waiting to happen.

After several trips around the nearly deserted streets I felt satisfied that there was no ambush awaiting me. I parked about a quarter of a block away, even though there was a parking spot right by the front door—again cautious—and walked slowly, still watchful.

I entered the Boys and Girls Club, walked up a small flight of stairs, and met the stare of Lady Q from across the room. She walked toward me without once taking her eyes off mine, and when she was close enough, she hugged me.

"Damn, so you're Reymundo Sanchez," she said.

"Yeah."

The weight of worry and despair we both felt lifted with that embrace. We spoke very few words. The Boys and Girls Club didn't offer the sanctuary essential for our talk so we decided to go to Sonia's apartment for more privacy.

As we walked toward my car, I soaked in the details of the great Lady Q today. She wore no stylish clothes or flashy jewelry. Her hair did not have the right-out-of-the-salon look that had been her norm; instead, while it was neatly combed, it was far from stylish. Her nails were short and unpainted. She wore very inexpensive clothing. Her face showed no trace of makeup.

During the drive to her apartment, Sonia reminisced about how exciting her days in the Nation had been, but she also told me that she had broken all ties to the Latin Kings and Queens, which included their leader, King Tino, who had been her man.

Our destination was a two-story apartment building; Sonia occupied the basement apartment with her ten-year-old son. As we walked in, Sonia's residence reminded me more of a dungeon than a home. It was a dark, humid place reeking of stale cigarette smoke, with boarded-up windows. The furnishings consisted of an old sofa, a coffee table, and a television on a stand that looked like it had been rescued from an incinerator.

Sonia turned on a light, which did nothing to improve the apartment's gloomy appearance. Instead, it highlighted the gray decaying walls and ceiling that gave an impression of desperation. In the far corner sat a small old stove and refrigerator. The apartment felt cramped. I sat on the sofa as Sonia walked into a room directly across from where I sat. I looked in and glimpsed her bedroom, which she shared with her son. There were two unmade twin beds arranged in an L shape along the wall, and clothes littered the floor. Sonia came out of the room and sat next to me on the couch with a lit cigarette in her hand. I asked if she could please put it out and she did so reluctantly.

I placed a digital recorder on the coffee table and asked Sonia to tell me about her childhood. No sooner had I made this request than Sonia broke down in tears. She hadn't spoken a single word, yet she cried uncontrollably. It was as if she had been waiting for years for someone willing to listen without making comments or giving opinions. She put her face in her hands and cried as I waited patiently for her answer. After about three minutes, Sonia collected herself and began to speak.

"I never knew my father, and don't know anything about him," she began.

AND SO I learned her story, of a young girl searching for love, belonging, and connection who thought she could find it in a gang. Little did she know that a gang is the last place she'd find what she was missing at home. The following pages detail Lady Q's story as she told it to me throughout the spring of 2005. During my conversations with Lady Q her tone of voice and demeanor changed drastically. The sad, weepy persona that was evident when she spoke about her early childhood was replaced by words that came out clearly, assertively, and rapidly when she spoke about her life after her transformation into Lady Q.

I hope her story helps parents open their eyes to the damage their abuse causes, helps young girls change their minds about joining a gang even when their home life is impossible and encourages them to seek healthier options, and helps convince young women who are already in the life to reconsider their choice and save themselves from a too-young death. I learned the hard way that if you don't learn from your mistakes, you're destined to repeat them.

1

TOUCH OF LOVE

SONIA RODRIGUEZ WAS born in 1967 in Puerto Rico in the middle of everything—the middle child of three girls, in the middle of an abusive home, and in the middle of the commotion that was her family life. Sonia's mother, Marta, was a stereotypical Puerto Rican woman: illiterate, uneducated, and unable to survive without a man—a welfare mother who had no ambition to improve her life. She was very petite, with the body of a little girl. She spoke no English, had a third-grade education, and began having children at age sixteen. Sonia and her older sister, Vivian, had the same father, who had died of pneumonia when Sonia was still a baby. Marta had quickly remarried, to a man named Carlos, and the couple had a baby girl together, Sonia and Vivian's younger sister, Jazmin. When Sonia was three, Carlos decided to move the family to Chicago, where he hoped to find factory work.

Sonia's older sister, Vivian, was born with a physical disability—both of her feet turned inward, which prevented her from being able to walk. This deformity required many operations to correct. Because of this, all of Sonia's mother's attention was reserved for Vivian.

Sonia was five years old when her stepfather began to physically abuse her. At the time, she was having consistent nightmares and walking in her sleep. Almost nightly Sonia dreamt
that a man climbed through her window, approached her while
she slept, and then touched her. She would wake up crying and
afraid. Ignoring Sonia's problem was one thing, but her mother
expressed her disbelief with a barrage of insults. She dismissed
both the nightmares and the sleepwalking as Sonia's attempt to
steal attention away from Vivian. From this tender age Sonia
was already filled with doubts about whether her mother loved
her.

Eventually Carlos left the family and returned to Puerto
Rico, which made an already difficult financial situation even
worse. Marta collected government assistance, but this hardly
took care of the needs of a family of four.

While the constant fighting and almost daily beatings
stopped, the lack of attention from her mother persisted.
Vivian's operations allowed her to walk, even though her feet
still pointed inward a little, and she therefore required less
attention, but that didn't seem to change the amount of time
her mother had to pay attention to Sonia. Additionally, although
the family was so poor that there was very little to break or lose,
Sonia was blamed for anything that turned up broken or missing. That would soon change, however, when Marta met
another man.

Sonia's new stepfather was named Juan. He was a short,
stocky Puerto Rican who seemed to have an endless supply of
money. Within months, Juan moved Sonia and her family from
a cheaply furnished, roach-infested, two-bedroom apartment to
a lavishly furnished, three-bedroom apartment near Humboldt

Park. Sonia, now six years old, welcomed the change because of how nicely her new stepfather treated her. Plus, there was now plenty of food in the house.

Juan spoke very little English although he'd lived in Chicago most of his life. His financial success came from selling heroin, in both large and small quantities. Because of this, the narcotics division of the Chicago Police Department raided the family's apartment about four times a year. Sonia didn't really know what was going on at the time, but she grew to dislike the police because of how they broke through either their front or back door with their guns drawn, screaming orders. All the adults in the house would be handcuffed and the children gathered and placed on the sofa in the living room. Sometimes the police released all the adults and took Juan with them, but mostly they just left without taking anyone into custody. The few times the police did take Juan into custody, he returned home within a couple of hours. To Sonia it seemed more like a game the police played with Juan than anything real. During each and every raid the police left destruction throughout the apartment, which Sonia, Vivian, Jazmin, and their mother cleaned up. These raids were Sonia's only contact with the police, and the episodes left her distrustful of them.

Despite all this turmoil and negativity in her life, Sonia was a good student at Von Humboldt Elementary School. Vivian was also a very good student, whose successes her mother readily acknowledged and bragged about to friends and family. But she didn't extend the same praise to Sonia. Trying to please her mom, Sonia worked even harder at school.

As Sonia tried to cope with the absence of her mother's love and the chaos that the drug dealing brought into her home, the fighting and violence within her family soon returned. Sonia had just turned eight years old when Juan ceased being a nice man. Almost overnight he became an abusive monster. He had always been loud and somewhat obnoxious, but his angry tirades were usually aimed at Marta and had never escalated into violence. Then suddenly it seemed that Juan grew tired of caring for the children in the family that weren't his own and started using them as punching bags. At first the physical abuse was aimed at Vivian, who now, at the age of eleven, Juan accused of being a little whore. When Marta came to Vivian's defense he redirected his attacks at Sonia. Juan would either slap Sonia across the face or go after her with a belt. Marta often took over the beating that Juan meted out, ironically, to protect Sonia from a more severe beating from Juan. All the while she was beating Sonia, Marta would scream obscenities in Spanish. *"¡Hija de la gran puta, desgraciada no sirves para nada!"* ("Disgraceful daughter of a bitch, you're good for nothing!") Jazmin, Sonia's younger sister, now five, with a dark complexion and nappy hair, was not usually targeted, but sometimes Juan beat her as well.

When Sonia was six, her mother had given her extreme spankings with occasional slaps to the face and kicks to the body depending on how angry she was. Now that Sonia was eight, Marta introduced household objects into her repertoire of pain. Anything Sonia's mother could get her hands on became a whipping tool—belts, shoes, extension cords, brooms, even books. When she caught Sonia in a wide-open space of the house, such as the middle of the living room floor, she usually followed whipping her with a handy object with frenzied kicking. Every time Sonia heard Juan raise his voice she knew that violence was headed her way. She tried hiding in closets and under beds but her mother always found her, and when she did, the beatings were brutal. Even becoming pregnant with Juan's first child didn't stop Marta from going on violent tirades.

On Christmas Eve when Sonia was nine years old, Juan thought it would be funny to have Vivian, Sonia, and Jazmin compete for money and shots of rum via games of bingo. The winner received a dollar, and the losers had to drink a shot of rum. The game ended when Vivian became rowdy due to her drunkenness and started to lash out at Juan. In Spanish she called him a bastard and yelled that he wasn't her father, and worse. In between the shots, Juan would roll up a fifty-dollar bill and throw it on the floor in the middle of the room to see the girls fight over it. Whoever won the fight won the money.

Over the course of the evening the girls ended up drinking six to eight shots of rum each. Jazmin became sick and made it to the bathroom, and Vivian vomited all over the place. Sonia can't recall if she became ill, but she woke up Christmas Day with a headache so bad it felt like her head was going to explode. Sonia did not include this festive holiday activity in the "What I did over Christmas vacation" paper she wrote after the holiday break.

In May 1977 Sonia turned ten years old. She had no friends and spent more time questioning her existence than she did playing with dolls, jumping rope, or playing hopscotch like other little girls her age. Mostly she watched them play with their friends. She felt left out and unwanted. She was convinced she was born to suffer.

This same year several events took place that changed the dynamics in Sonia's home. First, a baby boy was born into the family, Bobby, born on the same day as her own birthday. His arrival brought peace and quiet for at least a couple of weeks. Juan was overjoyed about being a father and focused all his attention on the newborn. Unfortunately, his joy wore off rather quickly and again he centered his anger on the girls. He'd always grown angry over any little thing. Now he simply added a "You're making too much noise for the baby" accusation to his senseless and unprovoked tirades.

Second, relatives from Lancaster, Pennsylvania, moved into the house. The relatives were Sonia's Aunt Teresa (her mother's sister), Teresa's husband Jose, and their teenage son Nito. They were avid Pentecostal churchgoers. Sonia's uncle Jose had been very close to the pastor of their church in Pennsylvania, and it was rumored that they had a falling-out after Jose made a pass at the pastor's wife. Sonia's Aunt Teresa was a small, uneducated woman who lived solely to please every whim of her husband and son. She had long hair, which she often wore in a bun, and an uncanny way of being sweet, quiet, and innocently mannered when in the company of other adults but absolutely wicked and authoritarian when left to care for the children.

Sonia's Uncle Jose had a medium build, black hair, and a mustache. He had served in the navy as a cook but had also seen action in the Korean War. Jose was quick-witted and carried a Bible everywhere he went. A chain smoker and heavy drinker, he also carried a flask of rum in the inside pocket of his jacket. Despite being such an avid churchgoer, Jose was a womanizer who routinely purchased and toted around pornographic magazines. Sonia's cousin Nito was tall and heavyset, with very fair skin and light-colored hair. Nito was neither Teresa nor Jose's biological son, nor was he Puerto Rican. He was the son of former friends of Jose's who were white and who had given Nito up for adoption. This fact was kept secret from Nito.

When this family arrived from Lancaster, they needed a place to stay until Jose could find a job and they could find an apartment. The only family they had in Chicago was Marta, so arrangements were made for them to come stay. Jose and Teresa occupied Vivian's room, Nito slept on the sofa, and Vivian slept with Juan and her mother. Sonia didn't want these relatives in the house further complicating her life, but she felt relieved that at least she didn't have to change where she was sleeping to accommodate them. She already shared a room and a bed with Jazmin. They slept at opposite ends of the same bed, each with their feet by the other's face.

Sonia's nightmares about a man coming in through the window and touching her while she slept had ceased about a year before the family from Lancaster moved in. She was no longer sleepwalking either. One night a few months after her relatives moved into the house, Sonia felt the sheets being pulled away from her as she slept. She opened her eyes slightly and saw the silhouette of a man sitting on her side of the bed. At first she thought her nightmares had returned. She pulled the sheets back over herself and turned toward the wall, away from the dark figure. She blinked her eyes in order to wake up completely, just as she'd done before to get rid of a nightmare, but this time it didn't work. Sonia felt the sheets being pulled away from her a second time and began to panic. The next thing she felt was a hand forcing its way under the sheets and onto her leg. She felt her legs being groped by this unidentified hand as it moved up to her thigh. The hand then tried to get in between Sonia's thighs.

Sonia felt completely paralyzed, too terrified to move or scream. She was still certain she was having the worst nightmare of her life and that was why it felt so real. She began to feel as if she was suffocating. Finally tears began to pour out of her eyes and she began to shiver and whimper uncontrollably. Her shaking and the noise she made caused the hand to stop, and the person pulled away. Sonia felt movement at the edge of her bed as the person got up, and as she came out of her state of shock she heard footsteps and turned toward the door just in time to see the outline of a man exiting her room. Only then did she realize that what had happened was no nightmare. Someone had been in her room touching her, and it was a man, so it had to have been Juan, Jose, or Nito.

Throughout the next day Sonia was full of anxiety, knowing that eventually daylight would end and she'd have to go to bed. She was afraid to tell her mother, fearing she'd be accused of creating the story to focus attention away from her new baby brother. And, she reasoned, even if she did decide to tell Marta and her mother believed her, Sonia couldn't identify who had been in her room the previous night. She decided to keep the ordeal to herself and to stay awake all night to see if the man would return so she could figure out who it was. She was afraid but also looked forward to catching the man who was trying to touch her so she could tell her mother.

That night, Sonia lay on her back instead of on her side as usual. She wrapped the sheets tightly around her body to make it difficult for them to be easily pulled off. Sonia was afraid but determined to follow through with her plan. Hours passed and no one tried to enter her room. She began to think that she'd been dreaming the night before or that the man wouldn't repeat his visit. She tried desperately to stay awake but kept dozing off and then waking up suddenly. Eventually, her eyes closed despite her best efforts.

Sonia was asleep when the man returned and again sat on the edge of her bed. She immediately awoke but pretended to be asleep as she held the sheets tight against her and tried to make out who the man was without completely opening her eyes. The man tugged on the sheets, but when he found them too tightly wrapped to remove, he proceeded to touch Sonia through the sheets. As he began to grope between her legs, Sonia immediately opened her eyes, lifted her head, and came face-to-face with Uncle Jose.

"It's you," she said. "I'm telling Mom!"

No sooner had Sonia spoken her mother's name than Jose put his hand over her mouth and pushed her back down against the pillow.

"*Callete*" ("Shut up"), he said in an intimidating whisper so as not to wake up Jazmin.

When Sonia struggled, he threatened to kill her. Jose held his hand firmly against Sonia's mouth as he pulled down the sheets and groped one of her breasts. Sonia struggled violently. Jose needed to use both hands to keep her from getting away.

"*Nunca voy a regresar pero te mato si dices algo*" ("I'm never coming back but I'll kill you if you say something"), Jose threatened in the same menacing whisper. Then he released Sonia and hurried out of her room.

Sonia lay in bed fighting to catch her breath. She could still feel the pressure on her face from being held so tightly. She felt frightened and confused; out of the three men in the house, Jose was the one she'd suspected least. After all, he carried a Bible and commanded respect from everyone in the household. Sonia's mother saw Jose as a great man because he'd served in the navy, and she looked to him for advice. Sonia wrestled with these conflicting thoughts for the rest of the night, failing to fall back asleep. She would convince herself that telling her mother about Jose was the right thing to do but then would think about his threat to kill her. She eventually decided it wasn't a real threat. But what would happen if Sonia told her mother and she didn't believe her? Sonia eventually decided that even if her mother didn't believe her, telling on Jose would prevent him from repeating his abusive behavior.

The next day Sonia worried about when and how to approach Marta to tell her about what had happened. At the same time she needed to avoid her uncle, who would surely try to stop her from telling. That afternoon Sonia found Marta in the kitchen getting dinner started and asked for a minute of her time. Predictably, her mom responded in a rude, uncaring way. *"¿Que quires?"* ("What do you want?"), Sonia's mom yelled at her. Sonia began to cry, but between sobs she told her mother what had happened.

"¡Que!" ("What!"), Sonia's mother screamed as she turned to face her.

"¡Tio Jose me toco!" ("Uncle Jose touched me!"), Sonia yelled, still hysterically crying.

Sonia looked up at her mother, wanting to be held, soothed, protected, believed. She didn't care whether Uncle Jose was kicked out of the house. All she wanted was for her mother to embrace and protect her. Instead, a veil of anger cloaked Marta's face, and fear overcame Sonia. Marta cocked her arm and slapped Sonia so hard with the back of her hand that she flew across the room. Sonia crashed against the refrigerator and fell to the floor. Her mother quickly ran over to her, grabbed her by the hair, and continued to slap her face. Sonia cried and screamed at the top of her lungs. The commotion attracted the attention of the rest of the family, who hurried into the kitchen. To Sonia's surprise, Jose came to her defense. He grabbed Marta and set her down in a chair in the kitchen as he told her to stop beating Sonia.

"Esa pendeja lo acuso de tocarla" ("That idiot accused you of touching her"), her mother told Jose.

"Esta vien" ("It's OK"), Jose assured her mother.

Jose said that Sonia was lying but that Marta should stop hitting her. Even with Jose there, Sonia continued to scream her accusations. Still she wasn't believed. Devastated, she finally managed to get up off the floor, then went to her room for the rest of the day and cried. No one came to comfort her.

Alone in her room, Sonia wondered why life had to be so terrible. Thoughts of suicide filled her head as she realized that everyone in her life caused her pain, either through abuse or by taking advantage of her.

Eventually Jazmin came into their room. Jazmin and Sonia rarely got along—too busy competing over the scant attention their mother had for either of them. Sonia was silent, and Jazmin didn't even acknowledge her presence, just climbed into bed and went to sleep. Sonia cried herself to sleep that night, only to be woken up again in the middle of the night by Uncle Jose, who had both his hands under her blouse groping her newly developing breasts. When he saw she was awake, he immediately told her to stay quiet because no one would believe her anyway. Sonia closed her eyes and cried while Uncle Jose continued to touch her. He pinched her nipples and tried to put his hands between her legs. Sonia closed her legs tight and Uncle Jose didn't try to force them open, knowing that would leave marks and evidence of Sonia's story. Instead, he pinched her nipples harder and told her he would stop if she opened her legs. Sonia was convinced that she wouldn't be believed regardless of whom she told, so she surrendered.

From that night forward, Uncle Jose had free access to Sonia without any fear of reprisals, and he took full advantage of this. Night after night he came into Sonia's room and molested her. Jazmin never woke up, never witnessed what was going on. Eventually he caught Sonia in a deep sleep one night and took the opportunity to grope her vagina and insert his fingers inside. Sonia awoke and suffered in silence.

The molestation continued every night for the three weeks that Jose, Teresa, and Nito remained in her home. During that time Sonia's mother excluded her from any activity where her uncle was present because of her accusations. Sonia's only relief from this unbearable situation came when her uncle found a job and an apartment and the family moved out.

Juan used Sonia's accusations as a reason to go on more tirades against her because now he considered her a liar. The tirades again ended with Sonia's mother beating her. Vivian and Jazmin often lied, stole money, and stayed out past curfew, but no matter what they did, somehow Sonia was always to blame, always the scapegoat.

A few months after Jose and his family moved out, they showed up at the front door one day to collect Sonia. Apparently either Marta or Juan had called them to complain about the constant problems they had with Sonia, and Sonia's Aunt

Teresa had convinced Marta that the devil was inside Sonia and that going to church would save her soul. Uncle Jose agreed that perhaps Sonia needed God in her life and proposed that he take Sonia to his home on the weekends so he could take her to church with them.

So when the family arrived at Sonia's door, her mother called out to her to pack a bag. Sonia cried and begged not to go. She screamed out the real reason her uncle wanted her in his house, but her pleas fell on deaf ears. She left with them that Friday night, and they brought her back home on Sunday night to go to school the next day. These weekend visits continued for a couple of months.

Of course when Sonia was back within her uncle's reach, the molestations in the middle of the night continued. Sonia slept in her cousin Nito's room while he slept on the couch. But after about a month of these weekend visits, Nito started complaining about this arrangement, and Sonia's aunt decided that it would be all right for Sonia and Nito to share Nito's bed in his room. This arrangement didn't make Sonia any safer. From the very first night Nito started to touch Sonia's breasts and force his fingers inside her vagina. Sonia complained about this to her mother once—reasoning that she'd prefer to be beaten instead of abused under her uncle's roof—but her mother told her to stop lying. Nito did just about everything a man could do to a little girl except penetrate her with his penis. This behavior and the abuse by her uncle was the so-called religion that was supposed to cleanse the devil out of her.

Nito continued to molest Sonia until Aunt Teresa decided that Sonia was no longer welcome in her home. The reasons she gave were that Sonia was too difficult to deal with and that money had started disappearing. Predictably, Sonia's pleas of innocence were ignored, and she was badly beaten again for something she didn't do. But this time she cared less about the beatings because at least she was in her own home once again.

Shortly after Sonia's eleventh birthday, her mother became pregnant with her second child with Juan.

Sonia discovered blood in her underwear when she was eleven and a half. Nervous and confused, she thought something was terribly wrong with her, but she didn't want to tell her mother for fear of being beaten. Eventually, though, she became so afraid that she called out to her mother from the bathroom. Marta came into the room, laughed at her frightened daughter, gave her a maxi pad, and told her to use it, and then told her to come out into the living room. Her mother explained that nothing was wrong with her and that this was a natural process that would now happen once a month. She said it meant that Sonia could now get pregnant—end of discussion.

Sonia didn't understand these physical changes, including growing pubic hair and developing breasts. She had so many questions but no one to give her answers. The changes made her feel uncomfortable, especially since boys who had previously teased her were now taking notice of her large breasts and approaching her socially. The trauma she'd gone through at the hands of her Uncle Jose and Cousin Nito remained vivid and made Sonia distrustful of all boys.

2

DAMAGED GOODS

BEING MOLESTED LEFT Sonia damaged in ways she was still, at age twelve, too young to understand. She already felt as though other kids her age didn't want her around them, but now she had an added reason to believe she was different. The molestation, added to the ongoing physical abuse, made her feel more isolated than ever. Sonia knew she was different, and she felt ashamed. She made little effort to reach out to others, including kids in her school, because she'd learned she would be hurt when she made herself vulnerable.

In school kids avoided her, except for one popular girl named Maritza, who was Sonia's only friend in sixth grade. Maritza lived across the street from Sonia and her family. She was a very pretty, cinnamon-colored Puerto Rican girl with long black hair. In contrast to Sonia's family, Maritza's family was tight-knit. She had four brothers, all of whom were into bodybuilding like their father had been when he was younger. Whenever there was an event involving one of Maritza's family members, whether a baseball game or a fight, they all showed up to support each other. Sonia often wondered why her own family didn't exhibit the same kind of togetherness.

Although Maritza talked to Sonia in school, mostly about schoolwork and school activities, she never invited her to parties at her house or to hang out with her and her other friends. Maritza also never came to Sonia's defense when other kids teased her about her clothes—always a few years out of fashion since she wore Vivian's hand-me-downs—or her well-worn shoes, or her hair that was out of style and less than perfect because Sonia had to fix it herself each morning. Her appearance, and how others treated her because of it, made her feel even more like an outsider and an ugly duckling. Once, at age thirteen, she attended a school dance and spent the entire time sitting in a chair waiting for someone to ask her to dance. Sonia loved school because it got her out of the house, but she loved little else about it.

Sonia's only positive outlet was education. She loved social studies the most, especially learning about wars. She was at the top of her class in all subjects and secretly rejoiced because she knew she was smarter than the popular kids. This was also her way of getting back at her sisters—to outperform them academically.

Yet bad luck continued to dog Sonia, and there was always something available for the kids at school to use against her. One day Sonia, Vivian, and Jazmin were at a Laundromat at Potamac and Western, near their home, washing the family's clothes—a chore the sisters regularly shared. Juan, for whatever reason, became irritated at how long it was taking the girls to finish doing the laundry. He showed up at the Laundromat screaming and ranting. Vivian made her way out of the Laundromat as she yelled at Juan. Jazmin and Sonia each grabbed a plastic bag full of finished laundry and walked toward the exit to get back home as soon as possible. As they passed Juan, he pulled off his belt and began swinging. The girls dropped the bags of laundry and took off running. Sonia, unfortunately, tripped over the bag Jazmin had been carrying and fell. Juan towered over her and began to whip her with his belt. Sonia's screams were so loud they could be heard blocks away, and a crowd soon gathered. Both children and adults witnessed this public whipping, but no one tried to stop it, and no one called the police.

The beating continued for several minutes. Juan would hit Sonia with his belt, then stop to curse at her while she tried to get up, and then he'd beat her again. Sonia cowered in a fetal position on the concrete sidewalk and tried to protect herself with the bags of clothes. She managed to cover herself with one of the bags, but Juan pulled it away forcefully. In the process, the plastic bag broke and laundry spilled all over the street. This further angered Juan and brought new energy to his beating. By now the crowd was large enough to block traffic. Sonia wore a dress that was now riding above her waist, exposing her underwear, but she was too busy trying to protect herself to even notice. The kids witnessing the spectacle certainly took notice and laughed at the sight. Minutes later, Sonia heard her mother screaming profanities as she made her way toward the scene.

The crowd parted, making room for Marta to join the spectacle.

"*¡Condena stupida!*" ("Condemned idiot!"), she yelled as she approached her daughter, who was on the ground begging for mercy. But instead of protecting her, she grabbed Sonia by the hair and shook her violently, then took off her sandal and beat Sonia's legs, arms, back, and head with it.

"¡Recoje esa ropa, hija de la gran puta!" ("Pick up those clothes, daughter of a grand bitch!"), her mother yelled, continuing to beat her. Juan walked away with a smirk of satisfaction on his face.

Marta tired of hitting her daughter after a few minutes and saw that Juan had calmed down. She made one final threat before walking away. *"Si no recojes esa ropa te mato como una perra"* ("If you don't pick up those clothes I'll kill you like a dog.") Slowly, ashamed, Sonia picked herself up off the concrete and began to gather the clothes scattered all over the sidewalk. Kids in the crowd continued to laugh and tease her as people left the scene. Sonia took her time gathering the laundry, hoping that by the time she was done there would be no one left to look at her. Vivian and Jazmin helped her retrieve the clothes, and after they were done Sonia buried her face in one of the bags as she carried it home. No one crossed her path, yet she still heard echoes of the laughter at her expense. She was alone, she thought; no one had come to help her or to stop the beatings. "I have to kill myself," Sonia thought as she walked.

Once home, Sonia went to her room to avoid any more violence. Marta was still muttering obscenities about her and would no doubt attack Sonia if she came within reach. Several items of clothing that had been on the ground were now dirty, and Marta blamed Sonia. Sonia listened carefully for the sound of her mother's footsteps, ready to crawl under the bed if she heard them approaching, but Marta never came into the room.

School became an even more agonizing experience the week following this public beating. News of how she'd been whipped by her mother and father in the middle of the street was the talk of the school. One kid even took off his T-shirt and threw it down on the ground while another kid pretended to be Juan and pretended to beat the first kid. Some kids were saying that she was lying in the street with her panties showing. The accounts became more embellished, and soon kids were saying that Sonia's underwear was dirty or smelled bad or was ripped.

Maritza came to Sonia's defense—a first. This was the only good thing that came from the whole episode—Maritza and Sonia became closer. Sonia had grown accustomed to the other kids' insults, but even the teachers hearing these stories did nothing to stop them. For Sonia, this was further evidence that no one could help protect her from or stop the abuse she endured.

3

THE BIRTH of A REBEL

SONIA STRUGGLED TO find a place in the world that labeled her a misfit. All the kids her age seemed so content and jovial. She knew of no one else going through the turmoil that she was. Her priority became to stay clear of the insults and violence that consumed her daily life. She started to think that maybe the answer was to develop a better relationship with Vivian.

Sonia had always been jealous of the attention Vivian received from their mother. She considered Vivian a thief who stole their mother's love and would not share it, and she believed that there would never be an opportunity to build a relationship with Marta as long as Vivian was present.

On the other hand, Vivian was developing into a rebel who questioned and challenged Juan's every word, and Sonia looked up to her and envied her courage. Because Marta usually came to Vivian's defense, Juan's habit of going on the warpath for no apparent reason became an exercise in frustration. As a result, Juan's temper tantrums became less frequent. Silently, Sonia counted on Vivian to come to her defense, at least when it came to Juan's abuse, if not their mother's. Vivian would defend Sonia but only if Juan attacked both of them together, never if the attack was directed at only Sonia.

Vivian was now in high school and experimenting with life as a party animal. She began coming home late at night and was never punished by her mother for this. Juan, however, began accusing Vivian of hanging out on the streets and having promiscuous sex instead of being in school, even though Vivian maintained decent grades. Juan yelled and screamed, and Vivian yelled and screamed right back.

Vivian attended the recently opened Roberto Clemente High School, which was located about six blocks from their home. Juan claimed that, along with drinking, Vivian also smoked marijuana and hung around with members of a street gang known as the Spanish Lords. But even that didn't seem to warrant any negative attention from their mother. Not that Sonia needed any, but this was further evidence to her of the double standard in her home.

Juan began claiming that money was coming up missing—a claim that would have been more reasonable if he didn't carry his money around with him at all times. Soon Marta claimed the same thing. Vivian's carousing until late at night with gang members and doing drugs made her the most likely suspect, but Marta always gave Vivian money, whether she asked for it or not, so they assumed she'd have no reason to steal it. That meant either Jazmin or Sonia was the culprit. Jazmin was the baby of the family and therefore above suspicion, so that left Sonia. She hadn't purchased anything new, and no money was ever found in her possession, yet they blamed her. She swore she hadn't stolen from either Juan or her mother and continued to maintain her innocence even through the beatings she received whenever there was missing money.

Being blamed for this crime she hadn't committed was a turning point in Sonia's life. She had had enough. No matter what she did or said, her mother and Juan thought whatever they wanted and punished her. She stopped trying to gain the approval she realized was out of reach, and she rebelled. She decided that since she was going to be punished for things she didn't do, she might as well do them and at least deserve the punishment. So she started stealing from her parents—regularly.

Sonia chose to rebel just as a baby girl, Jelly, was added to her family. As with the birth of Juan's first child with Marta, Jelly brought rare peace and tranquility into the household. Juan's euphoria at being a father lasted longer this time, but Sonia knew it wouldn't continue. By the time Sonia was thirteen she was completely lost—torn by sibling rivalry, being the butt of jokes at school, feeling suspicious about the intentions of the boys who now paid attention to her, and living with a family who didn't love her and regularly abused her. She had also developed into a bosomy teenager and was extremely self-conscious about it.

At least Vivian continued to challenge their stepfather as he lessened his physical attacks on the girls. Juan still screamed obscenities and caused their mother to throw angry fits, but otherwise he stayed away from them. But this reduction in Juan's hostility came much too late. The damage was already done by the time Marta became pregnant with Juan's third child.

Sonia took advantage of her mother's jovial mood during her pregnancy to steal money. When Juan discovered money missing, his curses could be heard a half block away. But what irritated him even more than the missing money was that no one paid much attention any longer to his tantrums. Not even Marta seemed to care whether Juan was angry or not, and she began to voice her displeasure. Suddenly Juan started talking about moving to Puerto Rico.

Juan grew increasingly distant from the family, including his own children. He began taking his rants out into the street, shouting demeaning words about Vivian, Sonia, and Jazmin. Inside the house he was defensive and avoided confrontation. Outside in the streets, neighbors eventually grew tired of hearing his rants, too, and many told him to shut up. Not even the birth of his third child and second son, named Peter, brought Juan out of his perpetual anger. Unfortunately, this change in Juan's behavior and the uniting of the rest of the family against him brought no harmony between Sonia and her mother and siblings.

Vivian continued her transformation into a rebellious young adult. She befriended an acquaintance of her mother's named Minerva and moved in with her after she'd finally had enough of Juan and the constant fighting. Minerva was a short, stocky, very streetwise woman with four kids of her own and a history of dating gang members and drug dealers. One of her kids was the child of one of the top generals in the Maniac Latin Disciples street gang. The father was found dead in the trunk of his car while Minerva was still pregnant with his baby. Minerva liked to drink, smoke marijuana, and wear skimpy clothing. She lived in an area inhabited by the Latin Kings, some of whom were close friends of hers. Her lifestyle didn't seem to bother Sonia's mother, who readily agreed to let Vivian live with Minerva and her kids.

Within the year Vivian dropped out of school and enrolled in a trade school to gain clerical skills and a General Equivalency Diploma. During that same year, Juan left for Puerto Rico.

In his absence, Marta supported the family on drug money he'd left behind, public aid, and government food stamps.

Initially Sonia was glad that both Vivian and Juan were out of the house. She hoped this was her chance to become closer to her mother. Unfortunately, even though Sonia helped Marta care for the three youngest children, her mother still had little time for her. Sonia didn't mind the presence of her half brothers and half sister, but her relationship with Jazmin, now age nine, grew sour. Each sister blamed the other for everything and anything happening around the house that angered their mother, no doubt to avoid whippings or to divert attention to the other. This change brought them to blows on more than one occasion. And because Sonia was older, and because she was Sonia, her mother usually directed her anger after these fights toward her.

Juan returned to Chicago after being away for a little more than two months. He immediately tried to reassert his position as head of the household by instilling fear back into the home. But now Sonia and Jazmin only laughed when he ranted, as did their mother, who was through with his obnoxious ways and argued with him constantly. Juan turned into a shell of his former self, grumbling under his breath.

Juan's stay in Chicago was brief. He collected enough money from his drug deals to return to Puerto Rico within six months. This time he left for good. His departure meant the end of his angry tirades and the police raids, but it also meant the end of the conveniences that the sale of illegal drugs afforded. He left his wife behind with no means of support for herself and the now five children in the home with her. The only way the family could survive was to move to a less expensive apartment and collect public aid.

After living out of the house for nearly a year and a half, Vivian rejoined the family once they moved into an apartment without Juan, even though the apartment was smaller. While living with Minerva, Vivian had obtained her GED, completed her clerical training, and was studying for the civil service test in order to apply for a government job. She was successful, and she started working for the Social Security Administration shortly after she moved back in with the family. As the solitary breadwinner, she quickly established herself as the head of the household and ruled with an iron fist. All decisions started and ended with Vivian. This didn't sit well with Sonia, who continued to be the primary target of abuse in the family—the one now receiving the brunt of Vivian's disciplinary actions.

Vivian handed out discipline as if she ruled the world. In fact, she was so devoted to her role as the family's dictator that one time she even struck her mother. Sonia was again accused of stealing money and was often the target of Vivian's violence, which was usually followed by attacks from her mother. Jazmin, however, now older, received a share of the beatings as well. Sonia soon began stealing money from Vivian to justify the beatings in her own mind.

The family's new apartment was located on Humboldt Boulevard, a block and a half north of Humboldt Park, between Wabansia and Bloomingdale streets. The stretch of Humboldt Boulevard starting on Chicago Avenue and ending four or five miles north at Logan Square was long known as the dividing line between rival street gangs. The portion of the boulevard where Sonia's family lived was especially rife with gang activity. The side streets east of Humboldt Boulevard were the turf of the Young Latino Organization Disciples (YLO-Ds), and the streets west of the boulevard were inhabited by the Almighty Latin King Nation. The boulevard was the location of choice for any and all confrontations between the two gangs, which took place almost daily. Oftentimes the encounters between YLO-Ds and Latin Kings consisted of only insults and yelling gang slogans at each other, but there were occasions when gunfire occurred.

Sonia remembers a gang-warfare incident that happened on a sunny day during the first summer her family spent in their new apartment. Her mother was sitting and looking out the front window down onto the boulevard. She noticed and commented on three young men in their late teens to early twenties sitting on the opposite side of the boulevard in the shade of the trees adorning the street, who were rolling and smoking joints. Her mother wondered out loud how these guys were able to break the law in plain sight. They sat on the Latin Kings side of the boulevard and stood up only to flash the Latin Kings hand sign at cars passing by. At one point they all left but returned soon thereafter, each carrying a forty-ounce bottle of beer wrapped in a brown paper bag. Moments after they returned from their beer run, two of the three young men got up and began shaking the hand of the third guy, who was still sitting against one of the trees. The handshakes ended with the Latin Kings hand sign being thrown up in the shape of the crown. Suddenly the two standing guys pulled out guns and opened fire on the guy sitting against the tree. There was nothing he could do but cower into a fetal position to protect his face. He was killed. The two shooters ran across the boulevard and into YLO-D territory and out of sight.

After this incident the Latin Kings' presence on the boulevard increased. Most of the Kings were from the Whipple and

Wabansia section, but members from the Cortland and Whipple and the Homer and Albany sections also hung around. The sections representing on the boulevard became known to Sonia and her family because it was customary for gang members to yell out their section name to announce their presence. The Latin Kings began to routinely cross the street into the YLO-Ds' side of the boulevard as a sign of strength. As a result the YLO-Ds almost disappeared from the boulevard. The few times they did come around they exchanged gunfire with the Latin Kings. But as a whole, gang warfare diminished with the Kings' constant presence on the boulevard.

Eventually some of the Latin Kings befriended Vivian and began to hang out in front of the building where she lived. Soon they were going into her apartment almost daily to visit with Vivian. Marta welcomed the Kings into her home and treated them well. Vivian would leave work, meet up with the Kings, and hang out with them in the 'hood. She came home intoxicated at all hours of the night but somehow always managed to get to work on time the next day. It amazed Sonia that Vivian was able to keep her job living the way she did. Sonia was jealous of the way her mother welcomed the Kings but failed to welcome her in her own home. Not only that, but the Latin King traffic in her home started to affect her reputation at school.

Sonia was now a freshman at Roberto Clemente High School, which was overrun by gang members who were predominantly rivals to the Latin Kings. About a month and a half into the school year she was pointed out by a Maniac Latin Disciples member, who'd seen Vivian walking out of the house with a Latin King, as having some kind of family connection to the Kings. Suddenly gang members started giving Sonia dirty looks and purposely bumping into her in the hallways. Sonia successfully avoided confrontation, but something always happened that lured negative attention her way.

Eventually some of the YLO-Ds approached Sonia in school about her supposed connection to the Kings. She sidestepped the accusation by pointing out that she hung out with a group of dancers who gathered on the YLO-Ds' side of Humboldt Boulevard. They called themselves the Richmond Street Dancers, and Sonia had met some of the members in her division class, the fifteen-minute class at the start of the day where school officials took attendance. None of the kids in the dance group were gang members, but several had relatives with gang affiliations, mostly YLO-Ds. It was these affiliations that kept Sonia from being jumped by gang members at school.

The Richmond Street Dancers met and practiced in the basement of the home of one member whose mother choreographed some of their routines. The father drove the members to performances and took care of lighting and sound. The house where the group gathered was on Richmond Street, one block east of Humboldt Boulevard near North Avenue—in YLO-D territory. When the rumors of Sonia's family's association with the Latin Kings began to circulate, the Richmond Street Dancers were apprehensive, but they eventually embraced Sonia as one of their own. Some of the dancers knew from personal experience the consequences of having relatives who were gang members—they were considered guilty by association.

The Richmond Street Dancers specialized in break dancing. Sonia couldn't master the difficult moves such as pop locking or spinning and didn't have the acrobatic skills required of break dancers. She did, however, possess a good ear for what songs best fit certain routines. She also had the creativity and imagination to put dance moves together. The group made Sonia their assistant choreographer, and she worked alongside the mother and father coaches. The group was well known and performed in the Puerto Rican parade and at night assemblies at Roberto Clemente High School. This was a great outlet for Sonia, who made new friends and was given responsibility and respect. Best of all, it kept her out of her home.

Sonia immersed herself into the break-dancing scene, which was taking off in the 1980s as a positive alternative to gangs for inner-city youth. Dance competitions sprung up all over the place. Local park districts and radio stations sponsored and heavily promoted these citywide dance battles. Freestyle dance-offs on the street were also common. The Richmond Street Dancers became known as one of the best break-dancing groups in the Humboldt Park area. Their acrobatic dance moves were outstanding, but it was the way they coordinated their moves with high-energy, bass-heavy music that made them stand out. Every move, be it a hand gesture, a facial expression, or movement of the entire body, had its purpose, and Sonia planned everything out in the choreography. Suddenly she was popular, and many kids, none of whom uttered insults about her looks or the way she dressed, wanted to be her friend. Sonia's newfound confidence helped her shed her ugly duckling moniker and develop into a very charismatic personality.

Things finally seemed to be going her way, and she had many things to smile about, but only on the streets. At home, when Sonia talked about her success with the Richmond Street Dancers, no one seemed to care. The only thing she did hear was to be careful about hanging out in the YLO-Ds' 'hood.

As Vivian's friendship with the Latin Kings grew, so did the danger in Sonia's attending Clemente. She tried to talk to Vivian about this, but Vivian couldn't care less. Making matters even worse, Vivian talked her mother into renting a small house on Homer and Albany streets, deep in the Latin Kings' 'hood. Not only did that corner have its own section of Kings, but it also was a short walking distance to two other major sections of the Latin Kings—Kedzie and Armitage and Cortland and Whipple. The area directly around the small house swarmed with so many gang members it resembled a beehive.

Sonia's small home became a clubhouse for some of the Latin Kings. Heavy drinking and drug taking among mostly underage kids at all times of the day and night became the norm. Cigarette butt- and joint-filled ashtrays, empty beer cans, and empty bottles of cheap wine now adorned the tables. Her home was also used to store some of the gang's weapons, including guns of all types. Mostly male Latin Kings hung out there, along with three or four female members known as Latin Queens. They were all friends with Vivian. Even when Vivian was at work they had an open invitation to come in and out of the house as they pleased. Sonia's two little brothers and little sister—ages one, three, and five at the time—also lived there, but their mother showed no concern about exposing the kids to the alcohol, drugs, guns, or violence that surrounded them.

Sonia had no say in what went on in the house and was verbally attacked by her mother and Vivian the few times she brought it up. She hated being around her home and consequently stayed out with Richmond Street Dancers members—watching movies, talking about their problems, putting together new dances, anything—to avoid going home. She was almost fifteen years old now. She still hadn't tried drugs but worried that it was only a matter of time given her reckless home environment.

This environment eventually began affecting Sonia's relationship with the Richmond Street Dancers. The Latin Kings who hung around her house were hard-core gang members and well known by their rivals. Also, there were many Latin Queens who hung out in the area, young women who were just as violent as some of the Kings. It got to the point where not even hanging out with kids who lived in YLO-Ds' 'hood helped Sonia avoid being tagged as a member of the Latin Kings and Queens.

The animosity toward Sonia at Clemente grew with every action the Kings and Queens took against the YLO-Ds or any other gang affiliated with them. The nasty looks and physical intimidation she experienced in the hallways as she walked between classes intensified. Gang hand signs were flashed in front of her face, and the bumps in the hall started to be hard enough to make her fall or to knock her books all over the place. Sonia weathered it all and continued to make it known that she had nothing to do with the Latin Kings and Queens. She told her mother once or twice about what was going on in school, but as usual she was met with indifference.

One day toward the end of her freshman year, Sonia was surrounded by a large group of male and female gang members who were rivals of the Latin Kings and Queens. They included members of the Insane Spanish Cobras, Maniac Latin Disciples, Latin Jivers, Latin Lovers, and others, all flashing their gang signs in her direction. She was verbally assaulted and caught a glimpse of a girl opening a pocketknife. There was no place to run and no way to defend herself against so many assailants. She just stood her ground and braced herself for the worst. But suddenly the crowd began dispersing. "Rios! Rios!" Sonia heard someone call out as kids began running every which way. Rios, the head of security at Clemente, was making his way toward the area with other security guards in tow. They asked Sonia several questions about the incident, but she stonewalled, not wanting to make matters worse by becoming known as a snitch. They put her on a bus and sent her home.

When Sonia arrived home, she told her mother what happened and was again met with indifference. Her mother didn't call Clemente or suggest Sonia transfer to another school. Sonia did try to return to school a few days later, but gang members were waiting for her a few blocks from the school and chased her back home. Sometimes she could make it to school for at least part of the day before gang members realized she was there. Then they would stand outside her classroom, wait for the end of class, and then run her off campus. Miraculously Sonia managed to finish her freshman year, but this was the end of her formal education. The following year no school official sought her return, and her mother did nothing to encourage her to go back.

The very real danger confronting her on the school's campus, and her consequent decision to stop attending, took away Sonia's only opportunity to escape her unhealthy and dangerous home environment. Hanging out with the Richmond Street Dancers was no longer an option because of the Latin King/Queen tag that hung around her neck. The mother who helped choreograph the group's dances explained to Sonia that her involvement with the dance group posed a threat to the safety of its members. Sonia understood, but she was heartbroken. She continued to see the dancers around the neighborhood and they never disrespected her, but this positive outlet was now firmly closed to her. And as it closed, Sonia began befriending members of the Latin Kings and Queens who surrounded her.

4

Loss of Innocence

SONIA'S INTRODUCTION INTO gang life was subtle and unexpected. Although she lived in a gang-infested area, she had never chosen to hang out with active gang members. It wasn't until her home became a Latin King/Queen hangout that she had unavoidable encounters with gang members and the gang way of life. And it wasn't until she attended Clemente High School that she really felt the power and intimidation of gangs. Sonia knew gangs were dangerous and that just hanging around them gave her the same label—she'd discovered this painful truth when she could no longer be involved with the Richmond Street Dancers—but so far she hadn't witnessed much criminal activity other than drug use. Otherwise she knew about gangs' hard-core violence only through urban myths and local news reports. What Sonia saw was just a bunch of people trying to fit in anywhere they could. She connected to this.

Although the Latin Kings and Queens were welcome in her home because they were Vivian's friends, her mother chastised Sonia when she started hanging out with gang members outside of her home. Again, she was in a no-win situation and continued to find her home an unwelcoming place. The streets were far more welcoming. She started staying out all day and most of the night with her new friends, coming home very late if at all. Her mother threatened to call the police and have her arrested for juvenile delinquency. Sonia found this humorous since Marta allowed—even welcomed—all kinds of illegal activity and delinquents into her own home because they were Vivian's friends. Although Sonia paid little attention to her mother's threats, she was wary that Vivian would talk her mother into following through on them.

One summer night Sonia came home after a night of hanging out and was immediately confronted by her mother. This was customary, so Sonia thought she would go through the usual routine of arguing with Marta and then disappearing into her bedroom. But this night was different. After exchanging insults with her mother Sonia headed toward the bathroom to bathe, change her clothes, and head back out onto the streets. Moments after Sonia entered the bathroom and closed the door, her mother came rushing in and took a swing at her that landed squarely on her face. The force with which Marta charged at her surprised Sonia and threw her off balance, and she fell to the floor. As Sonia fell, her leg thrust upward, kicking her mother in the chest and throwing her backward out of the bathroom. Before Sonia could pick herself up, Vivian and Jazmin appeared and screamed obscenities and hovered over her, accusing her of hitting their mother. When Sonia tried to get up, Vivian, Jazmin, and Marta began beating her. She made a feeble attempt to fight back but was overwhelmed by the number of punches and kicks. The attack lasted only twenty seconds or so but left a deep and permanent mental scar on Sonia.

After the attack Sonia remained on the bathroom floor, sitting against the bathtub crying. Her mind went blank. It was as if she had run out of hateful things to think about her family. She was exhausted from dealing with the bullshit, the double standards, the lack of concern for her well-being—all of it.

Sonia had experienced this family drama enough times to know that when she walked out of the bathroom everyone would pretend that nothing had happened. She bathed, trying to scrub the memory of the beating off her body. Then she changed her clothes and walked out of the house without saying a word and wishing she never had to return.

At about this time, Jazmin had become Vivian's pet sister and got away with all sorts of mischief and lies. Jazmin made it a habit to come home late from school, and this concerned her mother, so one day she sent Sonia to pick her up. Jazmin attended Stowe Elementary School, located about a half mile from Homer and Albany. Sonia walked to the school with a friend and got there just in time to see the students exiting the school, going every which way. There was no sign of Jazmin. Twenty minutes went by, the crowd disappeared, and there was still no Jazmin, so Sonia headed back home. As she entered her house to tell her mother that she hadn't seen Jazmin at school, she saw Jazmin sitting on the couch next to Marta. Jazmin's eyes were red and swollen from crying; their mother had an angry look on her face. Sonia assumed that her mother had beaten Jazmin for being late yet again.

Sonia closed the door behind her and stepped toward the living room, wondering why Jazmin was staring at her so hard. Before she could say a word her mother got up off the couch and lunged at her, landing a full-force, open-hand slap square on the side of Sonia's face. *"¿Hija de la gran puta, donde carajo estabas?"* ("Daughter of a great bitch, where the hell were you?"), Sonia's mother yelled as she hit her. The force of the blow snapped Sonia's head to the side and back so she lost sight of her mother, whom she knew would continue her attack. Sonia put her hands up to cover her face but wasn't quick enough. Her mother slapped her again. When Sonia turned her back to her mother and covered her face, Marta grabbed her by the hair and pulled her backward. *"¡En poquito abusan de tu hermana port u condena culpa!"* ("They almost abused your sister because of your damn fault!"), she screamed. Sonia stumbled, lost her balance, and fell backward. Her mother stopped hitting her but continued to call her all kinds of degrading names and blamed her for Jazmin almost getting raped. After things calmed down, Sonia discovered that Jazmin had told her mother that she hadn't seen Sonia anywhere near the school and was attacked on her way home. Jazmin's story was that she had been pulled into an alley by two big African American men who attempted to rape her. She fought them off and ran away. That's why she was late getting home from school. Sonia thought her mother was an idiot to believe such a bullshit story. Jazmin was barely four feet tall, there were dozens of kids all over the place at the time Jazmin claimed the incident occurred, and there wasn't a scratch on her to confirm any sign of a struggle—certainly fighting off two "big black men" would have left some kind of mark. No one attempted to notify the police of the alleged incident. Sonia concluded that her mother knew she was being lied to and took her anger out on her instead of Jazmin. This pissed Sonia off even more, although there wasn't a thing she could do about it.

Eventually Jazmin's truancy caught up with her when school officials informed her mother that she hadn't been to school in weeks. As a result, Jazmin was shipped out to Puerto Rico to live with her biological father, Carlos, a man she barely knew. Uncovering the truth about Jazmin was a bittersweet victory for Sonia because her mother never apologized for beating her.

Sonia started to gain popularity among a group of Latin Queens who hung out on the streets around her home on Homer and Albany. These Queens hated Vivian, and they knew that Sonia hated her, too. They admired Sonia's ability to survive and her toughness given how her older sister and mother treated her. Included in this group was a Latin Queen in her midtwenties named Reina. Reina was by no means an ordinary Latin Queen. She came from a family whose roots went back to when the Latin Kings were founded in the 1970s as a civil rights organization to protect Latinos against police brutality and help them improve their lives. By the late 1970s and 1980s the Latin Kings had become a violent street gang. Reina wanted the gang to return to the ways of the founders and believed in the original rules laid out by them, such as honor your mother and father, never disrespect any member of the Kings, never steal from your own 'hood, and "Die for your King brothers, for they are from the blood of your blood." But Reina was realistic enough to know that, while these words sounded good, it was hard for kids coming from abusive homes or addicted to drugs to follow them.

Reina had a pretty colorful history. She'd been in and out of correctional institutions since she was a preteen and was currently on parole for slicing up her boyfriend, who she was trying to leave because he was physically abusive to her. Reina's older brother was serving time in the penitentiary for attempted murder, and so was one of her younger brothers. Another younger brother was being held in a juvenile facility, and yet another had been murdered by the YLO-Ds. Reina's family had given their hearts and souls and some even their lives to the Latin Kings, and she talked about how others connected with the gang should do the same.

Reina was not fond of people who joined the gang mainly for protection or to be part of something larger than themselves. She knew how to identify these types, and she thought Vivian was one of them. Reina decided to take Sonia under her wing. In that neighborhood, if Reina warmed to you, you were the bomb and accepted by everyone. Sonia, starved for someone who cared about her and made her feel important, badly needed the attention Reina paid her. Whatever Reina's motives and whatever her beliefs, Sonia found a home in her company. And while their friendship grew, events in Sonia's "real" home pushed her out.

Vivian became romantically involved with one of the gang members passing through their home. Stone, in his early twenties, was an alcoholic, a drug addict, and a member of the Insane Unknowns, a gang allied to the Latin Kings. He was a tall, light-skinned, good-looking guy with a muscular body. He was also unemployed and seemed to have no future outside of jail. Shortly after they started dating, Stone moved in with Vivian and became another member of the family. Later that week, Stone took Vivian home to meet his mother and sister, who lived in a North Side project off Southport in Chicago. Vivian and Stone's sister, Gigi, hit it off right away. In fact they got along so well that Gigi went back to the house with Vivian and Stone and moved in.

Gigi and Stone's father was Puerto Rican and their mother Caucasian, but while Stone had obvious Latino features, Gigi looked completely Caucasian, with long stringy hair and a slim build. She was sixteen years old, very quiet and easygoing, and loved to get high. Overnight, Gigi became Vivian's best friend and confidant. She went everywhere with Vivian and shared her clothes and makeup. Vivian also protected Gigi and gave her money whenever she needed it. Basically, Gigi became Vivian's new sixteen-year-old sister. Gigi's presence made Sonia feel angry, sad, and further confused. Sonia looked at Gigi and saw her replacement—a girl who was the same age as herself, did nothing but hang around and get high all day, and who had Vivian's rapt attention and support.

A couple of months after Stone and Gigi moved into their home, Stone was arrested for drug possession. Gigi remained a part of the family, and her presence intensified Sonia's feelings that no one in her household loved her. The only people giving her time, attention, and respect were members of the Latin Queens, especially Reina.

Vivian quickly became romantically involved with another gang member whose prospects were similar to Stone's. Her new beau, RJ, was a carbon copy of Stone. In addition to being an unemployed drug addict and alcoholic, he was nearly illiterate. RJ also had a violent temper, which became especially evident when he was drunk.

As RJ became a regular member of Sonia's home, so too did his best friend, Baldi, another Latin King. Baldi was a short, chubby, fair-skinned Puerto Rican who held a steady job and had a wife and child and another on the way. But when Baldi wasn't working he was in the 'hood getting high, gangbanging, and preying on the young and vulnerable. As soon as Baldi laid eyes on Sonia, he made a move on her.

Sonia's feelings of being unloved and unlovable made her an easy target for Baldi. She knew Baldi's primary goal was to sleep with her, but she found his sweet words hard to resist. Baldi constantly told Sonia how beautiful she was, and when she confided in him about how her family treated her, he told her that she deserved better. He said he wanted to take care of her and give her the love she was missing. Sonia's defenses weakened, and when Baldi started inviting her to go out so that they could have some privacy and talk alone, she agreed. For the first time in her young life Sonia went to the lakefront, to dinner at restaurants, and to the movies. She and Baldi began exchanging passionate kisses and touches. Everyone in her house and in the 'hood began to recognize Sonia as Baldi's girlfriend.

In the middle of the afternoon one Friday, there was a knock at the front door of Sonia's house. She opened the door and there stood an attractive five-foot-two, twenty-something Puerto Rican woman who was obviously pregnant. She had caramel skin and a ferocious look in her eyes. She peered inside the house, saw Baldi sitting on the sofa in the living room, and immediately began screaming obscenities at him and Sonia. Sonia became upset and began to argue with her, saying things like "He's my man now, bitch, so get over it," and "Get out of my fuckin' house before I kick your ass."

Sonia didn't care that Baldi's wife was pregnant; as far as she was concerned, that was an issue between her and Baldi. Sonia went for the woman to fight her but Baldi stopped her. He forcibly led his wife out of the house as she exchanged insults with Sonia and tried to break free from his grasp. Baldi grew irritated and let go of his wife only to then grab her by her hair, pull her into his car, and drive her home. Her screams could be heard throughout the block. People looked on, seemingly amused by the spectacle. Sonia felt extremely proud over the outcome of this exchange because it validated all the sweet things Baldi had told her. She took this encounter as proof that Baldi was her man, and now the whole world knew it.

Sonia's mother became upset about the situation and attacked Sonia both verbally and physically. Sonia didn't care. This was nothing new to her and made no difference. Sonia simply walked outside and waited for Baldi to return after taking his wife back home. While she waited, a friend of her mother's showed up and asked her to babysit for the night. Sonia knew this woman liked to go out and party and went home with whatever man caught her attention, usually not returning until sometime the next day. Sonia agreed to babysit to get out of her house and away from her mother. About a half hour later, Baldi returned to be with Sonia, but he didn't stay for long because of Marta's anger. It was late in the afternoon, and he stayed only long enough for Sonia to tell him where she was babysitting and what time she'd be alone.

For the rest of the day Sonia felt pride, satisfaction, and contentedness—new feelings for her. No one had ever defended her. To Sonia this was a confirmation of Baldi's love; and further, she believed this love would last forever.

In the early evening Baldi met Sonia at her babysitting gig, which was about two blocks away from her home. The nine-year-old girl Sonia was babysitting was fast asleep by the time Baldi arrived. As soon as Baldi walked through the door the couple engulfed each other in passionate kisses and touches.

Sonia had been touched in her private parts before but never with the passion and reckless abandon that Baldi exhibited that night. He groped her violently as he kissed her; he licked her and gently bit her face and neck. Sonia, overwhelmed by Baldi's aggressiveness, became nervous. She wanted to stop him but was afraid he would no longer love her, would no longer stand up for her, would no longer want to be with her. She began to tremble. Baldi began pulling Sonia's clothes off, ignoring her now obvious fear. He laid her down on the sofa and continued to fervently claw Sonia's body. Sonia knew what was coming. She was scared and didn't want it to happen, but her fear of no longer being loved by the only person in the world who cared for her was even stronger. She turned her face and stared at the wall, not saying a word, not wanting to look at Baldi's face as he spread her legs and positioned himself to enter her. Sonia just wanted everything to be over. Her mind went blank as Baldi violently took her virginity. He ground into her for nearly a half hour while Sonia suffered beneath him in silence. During the act she felt like a corpse more than a woman sharing a moment of passion.

When it was finally over, there were no kisses or shared embraces. Sonia got up and went to take a shower, where it was difficult to know if the wetness came from the water spraying down on her or the tears she shed. After cleaning up she walked straight into one of the bedrooms to go to sleep. Baldi bathed and joined her on the bed without saying a word. Sonia didn't say anything; she couldn't look at him. The next morning he kissed her good-bye, said he'd see her later, and left.

Sonia was confused and angry with herself for allowing Baldi to take the only bit of self-respect she had left, but at the same time she felt confident that she would soon be sharing a home and many special moments with him. It was clear to her that Baldi was the only one who loved her, and therefore she felt a bit guilty for not enjoying sex with him and for not being filled with the desire to do it again.

In the weeks that followed, Baldi visited Sonia only twice and stayed only long enough to have sex. Although Sonia didn't enjoy sex with him, she conceded to the act in order to have him around. A few weeks later rumors began circulating around the 'hood that Baldi had a new girl in his life. She lived just around the corner.

Almost a month to the day after taking Sonia's virginity, Baldi disappeared from her life. Sonia felt used, dirty, and borderline suicidal—feeling that no matter what she did, no one would ever love her. She had lost all innocence about the world and realized that her desire—her desperation—for love had made her vulnerable. She vowed never to let it happen again.

5

LADY Q EMERGES

THE PAST YEAR of Sonia's life had completely changed her attitude toward the people around her and people in general. She had been harshly introduced to sex, her friendship with gang members had begun, and she had been replaced as a member of her own family by Gigi, who'd shown up only a short time ago and had already taken over as Vivian's new little sister despite her brother Stone's exit from the family. Then Sonia's home life had become even less stable when an opportunistic, freeloading gang member declared himself the man of the house. Sonia didn't think her family could get any more dysfunctional.

Sonia's attraction to Reina and the girls in the gang who hung out with her was wholehearted. Sonia felt accepted, and she believed their words of loyalty and their pledge to always defend her, as when Reina assured her that the righteous Queen sisters and King brothers would always be there for her. Acceptance, protection—these were the very things she'd always sought from her own family but never received. So Sonia's transition into gang life needed only an initiation to seal the deal.

WHEN THE ALMIGHTY Latin King Nation was still a relatively young organization, the induction of a new member was a highly dictated ritual. A prospective member had to be strong physically, mentally, and emotionally. These characteristics ensured that the Latin King Nation would be a Nation of leaders. Rarely was someone allowed to join if he didn't meet these criteria. When the Latin Queens were introduced, they adopted the same standards as the Kings when the benefits of having strong sisters by their sides became clear. But by the early 1980s only physical toughness remained of these initial criteria, and now potential members needed to exhibit a tendency toward criminal behavior, too. Committing hits (killings or other acts of revenge) against rivals and taking a beating at the hands of their own gang brothers or sisters became more important prerequisites than exhibiting leadership traits. Practically anyone willing to put on the black and gold colors was eligible to become a King or Queen. Many members were allowed to join without having to prove their toughness or loyalty at all. These were the foot soldiers who only had to deflect violence and police suspicion away from their leaders, who now led a drug empire.

This new way of doing things angered longtime members such as Reina who felt they had given too much of themselves to the gang to allow just anyone to wear the crown they had made so strong.

ON A BRIGHT sunny day in the summer of 1982, Vivian sat in front of her house with Gigi and two of their Latin Queen friends drinking beer and smoking weed when the subject of gang membership came up. Sonia came out of the house on her way out to the street but hung around when she heard the topic of conversation. Vivian expressed her desire to be a Queen and was quickly offered membership—no meeting to discuss her membership was held, no hit on a rival was required, and no approval by an elite veteran member such as Reina was needed. All a potential recruit needed to do was withstand a three-minute violation—a head-to-toe beating without any punches to the face—administered by those Queens loyal to her.

A small group of Queens gathered and egged Vivian on to officially become a member. Sonia needed no prodding—she readily volunteered to be violated into the Queens. As far as Sonia was concerned she had nothing to lose and a kingdom to gain. Four Queens from the Homer and Albany 'hood who were close to Vivian—China, Linda and her little sister Rosemary, and Smiley—assigned themselves the honor of initiating Sonia and Vivian into the Latin Queen Nation.

The nickname China was normally reserved for members who were Asian or resembled a person of Asian descent; her name didn't fit. She was an eighteen-year-old dark-skinned Puerto Rican with kinky black hair and a body built for trouble. Nothing about China's appearance gave even the slightest hint that she was a gang member, but she was known and respected for her reputation as a hard-core gangbanger. She loved guns and had an itchy trigger finger, and took part in more hits on rival gangs than most of the male members of the Homer and Albany section. On countless occasions China had used her drop-dead-gorgeous looks as bait to lead rival gang members into Latin King ambushes.

Linda was about nineteen, with a petite build, black hair, caramel skin, and deep brown eyes. She'd become a member of the Latin Queens on the South Side when she was thirteen. She found her way to the Humboldt Park area when she began dating a King from Cortland and Whipple and never left. Linda's days as a violent member of the Queens were all but over—her current status was party animal. Her little sister, Rosemary, was a fifteen-year-old carbon copy of Linda who also became a Queen at the age of thirteen, but she did very little gangbanging. Linda and Rosemary were of Mexican ancestry, born on the South Side of Chicago to hardworking and loving parents. They had no stories of abuse or neglect and no family history of gang involvement other than their older brother, who was a member of the South Side Latin Kings. Their parents still lived on the South Side, where they owned their own home, but they would come into the Humboldt Park area to beg their daughters to come home, offering to provide financial assistance. The couple was soft-spoken and seemed very understanding. They were the type of parents that all the truly lost children of the streets wished they had, especially Sonia. However, it was apparent to Linda and Rosemary that going home meant they would have to work, go to school, or involve themselves in other acts of responsibility they found unthinkable.

Smiley was a white girl with no real taste for gangbanging. The first impression Smiley gave was that she was a lesbian because of her masculine build and manner, her hairstyle, and the way she dressed. But Smiley was a party animal whose priorities were drinking, doing drugs, and having sex with whatever guy approached her. She was known around the neighborhood as the "Nation ho" who received her crown only because her brother was a longtime member of the Latin Kings. The odd thing about Smiley and her brother was that they were raised among Imperial Gangsters—the fiercest rivals of the Kings from Homer and Albany. Their parents still lived in an area controlled by the Imperial Gangsters; consequently Smiley rarely went home and preferred to hang out in the 'hood.

A crowd of gang members and nonmembers alike gathered as news spread that an initiation was about to take place in a public space. Performing this once-secret membership ritual out in the open for the world to see showed just how meaningless the Nation's rules had become and how trivial being associated with the gang really was.

Vivian was twenty years old, yet she was assigned Rosemary, a thirteen-year-old, as one of the initiators. Along with Rosemary, Smiley and Myra would also take part in making Vivian a member of the Queens. Linda would be the timekeeper. Vivian crossed her arms over her chest as she stood up against the chain-link fence lining one side of the empty lot. Sonia watched as Vivian was whaled on from all directions, but the blows didn't seem to do much damage and Vivian looked unfazed by the punishment she was enduring. Three minutes later Vivian was officially a Queen. It was now Sonia's turn.

Sonia was ready and confident. She considered herself much stronger and tougher than Vivian and had withstood worse beatings at her mother's hands than the one Vivian had just received. Sonia walked to the fence fearlessly, anxious to get her initiation over with. She crossed her arms over her chest and pressed them tight against her body for protection, knowing that the Queens beating her would not be allowed to hit her face. Linda, China, and Myra would again do the honors. Sonia worried about China beating her because of her reputation, but she didn't say a word. She thought about how there was no physical pain anyone could cause her that her mother had not already done.

Sonia braced herself for the onslaught of blows and concentrated on the crown she was earning and how proud she would be to wear it. Linda, China, and Myra began raining punches down upon Sonia's body. For a moment Sonia regretted her decision to become a Queen and feared she would not make it through, but after about thirty seconds she stopped feeling the blows. She couldn't believe how easy it all was and how quickly the three minutes went by. Sonia was now a Latin Queen. Now that she had ascended to the role of gang member, she proudly sat on her imaginary throne.

When Reina got wind of the initiations—how they'd been decided and how they took place—she was livid. She was elated that Sonia had decided to become a Queen, but she did not accept Vivian's membership. Reina confronted Vivian in front of their house and told her she would have to do more than take a three-minute beating to be a Queen. She wanted Vivian to prove her toughness and demanded that she fight Smiley until one of them was clearly victorious if she wanted to keep her crown. Reina selected Smiley because she saw her as one of the hangers-on and not a Queen in the true sense of the word. Because of Reina's rank, Smiley had no choice but to fight Vivian or face a much worse fate. Vivian was obviously intimidated by Reina and didn't seem to find the idea of fighting her friend Smiley too welcoming. But Smiley had been called out by one of the main Queens and so had to step forward to accept the challenge and show her loyalty to the crown.

Sonia saw that Vivian was not prepared to handle the fight and came to her defense.

"Leave my sister alone; I'll fight her," Sonia blurted out as she stepped toward Smiley and in front of Vivian.

"What the fuck are you waiting for?" Reina yelled at Smiley.

Smiley was not a fighter and came at Sonia halfheartedly. Sonia stepped to the side and threw three blows to Smiley's face. Each landed solidly, breaking Smiley's nose and causing her to stumble. Sonia kicked Smiley in the abdomen as she fell and continued to pound on her as she lay on the concrete trying to cover herself.

Sonia lost her mind, as if all the pent-up anger for all the beatings she'd received over the years was unleashed all at once. She attacked Smiley relentlessly, even though Smiley was clearly overwhelmed and defenseless. Smiley screamed in pain—one of her eyes was visibly swollen, and she was bleeding profusely from her nose and mouth—but Sonia kept beating her. Finally Reina, the one who had started it all, grabbed Sonia and pulled her off Smiley. This was the last night anyone in the 'hood saw Smiley.

"You see, bitch, this is a true Queen," Reina spit at Vivian.

Reina decided then and there that Vivian was not worthy to represent the Almighty Latin Queen Nation. She ordered China to make sure Vivian was initiated out of the Queens. Just two days after Vivian had been given her crown, it was taken away in the same fashion. Sonia, on the other hand, had earned the complete respect of one of the most respected members of the Latin Queens in the Humboldt Park area. Her reign had just begun.

Vivian did not like being initiated out of the Latin Queens, but because the decision had been handed down by Reina, a high-ranking member, there was little she could do about it. While she acted indifferent, she was hurt as the few Latin Queens who'd befriended her began to back away. Vivian no longer felt welcome in the Homer and Albany neighborhood. She almost immediately began talking about moving away.

Sonia didn't care one way or the other. She knew that, regardless of where her family moved, she would always return to the 'hood where her new extended family dwelled. The Latin Kings and Queens of Homer and Albany, and all the surrounding areas, accepted Sonia wholeheartedly as one of their own. They credited her with ridding their nation of Smiley, a member they considered a cancer. The news of Smiley's beating and subsequent departure spread throughout the Latin King and Queen Nation and earned Sonia the name Lady Q, which she was poised to make synonymous with toughness and loyalty.

The contrast between the person known as Sonia and the one who embraced the name Lady Q became apparent almost immediately. Sonia had been ignored, looked down upon, attacked, and blamed for all the ills that afflicted her family. Sonia was introverted, depressed, lonely, and harbored suicidal thoughts. Lady Q quickly became her alter ego. Lady Q stood tall and confident. She was welcomed, sought out, listened to, and respected by other King members. Lady Q felt powerful for the first time in her life, as if she held the whole world in her hands. Now the only time that Lady Q's complete supremacy over Sonia was interrupted was when she'd run into Baldi somewhere in the 'hood with other young conquests by his side.

As Vivian's plans to move out of the Homer and Albany neighborhood progressed, Lady Q got wind that these plans didn't include her, their mother, or their younger siblings. As it turned out, everyone did move out of the neighborhood, just not all to the same place. While Vivian, RJ, and Gigi left for an apartment building located about a half mile away from Homer and Albany (still in the Kings' 'hood), Lady Q was surprised to learn that she, her mother, and her other siblings would be leaving Chicago for the island paradise of Puerto Rico.

Lady Q didn't know exactly why Marta decided to move to Puerto Rico, but she suspected it had something to do with her mom's not liking or getting along with RJ. Seemingly out of nowhere, Marta contacted Juan and made arrangements to join him.

Despite her contempt for Juan, Lady Q felt thrilled that her mother was making such drastic changes and was adamant about including Lady Q. She was touched by what she saw as her mother's gesture of caring and looked forward to being the eldest child at home. She felt certain she'd now be counted on to head the family just as Vivian had done before her.

Surprisingly, Lady Q didn't give a second thought to leaving the streets of Chicago, the only world she knew. But as all brothers and sisters of the Latin King/Queen Nation who considered themselves righteous did, Lady Q made her rounds bidding farewell to those she considered her one true family. She swore her loyalty to the black and gold and to the crown she felt privileged to adorn forevermore, and she promised to spread the gospel of the Latin Kings and Queens wherever she went.

But on the plane on her way to a new life in Puerto Rico, Lady Q transformed back into the little girl named Sonia who dreamed of growing closer to her mother. Sonia's hopes were as high as the clouds that the airplane flew through.

As the airplane made its descent into San Juan, Puerto Rico, Sonia looked in awe at the deep blue color of the sea that surrounded the small island and the lush green miles that lay before her. Juan waited for them at the airport, and from the moment the family made contact with him, it was clear this would not be the best of times. There was a slight embrace between Juan and Marta, which was obviously more mandatory than heartfelt. No screams of joy exclaiming *"¡Papi, Papi, Papi!"* were heard from any of Juan's children. Their reception was mostly filled with indifference, not elation or acceptance.

As they walked through the airport to pick up their luggage and then made their way to his car, Juan walked ahead of his newly arrived family while mumbling "these bitches, they better behave." He probably thought he was talking to himself, but he could be heard by anyone within five feet of him. Sonia, her siblings, and their mother could hear Juan and, embarrassed by his behavior, dropped back farther behind him.

Their destination was the city of Aguadilla, located on the west portion of the island, but they made a detour north to the city of Arecibo where Jazmin now lived with her father, Carlos. Initially, Sonia thought that her mother wanted to spend time with Jazmin or pick her up and bring her along. But after a brief conversation among the adults while standing in the kitchen, Juan walked out to the car, grabbed Sonia's luggage, and placed it on the driveway. It was never clear to Sonia whether this had been set up with Carlos and his family beforehand or was a complete surprise to everyone but Marta, but either way, this detour was clearly meant to dump off Sonia— she wasn't part of her mother's plans after all.

As she watched her family drive away without once looking back, it became crystal clear to Sonia that her mother had no intention of taking care of her any longer. She watched in a daze, void of all emotion, as the car disappeared.

There was neither joy nor sorrow for Sonia that day. It was in fact more like a religious experience. On that beautiful, warm, sunny evening in the middle of a street in Arecibo, Puerto Rico, the ghost of the little girl called Sonia left her body and was replaced by a cold-blooded woman who would be known only as Lady Q from now on to friends and foes alike. No more bull-shit hopes, no more pussy-ass childish dreams, and no more illu-sions of a caring mother. Lady Q realized that the world was out to fuck her so she was going to fuck it first.

Lady Q felt apathetic about finding herself in the home of people who didn't care for her or she for them, including a sis-ter she hardly got along with. As long as they stayed out of her way, she would stay out of theirs.

Lady Q's domain was now the street, be it in Chicago or Puerto Rico. As Lady Q she felt strong, and her powerful new-found magnetism quickly opened doors. She soon discovered the same popularity she had left behind in Chicago, and Jazmin now clung to her because she wanted the same opportunities to party. Together they became the party animals of the neigh-borhood, much to the dismay of Jazmin's father and his fam-ily. Sonia was only sixteen and Jazmin thirteen, but that didn't stop them from obtaining a steady supply of alcohol. Their drink of choice was the good ol' Puerto Rican rum that flowed freely on the small island. The girls' suppliers were for the most part older men who mainly wanted a piece of ass from these wild adolescent girls in exchange. And they were wild, but not stupid. Lady Q and Jazmin were well aware of what attracted men to them and were wise enough to take precautions and not put themselves into situations where they could be raped or molested.

The girls became friends with a group of siblings living down the street who were also from a dysfunctional family. There were six kids in all, ranging in age from ten to nineteen, and most were the offspring of different fathers. When they met there was a stepfather in the home and a mother who had given up trying to deal with so many kids on her own. She was a small, frail, solemn-looking woman who didn't beat them but did neglect them. She would disappear at all times of the day or night and sometimes not return for days, leaving her children to fend for themselves. Without supervision her kids partied nonstop. Lady Q and Jazmin were a welcome addition to the around-the-clock partying and soon became involved with two of the boys who lived in the house. Lady Q's boyfriend was eighteen and Jazmin's was sixteen. Word of the girls' careless activities and rumors that they were sexually active got back to Jazmin's father. He tried to put a stop to their behavior by locking them in their bedroom at night and securing all doors and windows as best he could, but the girls were not deterred. Regardless of what Carlos tried, he could not keep the girls from sneaking out at night and into the waiting arms of their boyfriends and the bliss of alcohol.

UNPROTECTED SEX AND incredible amounts of alcohol became a normal part of Lady Q and Jazmin's daily life in Puerto Rico. They didn't think about sexually transmitted diseases or unwanted pregnancies. But during our interviews Lady Q was adamant that she did not sleep around during her time in Puerto Rico. "I only slept with three guys, OK? I'm not a 'ho,'" she protested.

I wanted to challenge her claim that a teenager having sex with three guys within a six- or seven-month period is not a bad thing, but I realized that three was actually a small number for the type of life she was handed. Her and Jazmin's conduct was in fact typical wherever abused and neglected kids gather to sulk in each other's miseries. In their world, what they were doing was normal, and caring was not important since tomorrow might never come. This is where young, uneducated, welfare-bound mothers usually come from, not to mention fatherless kids destined to grow up thinking that the idea of a tight-knit family and two loving parents is ludicrous and reserved solely for the weak.

JAZMIN'S FATHER, FRUSTRATED by the girls' carefree and careless ways, finally decided to put a stop to it. People around town referred to his daughters as drunks and whores, and his wife and her relatives harped on him to get rid of them. One early Saturday evening, Carlos paced up and down the front of his house, waiting for the girls to come back from the house down the street where they were once again partying. Lady Q awoke from a deep alcohol-induced sleep hearing screams coming from the street. She walked outside to find Carlos and Jazmin engaged in a screaming match that brought out spectators from all over the neighborhood. Jazmin's father threatened to beat her and turn her and her friends in to the police. Jazmin screamed that she would kill him and his entire family if he dared do anything to her. This bad scene lasted for about a half hour. It made an already untenable situation impossible.

At the end of the screaming match, Jazmin's father packed up their things and drove them to their mother's home in Aguadilla. He didn't say a word to either girl on the way there, while Sonia and Jazmin talked all kinds of shit in Spanish and

English, saying they didn't care what he was doing, that they planned to return to the home of their boyfriends, and that he couldn't do anything to stop them.

No one was at the house when they reached Aguadilla. Carlos simply unloaded the girls and their belongings and left them sitting on the driveway. He never made eye contact with either of them, and he never said a word. And then he sped away.

Lady Q found the whole ordeal hilarious, anticipating the looks on Marta and Juan's faces when they came home to find them sitting there. She knew Juan would hit the roof. They both expected him to load them into his car and drive them right back to Arecibo. Before Marta and Juan returned, Sonia and Jazmin decided not to stay in Aguadilla for long. They had invitations to a wedding reception the following weekend, and they had every intention of being there. If Juan didn't want them, they would welcome a ride back; otherwise, they knew they could find someone, especially some hard-up male, to give them a ride.

Lady Q and Jazmin waited outside the house in Aguadilla for about thirty minutes before their mother and Juan arrived. The girls had been gone a couple of months, but, as expected, Juan was still not at all happy to see them. He immediately began calling them bitches and whores, even before he got out of the car. Juan yelled things like *"¿Que carajo asen estas putas aqui?"* ("What the hell are these bitches doing here?") The girls responded in the same aggressive manner. Juan got out of the car and hurried inside, returning immediately carrying a machete. *"¡Cayensen, canyensen!"* ("Shut up, shut up!"), their mother urged the girls. Juan began pointing the machete at Lady Q and Jazmin, threatening to kill them. He intended to instill fear in the girls, but his plan backfired. Instead of cowering, the girls stepped toward Juan and called him a coward, letting him know they weren't afraid of him. Defiantly they demanded he drive them back to Arecibo if he didn't want them there, or he should use the machete and put them out of their misery. Marta responded as she had always done by arguing with Juan and physically attacking the girls. But this time the mother of Lady Q quickly realized that the girls no longer cared whether they were beaten. Neither was affected by the violence. She hit the girls but solicited no reaction from them. They merely deflected the strikes aimed at their faces. Neither Lady Q nor Jazmin tried to run and hide, screaming and crying from the pain, as they had before. Now they laughed at their mother's attempts to hurt them and simply told her not to worry because they didn't plan to stay long.

Three days later, Lady Q and Jazmin befriended a couple of guys who agreed to drive them back to Arecibo. They left with only the clothes on their backs. Lady Q figured that nothing could be worse than being threatened with a machete and chopped to death in her mother's home, so she wasn't afraid to drive across the island with strangers.

Although Lady Q and Jazmin were still minors, they were running their own lives and responded only to their gut instincts and personal drives in search of affection. Unfortunately, at sixteen and thirteen years old, Lady Q and Jazmin's instincts were those of irresponsible adolescents who wanted only to party. When they voiced their decision to leave, their mother said nothing—she gave no advice and made no protests.

Fortunately for Lady Q and Jazmin, the guys they decided to drive across the island with were just looking to party as well and didn't force them into anything they didn't want to do. Once back in Arecibo they attended the wedding they'd been looking forward to, reuniting with their boyfriends and now including their new chauffeur friends in their party plans. Their new friends partied with them through the night and then headed back to Aguadilla. Lady Q got incredibly drunk at the wedding party and later marked it as the beginning of a period that she was lucky to survive. Two young girls constantly out on the streets late at night with no supervision were bound to attract the attention of the local wolves. And they did—their party invitations became endless. So, too, was the supply of alcohol.

Now the only place Lady Q and Jazmin called home was their boyfriends' house. Of course this had more to do with their being sexually willing and available than being wanted there. They worried only about running into Jazmin's father. Being homeless never crossed their minds.

Lady Q turned seventeen in Arecibo at an all-night party thrown in her honor. It was the first time anyone had ever made a big deal for her birthday. But this night marked the beginning of the end of the girls' freeloading in Arecibo. A couple of weeks after the party the girls had worn out their welcome at their boyfriends' house. Now they were faced with the choice of roaming the streets and hooking up with the dirty old men who continued to line up for their attention, or returning to Aguadilla and battling Juan and Marta. While the girls loved their freedom and the partying, they chose to return to their mother's home.

This time Lady Q and Jazmin drove back to Aguadilla with friends. The girls knew they were in for an unwelcome reception, but they didn't care. As before, they would show up unannounced and force their mother to take them in, only this time they had no quick exit plans. Juan and Marta would just have to deal with Lady Q and Jazmin living with them.

The girls were tense as the car approached the house. They warned their friends about the dramatic reception likely to occur. When they arrived they saw their mom sitting in the carport watching her three young children playing. Surprisingly, she got up and hugged both Lady Q and Jazmin. Lady Q quickly realized that Juan wasn't home and so their mother was more relaxed, and she knew this would change once he returned. With that in mind the girls quickly said good-bye to their friends in order to spare them from the inevitable ugly scene that would follow.

As expected, all hell broke loose when Juan walked through the door of his home and saw Lady Q and Jazmin sitting at the kitchen table eating. At the top his lungs he screamed at the girls and demanded they leave immediately. Lady Q and Jazmin paid little attention to him, and this made him even angrier. He rushed past them toward the back of the house and returned moments later with his trusty machete in hand.

"Ain't this a bitch?" Lady Q said to Jazmin.

"Let's just go the fuck outside," Jazmin responded.

The girls went outside and Juan slammed and locked the door behind them. They sat on some chairs in the carport listening to the argument between Juan and Marta. About twenty minutes later their mother opened the door and told the girls to get inside. The day's events had exhausted them both so they found the room where they would stay and crashed for the night without any further confrontations with Juan.

Juan and the girls had many verbal and physical confrontations over the next few months. Their mother tried to reduce the opportunities for quarrels by enrolling the girls in the local high school. But whenever they came home from school Juan was waiting for them, machete in hand. He became obsessed with terrorizing them. He carried the machete around with him wherever he went and talked of chopping them up into little pieces to anyone who would listen. Many people warned Marta of Juan's threats, but she would dismiss them as all talk, clarifying that Juan would never dare hurt them or anyone else. But Lady Q didn't believe this. She felt threatened even though she wasn't afraid of Juan.

The war zone conditions in their house were well known throughout the small Aguadilla community, including at the girls' school. Some teased them; others accepted them. Their reputation for not hesitating to use violence, however, spared them from too much mockery. The girls understood very well that they lived in a microscopic civil war and took every necessary precaution to survive, including engaging the enemy when needed while attempting to disarm him.

But Juan knew about Lady Q and Jazmin's plan to take the machete away from him, and he never left it farther than a few inches away. A couple of weeks after they returned, Juan entered the house one day and found Jazmin in the kitchen. He began arguing with her. His overwhelming size compared to Jazmin's seemed to give him courage, and he put the machete down on the counter farther away from himself than usual, though he still stood between the machete and Jazmin. Lady Q entered the room, unbeknownst to Juan, and walked slowly up behind him. She took the machete off the counter before he could react. Juan froze as Lady Q stood before him with the machete, ready to defend herself. He stared at her. She stared at him. No one said a word. In an instant the hunter had become the hunted. Juan was noticeably nervous.

Jazmin broke the silence as she walked out of the kitchen purposely close to Juan saying *"Mira este pendejo. ¿Y ahora, hah, y ahora?"* ("Look at this coward. What about now, huh, what about now?") Lady Q stood tall and looked intimidating. She thought about putting the machete to use, but the longer she stared at Juan's nervous figure, the more she realized he wasn't worth her time. She'd always had an inkling that Juan would be powerless without his trusty machete at his side.

Lady Q walked outside and around to the side of the house and threw the machete as hard as she could toward the top of the roof of the house. In an instant the weapon and the threat it posed were gone. She walked back into the house and found Juan still standing where she had left him. She walked past him into the kitchen, and he didn't flinch or say a word. Juan left the house, got into his car, and quickly drove off.

In many ways Lady Q was proud of the way she'd behaved in this situation. But her euphoria was short-lived as soon as she realized that Juan would eventually come back home, likely to be carrying some new weapon. She also worried that the events of the day might embolden Juan to be more assertive. Perhaps the next time he would find the courage to use his new weapon. Lady Q shared her concerns with Jazmin and cautiously awaited his return.

Several hours went by and still no Juan. The girls told their mother what had happened. After a bit of yelling and screaming she assured them that Juan wouldn't do anything to harm them. She, too, believed that Juan was a blowhard.

As the afternoon gave way to night, a car drove up to the house and stopped in the driveway just short of the carport. Lady Q immediately went to the door to see who was there and saw a police car with two officers. The officers headed toward the door as Lady Q called out for her mother. The officers advised Marta that they would have to take Lady Q and Jazmin to the police station for questioning about the incident that had taken place earlier that day.

Lady Q asked why they had to go to that station if they were only defending themselves. She explained to the officers about the machete Juan carried around and threatened them with and how her only action was to take it and throw it on top of the roof so he couldn't use it against them. The officers took the lateness of the day under consideration and let the girls stay home but advised them they needed to come down to the station first thing in the morning. The police told Juan to spend the night at a relative's home to avoid further conflict.

Early the next morning, as the family prepared to present themselves before the authorities, a police car, again carrying two officers, drove up to their home. The officers talked briefly with Marta and then asked Lady Q where she had thrown the machete. Lady Q led the officers to the spot beside the house where she had thrown the machete up to the roof, and then she went back inside, now filled with questions. Anxiety engulfed Lady Q as the officers walked around the house looking for a way to get up on the roof. Minutes later they came back inside the house with the machete in hand, advised Marta that her daughters would have to come with them to the station, and gave her directions how to get there. Lady Q and Jazmin went with the officers without protest. They sat in the backseat without saying a word to the officers or to each other. Lady Q was scared about what could happen at the station, but she hoped the police would side with two terrorized young women over a machete-wielding maniac.

At the station the girls were taken to a room that seemed spacious only because there were no furnishings except a long table. One of the officers sat across from them as another left the room, then returned with a plainclothes cop carrying a file. This officer sat at the end of the table closest to the girls, opened the file, and began reading the accusations Juan had made against them: that Lady Q had threatened him with the machete on the day of the incident and that both girls had threatened to kill him since their arrival from Chicago. He claimed that the girls were the aggressors who carried the machete around as a means to attack him whenever he attempted to curb their unruly ways.

After the officer finished reading Juan's allegations aloud, the girls couldn't help but laugh. The officers weren't amused. The uniformed officer led Jazmin into another room, and Lady Q was left to talk to the plainclothes cop. She detailed for the officer their unwelcome reception upon arriving from Arecibo and how Juan was the one who'd carried the machete around with him from that day forward. Lady Q explained how Juan routinely made threats to chop her and Jazmin up and how this was a well-known fact around their community. She told the officer that the only time Juan called her by her name was to make direct death threats; otherwise he called her *puta* ("bitch"), *cabrona* ("asshole"), *desgraciada* ("disgrace"), and worse.

The officer sat there in disbelief at the monster Lady Q had painted. He left the room for about fifteen minutes and came back with Jazmin. He offered the girls a drink and something to eat and told them to sit and wait in that room until the officers had a chance to investigate their claims. They sent a squad car to the community where they lived to inquire about Juan's constant threats on the girls' lives. A sense of relief washed over Lady Q. She felt certain that many would bear witness to her claims.

Several hours later the girls were driven home by two officers. The investigation had uncovered nearly a dozen accounts of Juan declaring his plans to chop up the girls into little pieces. The insulting way he addressed the girls was also corroborated. Lady Q and Jazmin were vindicated. Now Juan was in hot water. They arrived in the police car just as the police were arresting Juan. His extended family quickly bailed him out, but a restraining order was served against him prohibiting him from going anywhere near the house or the girls until a judge heard the case.

Lady Q felt joy that there was finally peace in the house— no angry screaming, fighting, or fear of confrontations. There was plenty of money in the bank from Juan's illegal dealings, and there was no man in the house to come between the girls and their mother.

Lady Q became more relaxed and friendlier, which allowed her to gain confidence and develop camaraderie with girls her age. She became friends with other girls who were big fans, as she was, of the Puerto Rican singing group Menudo. Lady Q became so involved in the Menudo fan club that a teacher who knew someone involved with the group not only got her tickets for a concert but also backstage passes to meet the group. This was one of the happiest days of her life up to this point.

About a month after the incident with Juan, it came time to go before the judge. Lady Q didn't worry because she knew that the law was on her side. Juan's big mouth had pretty much guaranteed that the judge would rule against him. He would more than likely be asked to stay away from the house permanently—it wouldn't matter that it was his home.

As expected, the judge found Juan guilty of malicious behavior and ordered the restraining order to become permanent until Lady Q, who was now seventeen, and Jazmin, who was now fourteen, were either twenty-one or were out of the house and out on their own. After the verdict was given, however, Marta immediately dropped the charges against Juan and asked that the restraining order be removed since she planned to move the family back to Chicago. The judge granted her request, but Juan would have to stay away from his house until all other family members vacated the home.

Lady Q felt mixed emotions about the decision. She wanted Juan punished, but at the same time she welcomed the opportunity to return to Chicago, a place where her opinion mattered. Juan wasted no time and immediately purchased one-way airplane tickets back to Chicago for Lady Q and the rest of her family. Within two weeks of the judge's decision, Juan was back in his house and Lady Q and her family were on a flight back to Chicago. After eight months away, Lady Q was heading back to the 'hood to reclaim her throne among the Latin Queens.

6

THE BENEFITS of RoYALTY

THE FLIGHT ACROSS the ocean again conjured up many dreams of future happiness. Lady Q looked forward to seeing the members of the Latin King/Queen Nation and to taking her place within the gang without a thought to how she would be received. Deep down she understood that it didn't matter whether she returned with stories of success or misfortune. The gang would welcome her back and accept her. That, after all, was what made gang life so attractive. She felt empowered as the plane touched down at O'Hare International Airport. Not only did she feel like she was home, but also, now that the gang had accepted her as one of their own, she was in the only place in the world where nobody could hurt her without repercussions.

It was the middle of November when her family returned to Chicago, and although not officially winter yet, it was bitterly cold. Lady Q, her mother, Jazmin, and her three younger siblings would be staying with Vivian. Six people would be added to a one-bedroom apartment that was already shelter to three. Bodies were scattered all over the couches and floor that first night as Vivian and RJ occupied the lone bedroom. Marta scrambled to get on welfare and obtained winter coats for herself and her children from a local church. Even with these difficulties the holidays always included many Christmas presents for everyone. No matter how dire their circumstances, Christmas was always a day filled with abundance. It was a temporary joy.

The relationship between Lady Q and Vivian had not changed—it was as contentious as ever—so it wasn't long before Lady Q's primary residence became the streets. She went back to hanging out with the Queens and Kings since not even the worst winters kept gangs from hanging around outdoors. The comrades she'd left behind welcomed her with open arms, except for her mentor Reina, who was in jail again. Delighted that her absence hadn't depleted the respect she had earned from other gang members, Lady Q returned to being a role model to younger and older Queens alike, mostly girls relegated to the streets who had no choice but to join a gang for self-preservation. By all definitions Lady Q was the same kind of lost soul, only she hid it more effectively than the rest by standing up for those she considered her brothers and sisters and by always showing her willingness to endure punishment on their behalf when needed. This set her apart and brought her to the attention of Latin Kings who made decisions, created sections, or kingdoms, and appointed leaders to these kingdoms.

Lady Q was soon a regular figure at all major gatherings hosted by the Latin King/Queen Nation around the Humboldt Park area. She was asked to hold guns and drugs while she was on the streets and became one of the few Queens entrusted to accompany the Kings on hits. Many Latin Queens vied for this honor but few received it. Taking part in hits, even in the most insignificant of roles, separated the most trusted and respected Queens from those considered merely hangers-on. Lady Q was doubly honored because Kings sought her out to take part in hits without her even having to ask.

The first couple of hits Lady Q participated in were, for the most part, uneventful. They drove around in cars looking for rivals, and she held guns that weren't used or that she didn't witness being fired. Nevertheless, her willingness to take part in the activity and keep what happened to herself made her the first choice for hits where a Queen's presence was helpful. Two or more brothers in a car by themselves might arouse suspicion, but in the company of a woman, they became invisible to cops. Lady Q loved the role she played, and her joy in performing these duties only added to her rising stature within the kingdom.

In the 'hood people hurt one another, betray each other, even kill each other, but life goes on quickly. Resentments don't last. And what is the cause for strife one day is not expected to make a difference the next. The only unforgivable thing is when someone changes gang allegiances; this is cause for mortal retaliation.

Lady Q's allegiance was clear, and as her popularity grew Gigi and Jazmin began to accompany her on her all-night explorations of the streets. While Jazmin carried her own respect as a girl eager to fight, Gigi was more of a hanger-on. Wherever Lady Q went, Gigi was bound to follow; otherwise, she remained in the one-bedroom apartment that she was allowed to call home. But these all-night runs didn't sit well with RJ, not because he was concerned about their well-being but because he didn't like to get high alone.

RJ had become the dominant male figure that had been missing from this family for a long time, but unfortunately he had none of the qualifications required to fulfill this role. He imposed decisions based on self-gratification and not on the health and well-being of the family. RJ's main goal in life was to get high, and because he wanted to have someone there with him while he partied, he imposed a nine-thirty curfew on the girls. Vivian backed him up in this decision. Lady Q thought the curfew was ludicrous but went along with it mainly because she didn't want to create a fight between herself and her mother. She had not argued with Marta since Juan's dismissal from their home in Puerto Rico—a little shy of three months—and she wanted it to stay that way.

Lady Q hung with the Latin Kings and Queens of Kedzie and Armitage and found it difficult to keep the curfew RJ set. Inevitably she broke it, and this set off a series of events that would define the rest of Lady Q's life and make 1984 a year she would rather forget.

One night in the heart of winter, Lady Q arrived home just before nine-thirty and found that Jazmin and Gigi weren't home yet and would certainly be in violation of RJ's curfew. She knew that the girls kissed RJ's ass to stay on his good side and wondered if he would take any action against them. When Jazmin and Gigi arrived, RJ started giving them shit about breaking curfew. He sounded more like a father than a brother-in-law, and for some reason he included Lady Q in his attempts to discipline them.

Lady Q had never liked RJ and wasn't shy about letting him know it. When RJ scolded Lady Q she responded, "Fuck you, you swear you're my father." RJ demanded that Lady Q respect and obey the rules of his house. Tonight Lady Q could not hold her tongue. "Your house?" Lady Q began. "Motherfucker, this is my *sister's* house. She pays for everything. If it wasn't for her you'd be a homeless bum."

Lady Q truly believed that RJ was just a parasite leeching off Vivian and that if it weren't for Vivian's willingness to support him, he wouldn't be with her. Her words touched on RJ's most sensitive issue—his cherished manhood. His anger transformed into rage and he grabbed Lady Q by the neck, pushed her up against the wall, and choked her as he yelled obscenities and demanded that she respect him. When he let go Lady Q immediately ran out of the apartment, went to a pay phone, and called the police.

It took a couple of hours before the police showed up to investigate. This was the normal response time for a reported domestic dispute in Humboldt Park. The police responded much more quickly if a white person was involved or there was a report of a Puerto Rican with a gun. By the time the cops arrived, RJ was long gone and no one claimed to know where he was. Predictably Vivian and her mother took RJ's side and told the cops that it had been a personal skirmish that didn't require police intervention. Their excuses, also the norm when it came to domestic disputes reported in Humboldt Park, were also partly why the police typically responded so slowly. After the police left, the only thing that mattered to Vivian was getting Lady Q out of her house. Vivian kicked her out that night. She also told her mother she'd have to find another place to live for herself and the kids. Within the week Marta rented an apartment across the courtyard. During that time Lady Q slept in the homes of various Latin Queens and vowed to leave home for good when she turned eighteen in a few months.

While Lady Q waited to become an adult in the eyes of the law, she worked her way up the ranks of the Latin King/Queen Nation by taking part in hits. Chicago's cold weather helped to keep active gang members off street corners. Consequently there were few easy targets. Instead, they congregated in hallways, gangways, or in designated clubhouses. Despite the cold they weren't likely to pass up opportunities to deal drugs or kill a rival gang member in order to send a message of fear throughout the community. On one occasion when Lady Q was present, the Latin Kings did just that.

Little G, a Latin King from Pierce and Spaulding, and Green Eyes, a member of the Armitage and Kedzie section, came around looking for Lady Q to help them execute a hit on the Imperial Gangsters. The Imperial Gangsters had been very active against the Latin Kings that winter. Although the Kings retaliated countless times, they had not yet killed one of their rivals and continued to look for that opportunity. Both Little G and Green Eyes were in their early twenties and seemed destined for a career in gangbanging. Little G was a very handsome and well-known six-foot-plus Puerto Rican with light skin and straight stringy hair. Except for the same light tone of skin, Green Eyes was the total opposite of Little G in appearance. Green Eyes was short and chubby and had a chipped front tooth and countless jailhouse tattoos. But both were senior brothers of the Latin King Nation and were well respected for their ability to exact revenge on rival gangs at a moment's notice.

On the day of the hit, Lady Q was hanging out with a sixteen-year-old African American Latin Queen from Pierce and Spaulding called Cookie. Cookie looked much younger than her age. She was a child of the streets as were her brothers, also members of the Pierce and Spaulding section. Her family used to live in the 'hood but had moved to the South Side. At first glance Cookie looked like a sweet little girl, but she had a violent temper and was quick to take action whenever bodily harm was needed.

Little G and Green Eyes approached Lady Q as she and Cookie walked down Kedzie Avenue on their way to Pierce and Spaulding. Little G pulled up, called them over to the car, and invited them to participate in a hit on a rival gang that would enhance their ranks within the gang. In such situations, gang members really have no choice but to agree, except when they're already doing gang business such as delivering drug money or following through on orders delivered by a higher-ranking gang member.

The girls got into the car and were discreetly given handguns. The car then headed toward Palmer and Drake, the main section of the Imperial Gangsters. The day was cold and the streets were deserted, but the Kings were relentless in their pursuit of a victim and continued to drive around the Palmer and Drake area, expecting that sooner or later a Gangster would appear. Little G drove around so many times that when Green Eyes yelled at him to turn down an alley, Lady Q didn't know where they were. Green Eyes turned around and asked for a gun as the car neared the opposite end of the alley. He put the gun in his waistband, got out of the car, and hurried through a gangway. Little G drove to the intersection at the end of the alley, turned in the opposite direction, and drove the car around the block. A minute or two later he drove down the street where Green Eyes was headed.

Lady Q saw Green Eyes standing three-quarters of the way up the street. Walking toward him was a man in his midtwenties who seemed to be just minding his own business and showed no visible gang affiliation. As the car approached, Green

Eyes pulled out the gun and fired toward the man's head from about two feet away. Lady Q and Cookie began screaming as Green Eyes ran back to the car and got in, and Little G stepped on the gas to speed away from the scene. The girls continued to scream, and Green Eyes reached over the backseat and punched them, telling them to shut up. Seconds later they arrived at Homer and Albany, where the girls were dropped off and told that they would be dealt with for their "pussy-ass" reaction, which had put them all in jeopardy of being caught.

This was Lady Q's first time on a hit when a gun was actually used, not to mention her first close-up look at a person being gunned down in cold blood. She didn't actually see the bullets hit the man but assumed they'd done the intended damage. No retaliation from the Gangsters took place, which led Lady Q to conclude that the victim had been an innocent bystander—just someone walking down the wrong street at the wrong time. In the days that followed, Lady Q found out that the car they had used had been stolen and later abandoned in an alley between the Kings and the Cobra 'hood that was never frequented by either gang. She was also informed that she and Cookie would be punished with a three-minute head-to-toe violation for the way they'd reacted.

In a violation, a higher-ranking gang member chooses who will beat the offending gang member. In a head-to-toe, no part of the body is off limits. The head-to-toe violation Lady Q received was fairly painless as it was performed by girls who were afraid of really hurting her and falling out of her favor. They never touched her face. Cookie, on the other hand, wasn't so lucky. The three girls who violated Cookie pounded on her without mercy and left her face swollen. To

Cookie's credit, she took the beating and threw up the Latin King/Queen hand sign when it was over. She didn't stay away to recover or do anything to hide her wounds—they were battle scars she was proud of. Lady Q's violation taught her the limits of the gang's tolerance.

At about this time Minerva, an old friend of Lady Q's mother and the woman who had taken Vivian in as a teenager when she was at war with Juan, came back into their lives. Marta suggested to Minerva that she and her kids move in with Minerva so they could help each other out financially. Minerva had moved to Michigan for several years. Now three of her kids were teenagers, and only two of them had moved back with her to Chicago. Within the day the two women found and rented a three-bedroom apartment on St. Louis Street and North Avenue. Lady Q remembers how Minerva dominated and manipulated her mother and how Lady Q's disapproval of it made her feel unwanted in their apartment. It didn't matter one way or the other to Lady Q since she hardly ever stepped foot in that apartment and turned eighteen a few weeks after they moved in. Although Lady Q had pretty much already made good on her promise to move out from under her mother's authority, her eighteenth birthday made it official.

Lady Q's birthday marked her new freedom in a number of ways. No longer a minor, she was free to do as she pleased without fear of the cops hauling her back home. It also marked her introduction to drugs. Drugs and alcohol were always around, but up to this point she'd indulged in only alcohol. On her eighteenth birthday a group of Kings and Queens gathered in an apartment on Pierce and Spaulding to celebrate. There was loud music and plenty of beer and marijuana. Lady Q joked around with a King smoking a cigarette and asked him if she could have a hit. She took a long drag off the cigarette and got a head rush, prompting her to believe that it was actually a joint. The King began to laugh at Lady Q and provided her with an actual marijuana cigarette. Lady Q smoked it and within minutes could not control her laughter. She enjoyed this effect and continued to smoke throughout the night. From that night on smoking marijuana became a daily activity.

About a week after her eighteenth birthday, King Little G approached Lady Q with a proposition to become the president of a new section of Latin Queens. The Latin Kings had noticed that a group of kids had begun hanging around the intersection of Spaulding and Wabansia. Although the intersection was considered part of the Latin Kings 'hood, no active members hung out there. The Kings decided to open a new section of the gang on that corner to recruit those kids before another gang took the opportunity. The Latin Kings knew that once a gang won the loyalty of kids it was hard to make them turn their thinking around. So Little G was given the task of opening and maintaining a section on Spaulding and Wabansia. He would be the leader, or "Inca," of that section, and Lady Q would be the head of the Queens.

Becoming the leader of your own gang section is like being given franchise rights to a business. Little G was handed a drug business. He would be allowed to deal on Spaulding and Wabansia and was expected to recruit Latin King and Queen soldiers to defend his business. Little G wanted Lady Q to be the Inca of the Queens of his newly formed section. Lady Q considered this an honor and, after getting the OK from the leader of the Armitage and Kedzie Kings, who was her leader, readily agreed to take on the role. She recruited Cookie and four other girls to make up the Wabansia and Spaulding Latin Queens section.

Almost immediately static started in the 'hood over the creation of a new section, and it didn't come from King rivals. It came from the Whipple and Wabansia Latin King/Queen section located four blocks away. The Queens and Kings from this section protested the creation of a new section in an area they considered part of their kingdom. This new section infringed on their drug territory. A meeting took place to iron out the differences. The Queens from Whipple and Wabansia asked Lady Q to drop her title and to join their long-established section, along with her girls, but relinquishing her new rank and power was out of the question for Lady Q. The two sections reached a compromise—each section would stay within a narrowly defined area to maintain the peace and their customer base.

After the meeting, Lady Q made it clear to her girls that they would be under a microscope. She suspected that some members of the gang expected them to do something stupid that would get someone from the Nation into trouble with the law, or to back down when faced by a rival. Lady Q let her followers know that the only way to earn respect from other gang members was to prove their toughness on the streets and their loyalty to the Nation. It wasn't long before they had an opportunity to do both.

The Queens hanging around with Lady Q and Cookie were all teenagers. Slim was a fifteen-year-old Puerto Rican with a chip on her shoulder. She was attractive, popular, and had two loving parents who owned their own home. Slim was the oldest of three children whose parents gave them just about everything they wanted. Her parents weren't drug dealers, didn't drink or do drugs, and were never involved with gangs. But for whatever reason Slim chose to rebel against them. She spoke to them in a rude and obnoxious manner and snuck out of the house at night to roam the streets, where she was aggressive and actively sought out opportunities to engage in violence. Her ability to defend herself and her loyalty to the Latin King/Queen Nation prompted Lady Q to name her the *cacique* ("vice president") of her section.

Another of Lady Q's girls was a very large fifteen-year-old who was half Puerto Rican and half African American, called Pietra. She was about six feet tall and built like a linebacker. Pietra was a quiet person, but she held a lot of hateful feelings inside. Pietra never made it clear why she was in foster care, but she was quite vocal about hating every home she was placed in and about her nonstop efforts to find her brothers and sisters. Pietra was not yet a member of the gang but asked to be initiated. Lady Q began to make inquiries about this, and in the meantime Pietra became part of her section on a trial basis.

The other two girls were African Americans from the Pierce and Spaulding section. Since the new Spaulding and Wabansia Queens needed members, they were allowed to transfer sections. Their names were Carla and Isabel. Both were sixteen years old. They only came around once in a while, mostly for the meetings. Whenever Carla or Isabel came into the neighborhood they left no doubt they were members of the Latin Queens. If there was action to be taken they didn't hesitate. But overall it was questionable whether or not Carla and Isabel were true Queens or just there to hang out. Whatever their reasons, they were risking their lives.

Time flew by at warp speed for Lady Q. In a very short time she had purposely made the streets of Chicago her primary residence, started smoking marijuana, and earned a leadership position in her own section. She had to prove herself and prove that the section was worthy of existing. When Lady Q and her girls were not on Spaulding and Wabansia selling drugs, they roamed the streets intoxicated on one chemical or another. Lady Q's section quickly became the primary place to obtain LSD in the form of tiny pills called Purple Microdot. The first time Lady Q tried LSD she found that it made her feel as if she could conquer the world while laughing uncontrollably. With an endless supply at hand, tripping on LSD became a constant activity for her.

Oftentimes Lady Q and her girls would go to a restaurant on the corner of Kimball and North Avenue named Donald Duk's to hang out and look for rival gang members. On many occasions Kings would order food and the Queens would come in just as the food was placed into bags and set on the counter. Lady Q and her girls would order drinks and distract the employees, who were usually male, while the Kings walked out with the food without paying. No doubt on more than one occasion the employees knew exactly what was going on, but they weren't willing to risk their lives for a couple of cheeseburgers and fries.

One day close to the beginning of Lady Q's rule of her section, she sat with her Queens at tables just outside the restaurant eating food and smoking weed with several Kings. Everyone at the table was between thirteen and eighteen years of age, with Lady Q being the oldest. Two of the Kings started talking to a couple of thirteen- or fourteen-year-old girls who were walking inside to order food. No big deal; nothing out of the ordinary.

Then Little G drove up, got out of the car to talk to Lady Q, and identified the two girls as ones he had seen hanging out with the Imperial Gangsters, rivals of the Kings. They immediately suspected that the girls had been sent there to meet some Kings and lead them into an ambush. This would not be tolerated. Lady Q told Cookie and Slim what Little G had told her and they immediately took action. Cookie and Slim walked over to the Kings and the two girls and stood between them. Slim asked the girls where they lived and their gang affiliation. One girl made the mistake of saying "We live by the Gangsters but—" and that's all she could get out before Slim began to pummel her face. Cookie followed suit with the other girl. The girls fell onto the concrete and tried to cover themselves while Cookie and Slim stomped and kicked them from every which way. The brutal beating was witnessed by many passersby, none of whom tried to stop the fighting. It wasn't until one of the girls urinated on herself that the beatings stopped.

Slim stood over the girl, who was crying, bleeding from her nose and mouth, and lying in a pool of her own urine, and laughed and called for everyone to come see the spectacle.

"This bitch pee'd on herself!" Slim called out. "Get the fuck out of here and don't you dare come back!" she commanded while she let fly one last kick.

The girls finally managed to stand up and quickly walk away while continuing to cry and in visible pain. The Kings and Queens just laughed.

About ten minutes after the girls left the scene, a car pulled up and a woman who identified herself as one of the girl's mothers yelled out the window, "My daughter is not in a gang! Why did you do that to her?"

"Tell her ass to stay the fuck out of our 'hood and don't think we won't do the same to you," Lady Q responded.

The car pulled away without any further exchange of words. The Kings and Queens quickly left the restaurant expecting the cops to show up. For Lady Q and her young Queens it was a successful night. It helped establish them as a force to be reckoned with.

IT WAS NOW summer, and the Humboldt Park area prepared for the annual celebration of Puerto Rican pride. A carnival set up near the intersection of North Avenue and California, which would run for a week leading up to the Puerto Rican parade. This time of year was when gang violence was most expected and feared. Gangs that surrounded all sides of Humboldt Park flocked to the carnival, more to hunt down rivals than to celebrate their heritage or enjoy themselves. Everyone in the area knew that at one point or another a gang fight would break out; the most they could hope for was that an innocent bystander wouldn't fall victim to the violence. The Chicago Police Department expected gang violence in the days leading up to and including the day of the parade, and especially on the day of the spectacle called Three Kings Day. This year, 1984, they came up with the idea to involve gang members as part of the security team charged with keeping order as a means to control gang activity.

On the day of the parade, the Latin Kings and Queens of Spaulding and Wabansia eagerly anticipated the Humboldt Park festivities. They also chose this occasion to initiate a new member: Pietra would be formally crowned that morning and then everyone would go to the park to celebrate. Pietra was a large, tough girl, so during the three-minute beating that made her a Latin Queen she hardly flinched, and afterward there was no physical sign that the initiation had ever taken place. But this was just the beginning of Pietra's crowning day.

After the initiation, Lady Q and her crew headed to the park just in time to find out about a developing situation. The Chicago Police Department had handed out T-shirts to the gang members serving as security for that day's festivities—yellow shirts with black lettering, with a shade of yellow that very closely matched that worn by members of the Latin Kings. This offended half the handpicked security detail, who were rivals of the Latin Kings. By the time Lady Q arrived, the offended gang members had walked off angrily but were expected to return and challenge the security the Kings provided.

The Kings and Queens roamed the carnival as if it was their own private party as they waited for the crowd that would flood the park at the conclusion of the parade. The Puerto Rican parade began in downtown Chicago and marched up Division Street to the heart of Humboldt Park. Every year hundreds of people gathered along both sides of the street to watch the decorative floats, enjoy the performances, and then head to the park. The closer the parade marched toward its destination, the corner of Division and California, the larger and rowdier the crowd grew inside the park.

As daylight faded, tensions began building as rivals to the Kings began to arrive. Some of the Kings were easy to spot in the black-and-yellow security T-shirts, but many more weren't so easily identified. When a Spanish Cobra began to talk shit to one of the Kings acting as security, it was a King in regular street clothes who responded by coldcocking him in the face, which began a free-for-all. Many plain-clothed participants threw punches every which way. People scattered, and the police slammed combatants to the ground and handcuffed them. Lady Q gathered her girls to make their way back to the 'hood as the cops restored order. As she made her way through the crowd with Slim and Cookie, she found Pietra having what seemed to be a very animated yet friendly conversation with a member of the Latin Disciples, a rival gang to the Latin Kings.

"What the fuck?" Slim said.

"Don't say shit to her," Lady Q advised Slim and Cookie. "We'll deal with her in the 'hood."

Lady Q didn't let on that she'd decided in that moment that Pietra would endure a second beating that day.

A few minutes elapsed before Pietra finally caught sight of Lady Q, Cookie, and Slim and stopped talking to the Disciple. The four girls began walking back to Spaulding and Wabansia smoking a joint and joking around as if nothing were wrong.

When they arrived back in the 'hood, Little G called Lady Q over to him and told her that he had seen Pietra talking with a Latin Disciple, and he wanted to know what she was going to do about it.

"I know, she's got one coming, a head-to-toe," Lady Q told Little G.

Minutes later the Spaulding and Wabansia Latin Kings and Queens gathered in an alley and Lady Q read the riot act to Pietra.

"What the fuck were you doing talking to that flake?" Lady Q asked.

"I know him from when I used to go to school," Pietra answered.

"But you know he's a flake, right, and you're a Queen, so what the fuck were you thinking?" Lady Q demanded.

Before Pietra could answer, Lady Q gave her an ultimatum: "You can either take a three-minute head-to-toe violation so you learn to think twice next time or we can violate you the fuck out. What do you want?"

Right away Pietra said she would take the three-minute head-to-toe. She said she was sorry and that she understood why she was being punished. She also reaffirmed her commitment to the Latin Queens.

Little G was in the alley when Lady Q confronted Pietra, so Lady Q felt she was being judged, too. She believed Little G was assessing her ability to be a leader. She needed to put on a good show, a show of strength.

As the head of a new section of the largest Latino gang in the city of Chicago, Lady Q's role was not to give advice or to educate her girls about the dangerous realities of the streets. Her function was to fill her girls' hearts with hatred for rival gang members so they would defend their gang and their gang's honor without a second thought, even if it meant sacrificing their own life. Her job was to create street soldiers with blind loyalty to the Latin King/Queen Nation.

Lady Q knew her role. She stood before Pietra and called for Slim and Cookie to join her in administering the violation. As soon as Slim and Cookie were at her side, Lady Q punched Pietra squarely on her right eye and sent her stumbling back-ward. A flurry of kicks and punches followed until Lady Q, Slim, and Cookie were exhausted. Pietra lay bleeding and motionless on the dirty concrete in the alley. She was obviously in pain but shed no tears. Finally Lady Q caught her breath,

looked at Pietra, and called out, "She's a sister; help her up."
Wet towels and ice were quickly gathered for Pietra. Even
though she had two black eyes and a fat lip, and walked with
a limp, they walked away united. And from that day forward,
Pietra continued to be a presence in the 'hood and regularly displayed her loyalty to the Nation whenever called upon to do
so. The events of this night further cemented and expanded Lady
Q's reputation for being fearless. She gained prestige in this family of the streets, which fed on each other as much as her birth
family fed on its members. This way of life was familiar to her;
she knew how to survive in this kind of environment. As her
prestige continued to grow, Kings and Queens both young and
old sought her out and confided in her because they knew they
could trust her. The esteem in which she was held was new to
her, and she liked the way it made her feel. To Lady Q the five-
point crown and the black and gold colors represented peace
and equality that turned to violence only when provoked by
rivals. She developed the attitude of a hard-core gang member.

A couple of weeks after Pietra's violation, Popeye—a close
friend and former chief of Lady Q—was murdered by another
Latin King. Popeye's brother Tony got mixed up with a woman
named Rosa, who changed boyfriends every week. When Tony's
number was up and Rosa moved on to another man, Tony
became irate and argued with the guy—another Latin King—
in front of Rosa's apartment on the corner of Cortland and
Humboldt Boulevard. When word reached Popeye, he went to
lead his brother away from this potentially volatile situation.
Even with Popeye there, the other guy continued to talk shit and
hurl threats. Popeye told the King to shut up or face the possibility of having to deal with him. Unbeknownst to Popeye

another King, a friend of Rosa's new lover, witnessed the exchange from a window in Rosa's apartment and came down to help his friend, who he believed was about to be jumped. As Popeye led Tony away, Tony broke free and ran back to beat up the new lover. Popeye ran back to grab his brother and lead him away again just as the witness from the window came out the front door of the apartment building with a gun in his hand. Popeye was running at full speed to grab his brother, which gave the impression that both he and Tony were charging Rosa's lover. Popeye caught up to his brother, grabbed him, and pushed him to the ground just as the guy with the gun opened fire. Popeye took four bullets to the head and chest and died instantly.

The story of Popeye's death traveled fast. Lady Q cried when she heard what had happened. Popeye was a nice guy who, like so many others in the 'hood, had been handed a raw deal at birth. That night she decided to avenge his death by taking out the person she felt was responsible for it—Rosa. The Latin Queens from Whipple and Wabansia felt similarly and also took part in the hit. When they arrived at the scene, Popeye's body had already been carried off and the cops were gone. Rosa stood in front of her apartment building with her five-year-old daughter. She saw the Queens coming toward her and immediately grabbed her daughter and ran into her apartment.

Lady Q and Loca, a Queen from Whipple and Wabansia, followed Rosa into the building and ran up to her door, but Rosa had already locked it tight. Lady Q knocked and asked Rosa to come out, coaxing her by saying they only wanted to talk to her. Loca went to find a gun to shoot the lock off the door. As Loca walked down the steps, Lady Q heard Rosa's daughter begin to scream and cry hysterically. Lady Q kept knocking on the door, promising her that nothing would happen to her and that she only wanted to talk to her about Popeye's death to learn the truth. Moments later she heard Loca call out "five-oh!" (police) and then heard footsteps. Lady Q ran toward the back of the building, down the back stairs, and out the back door into the alley. She ran through the gangway and found herself on Whipple Street. Once there she casually walked back to her 'hood. The next day she found out that Queen Dimples from Whipple and Wabansia had been locked up for battery to a child. Rosa had beaten her daughter, then called the cops and reported that the Queens had done it. The police presence gave Rosa the opportunity to disappear from the neighborhood and never return.

To Lady Q's knowledge, the King who killed Popeye was never punished by the gang, even though Popeye had been a section leader. Because he was killed over a woman who was known to sleep around, the feeling was that Popeye should have known better than to let his brother develop deep feelings for such a woman, something that was disrespected among other gang members. Therefore little effort was made to extract revenge for his murder.

7

THE QUEEN of TALK

THE SPRING AND summer of 1984 brought about many changes in Lady Q. She replaced everything and everyone around her with those who were extremely loyal and devoted to promoting her well-being. She had her own Queen section and growing power within the King Nation, and she had no room in her life for family who didn't show her the respect she now required. Lady Q didn't give death or prison a second thought, even while gunplay and criminal activities were part of her daily life. Like so many before her, Lady Q felt untouchable as long she wore a crown, draped herself in black and gold, and surrounded herself with members of the Almighty Latin King/Queen Nation. Never once did she perceive a possible threat from those she believed to be most loyal to her.

As the summer wound down, Lady Q's mother's living arrangements grew sour when Minerva took in a man. Marta moved from the apartment on St. Louis and North Avenue to one across the street from Humboldt Park on North Avenue and Albany that she would share with Vivian and her posse. Along with Vivian, RJ, their son, Marta and three children, and Gigi now lived a woman named Nancy. Nancy, a coworker of Vivian's, had been abandoned by her husband and had a son about the same age as Vivian's son. She represented yet another reason for Lady Q to be absolutely livid at her family. Just about anyone could come and find shelter with her blood relatives except for her. She could only find it among the Latin King/Queen Nation. Every so often Lady Q would show up at her mother's with a major attitude. She usually argued with Vivian or with Jazmin if she was there. Jazmin, now age sixteen and pregnant, lived with her boyfriend, who was rumored to be a member of the Spanish Cobras, a rival gang to the Kings. Whenever Lady Q saw Jazmin, she'd warn her about bringing her boyfriend around, and Jazmin would respond just as aggressively.

About a year had passed since Lady Q and Jazmin had returned to Chicago from Puerto Rico. In Puerto Rico they'd been inseparable. Now, back in Chicago, Lady Q and Jazmin often fought because of Jazmin's boyfriend. Vivian always took Jazmin's side, so Lady Q was again on the outs in her family. She hid her hurt with her disrespectful attitude.

Summer gave way to fall, and Chicago began to display signs of the winter icebox to come. Lady Q took up residence among the Latin Kings and Queens of Pierce and Spaulding. She lived in an apartment one block over on Le Moyne and Spaulding that was a Latin King hangout rented by a twenty-two-year-old single mother on welfare named Flaca. The apartment served as a storage space for guns and drugs, where Latin Kings and Queens could find shelter at any time of day or night. While living there Lady Q became acquainted with the Inca of the Beach and Spaulding Latin Kings, named Cino. Beach and Spaulding, one of the original sections of the Latin Kings, was considered the kingdom above all other King sections, which made its Inca the leader above all other King section leaders on the street.

Through Cino, Lady Q met and became good friends with his sister Mildred. Mildred was unlike any other girl in the 'hood. Although she smoked weed every so often she was not a Queen, did not hang out on the street, and had finished high school and had plans to attend college. She also held a steady job. Mildred routinely encouraged Lady Q to curb her ways and go back to school, but Mildred's words made no impression on Lady Q. She listened out of respect but never considered taking the advice. Compared to her home life, Lady Q was living out a sweet fantasy and saw no reason to change it.

In October 1984 Mildred got ahold of some studio-audience tickets for *AM Chicago*, a live morning talk show hosted by the not-yet-famous Oprah Winfrey. It was this show that shot Oprah to stardom. Mildred invited Lady Q to attend the show with her and said she had a couple of extra tickets, so if Lady Q knew anyone else who wanted to come along she could invite them. On the morning of the show Lady Q, Mildred, Cookie, and Flaca headed downtown, excited about the possibility of being seen on television. They joked about being chosen to ask a question. Lady Q said she would throw up the Kings hand sign if she indeed was selected. On that day there was no reason for her to worry about being mistaken for anything other than a member of the Latin King/Queen Nation, since she was wearing black pants and a yellow T-shirt with black letters across the left breast that read SWALKQN, Spaulding and Wabansia Almighty Latin King/Queen Nation. Her comrade Cookie was styled in similar attire. All they had to do was remove their jackets and the whole world would know what they represented.

The girls arrived at the studio and waited in line outside in the cold. Finally the crowd began to move inside, and the girls settled in their seats waiting for the show to begin. The topic of that day's show was girls in gangs and featured an author from New York who had written a book on the subject. As they waited for the show to begin, one of the producers came by and struck up a conversation with Mildred. Mildred told the producer about Lady Q and Cookie's gang affiliation, and the producer asked the girls if they wanted to be part of the panel. If they participated, the show would treat all four of the girls to an all-expenses-paid luncheon. Lady Q and Cookie instantly agreed, and the producer took them into a small room where they were given release papers to sign. Lady Q signed the release but didn't read it. They were each fitted with a wireless microphone and escorted onstage to a couple of seats next to where the author would sit.

Lady Q and Cookie looked around the studio in awe as preparations continued and the crowd filled the seats. Lady Q was excited to be on television. The show was taped live, so she figured no one in the 'hood would see them because the show was on so early in the morning. Lady Q was excited but nervous because she didn't know what kinds of questions Oprah would ask. Moments later Oprah came out and stood between the rows of seats directly in front of the stage as she was introduced by an unseen announcer. It was time to start the show.

The book author had the first ten minutes of the show, and then Oprah turned her focus to Lady Q and Cookie. She asked Lady Q how the gang made money. Lady Q responded that it wasn't like the gang broke into anybody's house or cars to make their money. She simply replied, "We have our ways." She told Oprah and the audience how much the black and gold colors mean to the Latin Queens. She also talked about how any stranger in the 'hood would be stopped and questioned. They'd be asked where they were from and what they ride (their gang affiliation). She explained that if the person said the wrong thing, such as mentioned a rival gang, then that person would get moved on (beat up). She said anyone who came into their 'hood wearing black and blue (the colors of the Maniac Latin Disciples) or black and green (the Spanish Cobras) and especially black and pink (the Insane Gangsters—their archrivals) would get moved on. Lady Q talked up the Latin Kings/Queens' toughness and the need for others to respect and fear them.

While Lady Q and Cookie spoke, their real names, nicknames, and gang affiliations were displayed on the television screen for all Chicago viewers to see. Lady Q and Cookie didn't know the show's producers were doing this. They monopolized the show with their bragfest, so this identifying information was also displayed for most of the show. After the show Oprah thanked the girls, and the producer gave them her business card, told them to call her if they needed anything, and directed them to the five-star restaurant where they would receive their promised luncheon. No one from the show accompanied them to the luncheon. Mildred celebrated alongside the others.

Everyone in the restaurant was white, from the customers to the employees. The customers were high-society types wearing expensive clothing and expressionless faces. They looked like corpses to Lady Q. Even as the other diners stared at the four young ladies who were out of place in this elegant restaurant, they still had a vacant look. Their stares bothered Lady Q and she loudly voiced her displeasure, acting obnoxious while the other girls laughed at her antics and joined in from time to time. She mocked the table habits of the other customers. She ordered every item on the menu, knowing that they wouldn't be paying for any of it. The restaurant customers and employees were probably elated when the girls finally left. The feeling was mutual.

On the way back to the 'hood Lady Q felt like a movie star; she felt fantastic. She had just appeared on one of the most popular shows in Chicago. She and Cookie believed that their television appearance, and the way they boasted about the Nation, were cause for celebration. They expected to be showered with compliments and given special treatment for what they'd done. Lady Q noticed back in the 'hood that no Kings or Queens were out on the streets. Cookie and Flaca went to Flaca's apartment, Mildred went home, and Lady Q went to her mother's to see if anyone in her family had watched the show. When she arrived, no one seemed impressed by her appearance, and RJ told her flat out that she was stupid. He warned her that she had broken a law of the Latin Kings and would probably face severe consequences because of the things she had said on *AM Chicago*.

Lady Q's generation of Queens and Kings hadn't been taught the gang's laws, yet when they broke one of these laws, they still faced the consequences. One of the laws was not to set yourself out to the media. No gang, especially one as large as the Latin Kings, wanted to call attention to itself.

Lady Q became very upset at the idea that her adopted family, the only people who showed her any type of caring, would hurt her for representing them proudly in front of the entire city. She argued her point with her family and then left angry. She dismissed their words as yet another instance of her relatives failing to support her or anything she did. In her mind the Latin Kings were her true family and would honor her for what she'd done.

Lady Q rapidly walked through the park to her own apartment, still furious over the encounter in her mother's apartment. When she arrived she found Cookie there and told her what her relatives had said. They laughed about it and decided that jealousy explained their reaction. Cookie's brothers and Flaca congratulated them but in a subdued way. There was no fanfare, no big celebration. A bit disappointed, Lady Q quickly returned to her regular routine of sitting around and getting high.

By about seven o'clock that night it was dark and chilly outside and not much warmer inside. Lady Q continued smoking. She was joined by Cookie, Flaca, and Cookie's brothers, while Flaca's kid played in the same room breathing in the marijuana smoke. They listened to WBMX's Friday Night Dance Party. At the start of a song Lady Q really liked she went to turn it up. The radio was up against the front wall of the apartment. Flaca left the room with her kid to put her to bed. While Lady Q bent toward the radio she heard a clicking sound on the window, as if someone had thrown little rocks at it trying to get her attention. Before she knew what was happening, the window shattered. Everyone left in the room ran into the back of the apartment except for Lady Q, who fell into and was now trapped in her chair by the window. She couldn't move. Everyone waited for the shooting to stop. Finally, one of Cookie's brothers got up carefully and looked through the completely destroyed front window. There was no reaction from the street. He announced it was safe for everyone to get up.

As they inspected the window frame and walls near the front of the apartment, it became apparent that the booming noises had come from a sawed-off shotgun that had shot pellets into the apartment. They'd heard no car driving up or speeding away so they knew the shooter was local. And if the shooter was local, then the shooter had to be a Latin King. Everyone immediately concluded that the attack was payback for Lady Q and Cookie's appearance on *AM Chicago*. Cookie's brothers grabbed her and headed out the back door to lead her out of the 'hood and to safety. Lady Q followed close behind. When they reached North Avenue, a bus was just pulling up. Cookie and her brothers jumped on the bus while Lady Q ran like a bat out of hell toward her family's apartment. As she ran she decided that the shots were more than a warning. She felt certain that more reprisals would quickly follow, and she had to get out of town. She hoped her family would drop everything and do what they could to get her to safety.

Lady Q reached the first-floor apartment and knocked frantically. Her little brother opened the door, and she pushed past him and ran inside looking for her mother. Her face was flushed, her eyes bloodshot, and she couldn't contain her tears. Lady Q found her mother sitting at the dining room table with Vivian and her friend Nancy.

"*¿Que te pasa?*" ("What's wrong with you?"), her mother asked.

"*¡Me quieren matar!*" ("They want to kill me!"), Lady Q yelled.

"The Kings came after you because of the show, right?" Vivian asked matter-of-factly.

Just then RJ entered the room. "I thought your people were going to take care of you?" he said sarcastically. "I told you, you had one coming." Lady Q was too hysterical and scared to give a second thought to RJ's tone or words.

"I need to get out of Chicago," she told Vivian. *"Me tengo que ir para Puerto Rico"* ("I have to go to Puerto Rico"), she told her mother. She told her family about what had happened at Flaca's while she sat with her face in her hands, crying and trembling.

The family realized the seriousness of the situation and scrambled to various places in their homes to gather enough money together to get Lady Q out of town. Lady Q remembered that the *AM Chicago* producer had told her to call if she needed anything. She reached into her pocket for the business card. "Call this lady! Call this lady; she said they would help!" Lady Q yelled as she held the business card out at arm's length. RJ took the card and went to the nearest pay phone to call. He reached the producer and told her what had happened and that they didn't have the funds to get Lady Q out of town. The producer apologized and said that unfortunately the show could do nothing to help.

It became evident that there was no way for Lady Q to leave immediately for Puerto Rico. Vivian came up with a more financially reasonable solution—a bus ticket. Marta had a sister and brother who lived in the Amish area of Pennsylvania, in a little town called Lancaster. She called them and begged them to take Lady Q. The family in Pennsylvania agreed. Lady Q's family pooled the money they had on hand for a Greyhound bus ticket. The bus left in the very early hours of the next day, which was Halloween. It would be a long and uncomfortable twenty-hour bus ride, but Lady Q didn't care. If this was her only way out, she would take it.

For the rest of the evening and well into the night, Lady Q jumped at every sound she heard outside. She felt that she was relatively safe because RJ was a Latin King, so the chances of them attacking the apartment were slim. She tried to stay calm and control her fear by smoking marijuana with RJ. She tuned him out while he talked shit to her about the whole incident. Finally at four in the morning she hopped into Nancy's car with a few possessions in a paper bag and a little money. Her mother went with them, too. Nancy drove them to the downtown Grey-hound station. All the way to the bus station she ducked so she couldn't be seen. She couldn't believe what her so-called friends had done to her. If Mildred hadn't supplied the tickets, this whole situation wouldn't be happening. Lady Q knew it was her own big talk that had threatened her safety, but she still felt alone and unsure who she could trust or what this place called Lancaster or her relatives there would be like.

When they arrived at the bus station, Lady Q was thrilled to learn that her bus was already loading. She hugged her mother and Nancy, boarded, and walked to the back of the bus, checking out who was sitting in each seat. Once she assured her-self there were no Kings on the bus, she sat down. It wasn't until she was an hour inside Indiana that Lady Q began to feel safe and her survival instincts returned.

As fear left Lady Q's mind and body, reality set in and she began silently crying. She couldn't understand why the Kings had betrayed her or why they would try to kill her for representing them proudly on live television. She believed if anything they should have been happy to know how loyal and dedicated she was to the Nation. The Latin Kings no longer wanted her around and this hurt Lady Q deeply—more than anything her blood family had ever done to her. She realized that when the shit hit the fan a gang member, no matter how loyal, stands alone. She also came to terms with the reality that even within the family of the gang she was ultimately on her own. It had been less than one year since she had been made Queen of her own section. She had failed and was leaving her girls behind to fend for themselves. Lady Q cursed Oprah Winfrey and her staff for not helping her in her hour of need.

As she replayed the events leading up to her appearance on the show, she decided that it wasn't merely chance that had made those tickets available, and there wasn't any chance involved in how she was picked out of the crowd to be interviewed. She realized that Mildred must have had some kind of connection to that show and had agreed to bring some ignorant victims from the 'hood to serve her needs. Lady Q felt betrayed and thought that Mildred needed to be dealt with for putting her and Cookie in that dangerous position.

But Mildred was never dealt with because she wasn't in the gang, and Mildred was also the sister of Cino, the Inca of Beach and Spaulding, so she was protected.

8

ALL IN THE FAMILY

LADY Q HAD plenty of time on the bus to clear her head from the series of events that had spiraled out of control, forced her out of Humboldt Park, and led her to a place completely foreign to her. She wasn't able to sleep on the bus and never got off to get something to eat when it stopped for fuel, so when the bus pulled into the terminal in Lancaster, Pennsylvania, around noon, she was exhausted.

Two uncles met her at the terminal. She didn't know them and they didn't know her, so connecting in the terminal was a bit of a challenge. On the drive to her aunt's home, Lady Q stared out the window at the new place she'd call home; no words were spoken. Nothing looked remotely similar to the urban environment where she'd spent her entire life. Here she was in a small town best known for its Amish community. There were rolling green hills and trees all over the place. Here she would be known just as Sonia again—not as the tough Queen Lady Q. The only similarity to Chicago was the cold.

Sonia arrived to a houseful of relatives she had never met. It was a small two-story home owned by her aunt and uncle, who had lived there for many years. Maria, Sonia's aunt, was a short woman with a medium build and graying hair who wore glasses. Luis, Maria's son, also lived there. Flora, Maria's daughter, and her four children who lived down the street were also there to greet Sonia. Also in the greeting party—and a resident of the house—was another aunt of Sonia's. Her two sons and daughter were visiting from Puerto Rico and were also there. Altogether there were nine people living in this small home— Sonia made it ten—so she was quite relieved when she learned that a small maid's chamber–like bedroom on the first floor by the kitchen was reserved for her. Sonia needed time and space to fully evaluate the circumstances that had brought her to this place. She was grateful for the room away from everyone else.

Sonia's first day in Lancaster went by uneventfully and quickly. She met a lot of her extended family for the first time and felt welcomed by everyone. She quickly realized that there would be no shortage of beer in this house and no shortage of marijuana as long as she hung out with Flora's son Pedro, who was Sonia's age. That first night, after everyone had gone to bed, Sonia lay on the twin-size bed in her room, which was only slightly larger than the bed itself. She stared at the ceiling while listening for the familiar street sounds of the city, but heard nothing. No cars drove by, no one was shouting, and there was no echo of gunshots to break the silence of the night. A feeling of peace that she was unaccustomed to overwhelmed Sonia. She thought about what the future held for her and knew this was an opportunity for a new start if she was ready to take advantage of it.

For the next couple of months, however, Sonia did very little other than help her aunt around the house and hang out with Pedro and his friends smoking weed. At first she had second thoughts about joining Pedro in his daily activity because she worried she was heading in the same direction that had almost gotten her killed. But the drinking in her aunt's home was constant. It wasn't long before her two male cousins visiting from Puerto Rico, Julio and Pablo, made her uneasy with the way they'd stare at her in a sexually intimidating way. She thought about telling her Aunt Maria about her discomfort, but she'd noticed that Maria was in many ways not just their aunt but also their drinking buddy, so she thought better of the idea.

Soon Julio began knocking on Sonia's bedroom door after everyone had gone to bed, saying he wanted to talk to her about the family. Sonia was skeptical but initially all her cousin did was ask questions about the family back in Chicago and tell her about Puerto Rico. As his nightly visits continued, however, his true intentions were revealed as he started to lace his conversations with sexual innuendo. Coming from the streets and being wise to the ways of men, Sonia wasn't fooled for a minute and refused to go along with any kind of verbal sex play he introduced. Julio became frustrated with her lack of response and finally flat out suggested that they have sex. Sonia asked him to leave her room or else threatened to make a scene loud enough that everyone would come running. This was the end of Julio's pursuit of her but not her wariness of him and Pablo. From that point on, every time she saw either of them she was reminded of the sexual abuse she'd suffered at the hands of her uncle and cousin. She'd been a little girl then, unable to defend or protect herself. But things were different now, and she wasn't about to let anyone hurt her in that way again. The sight of them now disgusted her. The only way she found to avoid them was to befriend Pedro.

Pedro belonged to a crew who called themselves a street gang and congregated in the basement of one of its female members. The crew consisted of eleven or twelve teenagers who got together to drink and get high and tried hard to emulate the gangster rappers they saw on television. But Sonia knew this wasn't a real gang. For one thing, there were no rival gangs in Lancaster to define them or their territory. Without an outside enemy, they regularly fought among themselves. Sonia enjoyed their company and saw through their feigned toughness. She realized each member of the crew needed to belong to a group to avoid loneliness. In this way they were no different than the real gangs back in Chicago.

Two months after Sonia arrived at her Aunt Maria's house, the welcome mat began to wear thin. Her aunt and uncle demanded that she either start going to school or get a job, and Sonia knew that it was in her best interest to do something other than drink and get high all the time. She decided to get a job but was full of anxiety at the thought. Although she was now nineteen years old, she had never filled out a job application before. She'd dropped out of school at fifteen but had been a good student, so filling out the applications wouldn't be difficult. She just had to steel her nerves to do it. She figured employers wouldn't expect her to have much job experience anyway, given her age. She decided to apply almost exclusively at fastfood restaurants, where she assumed they were more likely to consider hiring a young woman with no previous employment history.

Sonia was lucky. She was hired at a burger joint right away—first application, first job—and then was hired for a second position as a dishwasher at a fancy restaurant three weeks later. Suddenly Sonia found herself making friends who did nothing but work as they planned their future. That attitude rubbed off on her and she began to enjoy having her own money to spend, being treated like a respectable young adult, and having responsibilities. She was extremely happy with how things were shaping up for her in Lancaster and began to think of it as the place she wanted to spend the rest of her life. But Sonia continued to hang out with Pedro when she wasn't working and consequently was still drinking excessively and smoking marijuana.

Because of her friendship with Pedro, Sonia also became close to his mother, Flora, and divided her time between Flora's home and her Aunt Maria's home. Staying at Flora's allowed Sonia to get away from her drunken cousins but not away from alcohol altogether since Flora also drank. Sonia enjoyed hanging out at Flora's house because there were other kids around her own age, but she was closest to Pedro, who had taken the time to show her around when she'd first arrived and had introduced her to his friends.

Sonia had arrived in Lancaster in October. By February of the following year she had settled into a comfortable routine and continued to hang out with Pedro. One day Sonia and Pedro were at his house watching television and drinking beer when he invited her to take a walk so they could smoke a joint. They started walking and smoking and when they were about two blocks away from his house and out of sight from anyone who knew them, Pedro stepped in front of Sonia and kissed her. Sonia was surprised, but she also welcomed the kiss because she had begun to feel things for him. From that point on the two of them looked for opportunities to be together without being seen by other family members. They were second cousins, and although this extended family was dysfunctional in numerous ways, they would not accept a relationship between cousins. Incest was one of the few remaining taboos.

Pedro and Sonia were a couple for almost two months without anyone else knowing. But as they spent more time together their passion grew, and they became increasingly daring. One day they were in Pedro's room involved in some heavy petting. They thought they were alone, but Pedro's little sister walked in and caught them. Pedro threatened her with bodily harm if she said anything, and Sonia pleaded with her to stay quiet. She agreed to keep the secret, but ten-year-olds don't always see the importance of keeping secrets and later that day she told her mother, Flora, what she'd seen. By the time Sonia returned from work and entered her Aunt Maria's home, her aunt, uncle, and all the other relatives in the house had worked themselves into a frenzy. She walked through the front door and was immediately bombarded with the same question in both English and Spanish: "How could you?! He's your cousin!" Sonia was shocked at the intense reaction and didn't know what to say or do. Soon her relatives began hurling insults. The fact that many of them had been drinking only made things worse.

In the end too many hurtful words were thrown back and forth, and Sonia was kicked out of Maria's house. Meanwhile Pedro received the same treatment in his own home and he, too, was kicked out of his house. Pedro and Sonia agreed that they didn't care what other family members thought and felt that being second cousins shouldn't prevent them from loving and caring for each other. Further, no one had the right to keep them from being together. Pedro took Sonia to his friend's house, where they decided they'd stay until they could get their own apartment.

While Pedro and Sonia had engaged in heavy petting, they hadn't had intercourse. So far Sonia had only been with assholes—and had been abandoned by the same—so she moved more cautiously before deepening this relationship. But the excitement and anxiety over the circumstances that now forced them together unleashed a passionate excitement that led them to start having sex the day they moved into their friend's house. The sex wasn't planned and it wasn't protected.

After several weeks together, Pedro went for a walk one day and never came back. His family had accepted him back home—but Sonia was no longer welcome. Suddenly she found herself in the home of a man she didn't know, with nowhere else to go.

Sonia was still working. She befriended a young woman named Millie who lived next door. Millie was a tall, slender, attractive twenty-six-year-old single mother who held her head high and carried herself with respect. Millie's husband had been unfaithful, and she'd left him after deciding that she could provide for her little two-year-old daughter without the help of a man. After Pedro walked out on Sonia, Millie asked her to move in, suggesting they could help each other and share expenses. Sonia accepted the invitation with relief. Millie didn't smoke cigarettes or anything else and drank only socially. In all, Millie was a good influence and role model. Sonia didn't need Pedro and didn't need her relatives. As far as she was concerned they were a bunch of hypocritical alcoholics who readily demonized the mistakes of others while making excuses for their own behavior. She made it her goal to succeed to show them all.

Sonia continued to work her two jobs. She was not around her extended family and hadn't heard from Pedro and had no regrets. She stopped drinking as much and smoked weed less often, too. But soon Sonia noticed she was gaining weight around her midsection. She attributed this to the junk food she ate at her fast-food restaurant job. As the months passed she continued to gain weight and began to feel changes in her body. She continued to get her period on time every month, so the thought of being pregnant never crossed her mind. Then one day at her fancy restaurant job she saw that frog legs were being prepared. She had seen this dish prepared daily for nearly four months and had never had a problem. But now she became nauseated, light-headed, and dizzy and finally fainted. She was lucky she didn't hurt herself fainting in the middle of a busy kitchen with blunt objects all around. When she came to, coworkers were hovering around her trying to revive her. She declined medical attention and decided to go home.

As Sonia walked outside and away from the restaurant she still felt weak and sick, but the outside air made her feel better. She made it home safely, but she didn't understand why she had fainted or felt poorly and started to worry about her health. Getting fat was one thing, but fainting at work was quite another, so she made an appointment to see a doctor two days after the incident.

For the next couple of days Sonia only went to her burger-joint job where, thankfully, the food being prepared didn't affect her. Otherwise, she stayed home caring for Millie's daughter. By the day of the appointment she was on edge and fearing the worst. While she waited she silently prayed that there was nothing seriously wrong with her. At the end of the exam she was given good and bad news—the good news was that she was in very good health; the bad news was that she was pregnant. Sonia was shocked, then she completely denied it was a possibility and questioned the doctor's diagnosis.

"I'm still getting my period, I can't be pregnant," she insisted.

"It's possible for women to be pregnant and continue to have their period," the doctor responded.

Regardless of how Sonia tried to deny the obvious, it was no use. She was going to be a mother, and Pedro was the father. Sonia didn't believe in abortion so she never considered this option. She contacted Pedro to give him the news, but he didn't care and neither did his family. No one wanted to talk to her.

Six months into her pregnancy, Sonia stopped working altogether and applied for and received public aid and food stamps. Millie didn't mind that Sonia had stopped working because she was still able to help out financially and was always available to babysit Millie's daughter.

Sonia's pregnancy progressed without complications, and in the fall of 1985 she gave birth in the local hospital to a beautiful baby girl she named Lisette. She hadn't heard from Pedro or anyone in his family throughout her pregnancy, but after the delivery Millie made it a point to let them know about the baby. Flora forgot her anger and showed up at the hospital to embrace her granddaughter. She also insisted that Sonia move back to her house so that Pedro could be a father to his child. The miracle of life has a way of blinding evil eyes and warming cold hearts.

When Sonia and her newborn child arrived at Flora's, a wellspring of goodwill erupted. The whole family came to see the baby. It seemed as if the shame of cousins being romantically involved had been forgotten. Pedro warmed up to his daughter and to Sonia and talked of a great future for his child. Unfortunately, he didn't understand that to guarantee any kind of successful future for anyone, he had to get and keep a job. While Sonia supported herself and the baby with the aid of the government, Pedro did nothing but leech off her and his mother. As the days and then weeks passed, the initial joy of a new baby in the house wore thin, and battles between Sonia and Flora ensued. Flora would get drunk and bitch at Sonia about not doing enough to get an apartment for herself, the baby, and Pedro, and Sonia responded by reminding her that her son wasn't doing a thing to help make that happen. On top of Flora giving her shit, Pedro began using Sonia's welfare money to support his drug habit. He became enraged whenever she brought up the subject. She suspected that he was involved in something more serious than just smoking marijuana and eventually caught him in the act: Pedro was a heroin addict.

Sonia had seen many heroin junkies on the streets of Chicago and knew how desperate they could get when they needed a fix, so she began taking precautions to ensure that Pedro didn't use what little money they had to get high. Pedro had no clue how to survive without drugs, and being an addict just made him that much more helpless. The only way he could pay for his next fix was to get ahold of Lady Q's money. When he couldn't get it, he began beating her. Day after day Pedro would become sick when his body craved heroin. He would become insane with anger and attack Sonia. She did her best to defend herself and fight back, but she was no match for a man driven into a fury by his need for heroin. The more Sonia fought him, the more ferocious he became and the worse he would beat her. Pedro would leave her crying and bloody, with her face swollen, but she still wouldn't give him her money. She needed it for the baby.

The situation grew worse when Flora, who ignored her son's abuse of Sonia, escalated her verbal assaults on her from once or twice a week to two or three times a day. Sonia wasn't the type to back down from any confrontation, especially when she was positive that she was being attacked unjustifiably. A little more than two months after Sonia had been welcomed back into Flora's home, she was kicked out into the streets, baby and all.

It was November 1985, nearing Thanksgiving, and Lady Q found herself homeless on the streets of Lancaster with a two-month-old child. She had many relatives in that small town, but no one came to her aid. Her friend Millie had moved, and Sonia had no idea how to find her. The bitterly cold winter months were setting in, and the realization that she was homeless was more than Sonia could handle. She found herself in desperate straits with nowhere to go and not knowing what to do. She didn't know if Lancaster had shelters, and even if they did she didn't know how to find them. The only thing she could think about was keeping her baby warm. She wrapped the few items of clothing she left carefully around her.

For the first week, Sonia and Lisette slept in hallways and then walked the streets looking for somewhere to warm up the baby's formula. Sonia breast-fed her daughter as much as she could, but she didn't eat often enough to produce much milk. She found that warm water was easier to come by than a stove to warm up liquid formula, so she began buying powdered formula and mixing it with the warm water to feed her daughter.

Night after night she huddled over her little girl as she struggled to find a place—any place—out of the cold. Eventually Sonia couldn't feel her own toes and was certain she had frostbite. But she didn't care about her own physical well-being as long as her daughter stayed warm.

Sonia began to run into young women she'd met while working. They, too, were single mothers with no support from the fathers of their children. They took pity on Sonia and allowed her to stay with them for a day or two before whichever family member owned the place asked that she and her child move on.

The closest Sonia came to a permanent shelter that winter was a room she rented at a boardinghouse. But she could only afford to pay for one week. After that she would leave the room early in the morning and come back late at night to avoid the landlord. She felt like a criminal, but her welfare check wasn't enough to both pay rent and buy diapers and food for herself and her baby. She knew that she wouldn't be able to avoid the landlord forever, so she wasn't surprised to find the locks changed when she returned to the room one night. There was no Thanksgiving dinner for Sonia and Lisette that year. There was no Christmas either, and no New Year's celebration. No family, no friends, no gifts. She spent the holiday season wondering if someone would find it in their heart to give her a warm place to lay her child down for at least one night. She walked the streets in desperate need of help while Christmas shoppers turned their faces away so they wouldn't have to see her. She spent New Year's eve in a cold, dark hallway listening to the echoes of those who had something and someone to celebrate. Sonia looked at her baby girl and softly apologized.

Sonia and her baby survived that winter, but it left her with a bad taste in her mouth about humanity. She promised herself to never forget all the so-called Christians who passed her by as they acquired their tokens to celebrate their faith while she was left to suffer with a newborn baby on the streets. No one had offered her any charity, and she was bitter.

The weather began to grow warmer by March, which made Sonia's condition more tolerable but no less desperate. As spring approached, she had had more than enough days on the street and finally went to her family to beg for the phone number of her relatives back in Chicago. She called her mother, told her about the situation she was in, and begged to come home. Certainly hearing that her daughter was living on the streets with a child would warm any mother's heart, but it wasn't so. Marta told her she wasn't sure what she should do and asked her to call back in a couple of days. When Sonia did so, her mother told her that she would not be welcome in her home because she had a houseful of people already. Sonia's heart fell to the soles of her feet. She wanted only to stomp on these excuses to extinguish her pain. When she hung up the phone she held her baby tightly and began to cry. She demanded that God tell her what she had done that was so wrong that he would punish her in this way. After she had shed all her tears she became angry, and grew angrier until she became determined to go back to Chicago and show up on her mother's doorstep whether she liked it or not. She reasoned that the worst that could happen was that she'd be left homeless there as well. Maybe the Latin Kings would catch up with her and put her out of her misery, just as long as they spared her daughter. That, Sonia reasoned, would be a perfect ending to a fucked-up life.

It took Sonia a little over a month to save enough money from her welfare check to purchase a one-way bus ticket back to Chicago. Other than her daughter, she left Lancaster with less than she'd arrived with. She didn't bother to say good-bye to anyone.

Another long bus ride brought on by hopelessness and the need to run away from her life took Sonia back to Chicago.

9

THE QUEEN OF KINGS

AFTER BOUNCING FROM pity place to pity place and sleeping in hallways and anywhere else she could cuddle up with her daughter, Sonia arrived in Chicago unannounced. Back around those who knew her as Lady Q, she was still afraid for her life. Lisette was now seven months old. Lady Q would have to move through the 'hood in a way that would protect not only herself but also her infant daughter. Because no one knew of her impending arrival, she wasn't greeted at the downtown bus station and spent her last few dollars on a cab back to the 'hood. It was a clear spring morning, and as the cab moved through the city all she could think about was how and if her family would receive her.

Finally Lady Q was back in the Humboldt Park area for the first time in nearly two years, during which she'd hardly communicated with her family. Lady Q's mother and three younger siblings still lived in the same building but now on the third floor. A family of career Latin Kings from Whipple and Wabansia now occupied the first-floor apartment—not exactly the ideal neighbors Lady Q wanted. She figured word would get back to the Kings in no time at all that she was back in town.

But Lady Q had nowhere else to go, and besides, she had come back to Chicago to prove a point.

The cabdriver removed her bags from the trunk, placed them on the sidewalk, collected his fare, and drove away. Lady Q quickly scanned the surrounding area for anyone she didn't want to run into as she carefully held her baby in her arms. At that moment a young man exited the first-floor apartment and instantly recognized her. He was a Latin King who knew very well why Lady Q had disappeared. Papo was tall with olive skin, black hair, and a well-built physique. He shared the first-floor unit with his mother and other family members. Papo was the brother of the chief of the Latin Kings of Whipple and Wabansia. When Lady Q saw Papo coming toward her she stiffened, but he immediately put her at ease by joking with her about her time away. He also grabbed her bags and carried them to her mother's third-floor apartment.

After Papo placed the bags in front of Marta's door, Lady Q thanked him for his help, took a deep breath, then knocked on the door and awaited her fate. From inside she could hear laughter and salsa music playing, but no one answered the door. She knocked again, harder. This time she heard footsteps coming toward the door. She braced herself for the worst. The laughter and music continued as she heard the locks on the door being unlatched, and then she was face-to-face with her mother. Lady Q froze, expecting to hear *"¿Que carajo ases aqui?"* ("What the hell are you doing here?") as a greeting. She had prepared herself with a handful of insults and arguments to get her and her daughter safely inside but was immediately disarmed when her mother screamed her name with joy and reached into the hallway to hug her long-lost daughter. *"¡Mira que bonita esta la nena!"* ("Look at how pretty the little girl is!") And with these words Marta carried her granddaughter inside to show her off to a visiting friend.

Lady Q was shocked by the reception. She grabbed her bags and closed the front door behind her. She knew that now that she was there with her daughter she would not be put out on the street, but she wondered how long the warm reception would last.

After showing her granddaughter off to her friend, Marta carried Lisette into her bedroom, laid her in the middle of the bed, and began preparing food for Lady Q. It had been a long time since Lady Q had eaten a hot, home-cooked meal, so she anxiously awaited the rice and beans with fried chicken her mother was making. While Marta cooked in the kitchen, Lady Q met her mother's friend, who turned out to be Gloria, one of RJ's sisters. Gloria was a heavyset woman in her midthirties with short hair. Her boyfriend was a Cuban refugee from the Mariel boatlift of 1980. He was also a cocaine dealer. Lady Q ate while her mother and Gloria sat with her and asked questions about her stay in Lancaster, all the while condemning the relatives who'd thrown her out on the street. After eating, Lady Q enjoyed a cold beer as the three women chatted about the alcohol problem eroding the family in Pennsylvania.

Lady Q got up to check on Lisette and then walked to the front windows and looked out at Humboldt Park. Nothing had changed. She saw the same old losers (or their younger and greener replacements) standing on the same street corners where they were still doing the same old drug hustles waiting to get killed or locked up in jail. Lady Q strained her eyes looking as far as she could see for the Latin Kings who worried her most—

the street soldiers. The rhythm of a popular salsa tune broke her daydream. Although it was the first time she'd heard it, it was catchy and she started singing along. The song was by Tommy Olivencia y su Orquestra, a world-renowned salsa band, and the song was "Periquito Pin Pin." On the streets of Chicago *periquito* was Spanish slang for "a little cocaine."

Lady Q waltzed across the room singing the catchy chorus "Periquito pin pin, periquito pin pin." As she walked past Gloria singing on her way to the bedroom where her daughter slept, Gloria threw out "*¿Quieres un pase?*" ("Do you want a pass?")

"*¿Que?*" Lady Q didn't understand the question.

Gloria got up and went into another bedroom and motioned for Lady Q and her mother to follow. She picked up a small round mirror on top of the dresser that contained a white powder neatly arranged in eight lines, each about an inch and a half long, with a razor blade on the side and a straw cut down to about the size of an adult pinky finger. Gloria picked up the straw with one hand as she held the mirror with the other, brought the straw up to a nostril, and inhaled a line of the white powder. She repeated this with her other nostril. When she was done she stood straight up and blocked one nostril, sucked in air, and then did the same on the other side. As Gloria did this, Lady Q's mother took the mirror and straw, sat down on the bed, and snorted a line of white powder up each of her nostrils, too. Lady Q was shocked by what she saw. It wasn't the presence of cocaine that left her bewildered and speechless; she had seen it many times. Seeing her mother use it, however, was astounding.

Marta nonchalantly handed her daughter the mirror containing the cocaine and the straw. Lady Q had never used cocaine and was reluctant but also curious. Gloria noticed her hesitancy and said something to the effect of "Why did you ask for it if you didn't want it?" Lady Q responded that she had not asked for anything.

"*¿No estabas pediendo perico?*" ("Weren't you asking for cocaine?"), Gloria asked.

Lady Q realized that her singing along with the song on the radio had prompted Gloria and her mother to think that she was asking for cocaine.

"*Yo no mas estaba cantando*" ("I was only singing"), Lady Q replied.

"*Pues ya que estas aqui, metete un pase*" ("Now that you are here, take a pass"), Gloria urged.

Lady Q glanced at her mother, who sat on the bed glassy-eyed and quiet. Then she brought the straw up to her nose, bent down, and snorted a line of cocaine into each nostril.

The next night Marta's home filled with people including Vivian, RJ, Gloria and her boyfriend, RJ's brother and his wife, and another one of RJ's sisters and a male friend of hers. Salsa music came from the stereo and just about everyone had a cold beer in their hand as they sat at the dining room table playing dominoes. While the kids ran in and out of the house, the small round mirror with white powder lines was discreetly passed among the adults. The shock Lady Q had initially felt quickly wore off as she began regularly indulging in the drug herself.

The effect cocaine had on Lady Q was common for most users of the drug. Her heart raced, she felt alert and upbeat, and the more she snorted the more she wanted. She wanted to go outside and release all that energy, but every time she looked out the window she experienced a paranoid rush. She was certain the Latin Kings already knew she was in town, so she panicked whenever someone she recognized entered her field of vision in the park or in a car passing by. She knew she wouldn't be able to stay inside her mother's home forever.

Four days had passed since Lady Q's arrival from Pennsylvania, and she had yet to set foot outside. She knew she was well within the domain of those she feared most, and the streets of Chicago, especially in the area she once called her kingdom, now made her cringe. She knew that whenever she finally stepped onto the city's sidewalks, a confrontation was inevitable, no matter how many precautions she took. On this fourth day after her return, Lady Q decided to seek out Cino, the Inca of the Latin Kings of Beach and Spaulding. She took along her daughter and a young Latin King she found sitting on the steps of her mother's building. She had never seen him before, but he knew who she was and where to find Cino.

Lady Q felt anxious as they walked the one block to the corner of Kedzie and North Avenue to a gym the Latin Kings had opened. Her heart raced and she struggled to conceal her nervousness while she spoke during their walk. She knew when she met up with Cino she wouldn't be able to control her stutter.

As soon as she entered the gym, all movement stopped. Immediately all eyes focused on her. Everyone obviously knew she was back in town and why she was there. Toward the back, with his shoulder-length hair gathered in a ponytail and wearing a tank top that showed off his muscular physique, Cino sat surrounded by three of his top officers. Lady Q almost peed in her pants from fear when her eyes first met Cino's. She prayed the presence of her baby girl would plant a seed of mercy in his heart.

Cino walked toward her with a smile on his face as if he were about to greet an old dear friend, but that didn't help her overcome her feeling of doom.

"You ain't shit," Cino said as he reached out for her and gave her a hug. "You've been here for four days; it's about time you come see me."

"Why would I come see you?" she replied with as little attitude in her voice as possible. "It was because of you that I had to leave."

Cino laughed. "You didn't have to leave. What was done had to be done. You of all people should know that."

Lady Q walked with Cino to the back of the gym as everyone greeted her and then continued their workout.

Cino was surprised that Lady Q had become a mother in the short time she'd been gone but was happy for her and asked to hold her baby. They sat down alone in the back of the gym, facing each other with Lady Q's daughter in Cino's arms. It didn't take long for him to explain that her appearance on *AM Chicago* had broken a major rule of the Latin Kings, which required the gang to retaliate. He told her that, although he knew about what was happening, it was his *cacique*, Spade, who had actually made the decision to take the action to teach her a lesson.

Cino told her to come back and talk to him the next day. In the meantime, he wanted her to go back to her mother's apartment and not do anything until he had a chance to talk to Spade. Lady Q left the gym somewhat relieved but still skeptical about the intentions of her old comrades. But she felt she'd taken a step in the right direction because of the way Cino had received her.

The next day Lady Q went to the gym by herself. She felt more confident and relaxed while knowing that if something was going to go down against her, it would happen on this day. This was the reason she decided to leave her daughter with her grandmother. When Lady Q walked into the gym there was little reaction this time around. Cino and Spade were at the back of the gym, and neither one of them showed any noticeable emotion when they saw her. Lady Q took this as a good sign since it appeared that she was being welcomed in a casual way, once again as an everyday member of the gang, she hoped. She walked to the back of the gym and sat in the presence of these two top members. Spade welcomed her back to the city and began to explain what had led to the gun blast. He explained to her that, although she hadn't said anything critical about the Kings on *AM Chicago*, her real name and nickname had been displayed for all the world to see during her appearance. They had to send a strong message to keep other young brothers and sisters from setting themselves out in this way. Spade also made it clear that there had been no intention to hurt her or anyone else in the apartment when the Latin Kings shot out the windows. As he put it, "If we wanted to kill you, we would have just killed you"; that is, had the Latin Kings wanted to take her out, they would have done so without a big production. Nonetheless she was extremely upset.

"Motherfucker, I was standing by the window when that shit happened," Lady Q snapped. "There were kids in that fuckin' house!" Cino and Spade didn't physically or verbally respond to her anger.

"But you'll know better next time, won't you?" Spade said after letting Lady Q's anger simmer for a few minutes.

"The order came from *el jefe* ("the chief")," Cino added. "So it had to be followed."

"Who the fuck is the *jefe*?" Lady Q asked.

"The *jefe* is the Inca of all Incas, the King of all Kings," Spade said.

"Fuck him," she yelled. "Where the fuck was he when I was on the streets holding up the crown? How the fuck did he help me while I was homeless in the streets with my daughter? The *jefe*, my ass! How the fuck can he be the King of Kings if he's never around to do shit?"

Lady Q continued to rant. Cino and Spade laughed as everyone in the gym looked back in shock at Lady Q's words.

"You haven't changed a bit," Cino told her. "*El jefe* has long ago done what he needed to do for the Nation and is locked up, so you better watch what you say about someone you don't have a clue about."

With that, both Cino and Spade got up and left the gym, leaving Lady Q to think about the events of the day. She walked out moments later, satisfied with the knowledge that she could retake her place among the Almighty Latin King/Queen Nation of the Humboldt Park area.

From that day on, Lady Q once again became a regular in the area gang scene, only this time she had her daughter in tow. Lady Q found that, along with the gym, the Latin Kings had opened up a GED (General Educational Development) center on the opposite side on the street on Kedzie and North Avenue. This is where she began to hang out daily, though she doesn't recall witnessing any learning going on. Lady Q was offered a position as the top Queen of a section by Cino, which she declined, feeling insulted that the Kings would even consider the idea knowing that she was now a mother.

About a week after Lady Q's talk with Cino and Spade, a call came into the GED center. It was the chief of all Kings—the Inca—and he wanted to speak to her. Now. Lady Q took the phone and listened as a man with a deep voice spoke.

"Do you know who I am?" the voice demanded.

"No."

"I'm Lord Tino, your Inca," he continued in a commanding manner. "I understand you have some words to say to me."

Lady Q thought for a second and then let him have it. "You call yourself my Inca and call violations on me, scare the shit out of me, and I don't even know who the fuck you are. I had to live on the streets because of you and I'm supposed to call you my chief? Hell no."

After she finished, there was silence. Finally, Tino spoke in the same calm and direct voice he had used since the start of their conversation.

"I've heard a lot about you and admire that you don't take shit from no one. You want to meet me? That's not a problem; it will be arranged. Anything else you want to say to me?"

"No," Lady Q replied.

"We'll talk again," Tino assured her, and with that the conversation was over.

Whenever Lady Q heard anyone talking about having a conversation with Tino, they described it as a special event. She couldn't understand what the big deal was and didn't share in the excitement that others thought she should feel when they found out she would be meeting him. Few of the thousands of

Kings and Queens ever had the opportunity to speak to the Inca directly; most would consider themselves lucky to even hear the words of the Inca passed down by one of his trusted soldiers.

At the GED center Lady Q met and became close friends with Tino's wife, Tammy. She was a heavyset white woman with expensive tastes, an expensive cocaine habit to match, and a bossy attitude. Tammy was not well liked, mainly because she used her status as the *jefe*'s wife to dictate orders to Latin Kings and have them wait on her hand and foot. Tammy was well aware of how the Kings and Queens felt about her but didn't give a fuck. What she did was align herself with those in power in order to manipulate those who didn't have any. This is where Lady Q came in.

Tammy had noticed how brothers and sisters of all ages flocked to Lady Q and adored her, so she quickly befriended her. Everywhere Tammy went she took Lady Q and her daughter along. She bought Lisette many gifts and funded a lavish party for her first birthday to suck up to Lady Q. In just five months since Lady Q's return to Chicago, she once again had a major presence in the 'hood, mainly because of Tammy's friendship and because word got around she had spoken to the Inca. The birthday party was held in Humboldt Park right across the street from her mother's apartment. Everyone in Lady Q's family was invited, and there were more Kings there than kids.

As time went by, Tammy confided in Lady Q, telling her everything. This didn't please Lady Q, especially after she met Tino.

Tino had been in jail since he was seventeen years old. He had worked up the ranks of the Latin Kings as it grew to become one of the most—if not *the* most—powerful prison gangs in the Illinois correctional system. In prison Tino made acquaintances that increased the Latin Kings' drug trafficking and therefore intensified the power the gang had on the street. Although Tino's influence on the street was diminishing, many there took action on his command. At one time the Latin Kings didn't make a move without Tino's blessing, but as the demographics and attitudes of gangs changed, and street soldiers struggled to make a name for themselves, his domination began to fade. But there was no doubt that if Tino wanted something done, many loyal to him were ready and willing to respond. It was also well known among gang members that their actions on the street could determine their fate should they end up in the penitentiary, and this did keep some in check.

Inside the Illinois correctional system, Tino's power was so vast that it was rumored he ordered the murder of guards as well as fellow inmates. Not only was Lady Q going to meet this man, but she was going to do so via one of his high-ranking officers who carried out his direct orders on the street, not by an order passed along by Tammy or anyone else.

Lady Q's visit to Tino was set up to be an indirect meet. She was placed on the visiting list for a Spanish Lord named Juni. JC, who was a top general in the Latin Kings, would escort Lady Q to the prison and call out Tino for a visitation.

Generals such as JC were rarely seen; when they were seen, something big was happening. JC was short and stocky, had a bulldog flamboyance, and didn't take shit from anyone. Many Kings disliked him for several reasons but mainly because of his business practices. JC's only true loyalty was to money. Certainly he was a Latin King first and foremost, but his devotion to the almighty dollar gave him no scruples when it came to expanding his narcotics dealings, including working with rival gangs. Many gangs were sworn enemies of the Latin Kings, such as the Maniac Latin Disciples, Insane Spanish Cobras, and the Imperial Gangsters. JC was their main drug supplier. These gangs sold the drugs on the street to make money to buy guns that were then used against the Latin Kings. JC's son, in fact, was one of the top leaders of the Imperial Gangsters, one of the Kings' deadliest rivals.

Lady Q met JC a couple of days before she went to visit Tino. He came to the GED center looking for her. He introduced himself and then gave her details about the meet-up. He told her that Tammy was not to know a thing about the visitation. A couple of days later, JC picked up Lady Q in front of the apartment building where she was staying with her mother and drove her the two hours it took to get to the Statesville Maximum Security Correctional Center in Joliet, Illinois, where Tino was imprisoned.

Once they entered the prison, Lady Q and JC were patted down and had their purses and bags checked and their official state identifications reviewed. Once they cleared security they were taken into a room with rows of tables with one chair on either side every few feet. JC was escorted by a guard and asked to sit at one table, and Lady Q was taken to a different row of tables and asked to sit as well. After about five minutes, Juni from the Spanish Lords was escorted to the table where Lady Q sat. Shortly thereafter, Tino was brought into the visiting room and was taken to the table where JC waited.

Lady Q made small talk with Juni while placing most of her attention across the room where Tino sat. Tino was nothing like she had pictured him. She had thought he was probably old, bald, and physically wasted from all the years he'd spent in the penitentiary. Instead, Tino was a tall, fair-skinned, and very well-built Puerto Rican who turned heads when he walked into a room. He was by far the handsomest man Lady Q had ever seen, and she was instantly infatuated.

About ten minutes into the visit, Tino got up and walked over to the table where Lady Q sat. He stood before her and said, "You're not so tough in person, are you?"

"I just say what's on my mind," Lady Q responded, looking Tino straight in the eyes.

Before they exchanged any more words, a guard approached Tino and asked him to go back to his table. Tino told the guard that there was no need to go back because he was done with his visit. Tino walked away and Juni followed. Minutes later Lady Q and JC were on their way back to Chicago.

On the drive back, JC explained to Lady Q that Tino was going to add her to his list of approved visitors and from that day forward she was to meet with him, alone, every visitation day, which meant weekly. Tammy was not to know anything about it. Lady Q felt somewhat uneasy going behind Tammy's back to visit her husband but concluded that it had something to do with Tammy's attitude and the way she did things.

SINCE SONIA HAD returned from Lancaster, her periods had become irregular. She wasn't sure what was going on—maybe her time on the streets or poor nutrition had messed with her system. She went to get a Pap smear and it came back abnormal. She spoke with a doctor who warned her it could be cervical cancer. He told her to get a biopsy and instructed her to make an appointment to have this done. Lady Q never made the appointment.

As LADY Q became acquainted with the upper echelon of the Latin King hierarchy, the welcome her mother had given her on account of Lisette suddenly disappeared. A few months after Lady Q started visiting Tino, Marta told her that she would have to find another place to stay—she was returning to Puerto Rico. Lady Q didn't believe her mother was actually going to leave and thought it was just a ploy to get her out of the house, so she countered by getting a job to help out financially. She already gave Marta money here and there from the cocaine trade she was slowly getting involved in, but she thought that getting a job would make her mother chill out with the Puerto Rico claims.

On the corner of Troy and North Avenue, one block away from where Lady Q lived, was a bar named Rhythm of the Night that was a primary hangout for the Latin Kings. In that bar, more cocaine was sold than alcohol. Lady Q inquired about getting a job there, and because of her status with the Latin Kings she was quickly hired as a waitress. Lady Q loved this job because she could socialize and party all night long.

In the meantime, Tammy was sharing parts of her life that made Lady Q uncomfortable and left her confused about what gang life was really about. A prime example was Tammy's connection to the Latin Jivers, a rival gang of the Latin Kings. Tammy took Lady Q into the Jivers' 'hood at Evergreen and Talman, to an apartment where all the gang members hung out. When she entered, the Jivers immediately knew who Lady Q was because of Tammy, but they were powerless to do anything but share their drugs and alcohol with her. There was one particular Jiver who Tammy was inseparable from who often came to the GED center. In turn, the Latin Kings were powerless to do anything about his appearance there because of Tammy. The Jiver was said to be a relative of Tammy's and therefore could not be touched, but Lady Q soon saw that he was actually Tammy's lover.

Lady Q was no stool pigeon. She would never backstab someone she hung out with regardless of how asinine she thought her actions were. During her visits with Tino, he sometimes asked about Tammy and what she was doing. Lady Q responded that he would have to ask his wife about her business since it was none of hers. This stance—her loyalty to a friend—impressed Tino and prompted him to trust Lady Q even more. She became one of his closest friends.

But eventually the shit hit the fan over Tammy's behavior. News got around that she was screwing the Latin Jiver she was pretending was her relative, and it got back to Tino. Word on the street was that she should be taken out on sight. Many soldiers looked forward to doing it after having put up with her for so long. Tammy knew the street well and was aware of what was coming, so she disappeared. The Latin Kings sought her out but she was nowhere to be found, and neither was a valuable commodity she'd been entrusted to safeguard: the Latin Kings manifesto. The document contained everything that defined the Almighty Latin Kings and Queens, from rules and prayers to secret handshakes and hand signs. It could be used by the Kings to identify a true member; therefore it was a very secret document. The manifesto had no doubt fallen into the hands of the Latin Jivers, the enemy, and the Latin Kings were pissed off.

Neither Tammy nor the manifesto were ever seen again in the 'hood.

With Tammy out of the picture, Lady Q became the only woman in Tino's life. She was the only one who was there to listen to him, and he vented to her about his wife's betrayal.

As Tino filed for divorce, Lady Q became known as his new girlfriend, and many street soldiers were excited and happy for her.

Lady Q and Tino's relationship didn't become physical until a year after her weekly visits started. He'd been transferred downstate to a correctional facility in Menard, Illinois, and that prison held biannual barbecue picnics where family members could visit the prisoners, play basketball, and just hang out. Everyone walked around with a towel, to keep cool or wipe the sweat away after a game. While others kept watch, Tino and Lady Q had sex while sitting on a picnic table. Lady Q feared they would get caught, which would result in her losing her visitation privileges for a year, but they didn't get caught. Either time. She did it for Tino. She would have done anything for Tino.

LADY Q BECAME close to Spade's wife, who cared for Lisette while Lady Q was at work or visiting Tino. Sometimes Lady Q stayed over at Spade's house with her daughter, and other nights she'd pick up Spade's daughter and take them both back to her mother's apartment. One night she picked up Lisette and went home to discover an empty apartment. The landlord told her to turn in her keys and vacate that night. Again homeless, this time Lady Q had a support system that guaranteed she'd be taken care of.

For the benefit of her daughter, Lady Q sought out family to live with before she would accept living arrangements anywhere else. She approached Vivian about the possibility of living with her and Vivian accepted, mainly because Lady Q could provide some financial assistance along with discounted or free cocaine to the household. Vivian and RJ were now crack addicts. RJ also drank heavily, which made it difficult for him to control his explosive temper. Lady Q was almost oblivious to the state of their relationship as she was always either working at the bar or doing her own cocaine deals for the Latin Kings. Only a couple of weeks after Lady Q moved in, Vivian told her she was going to the store with her downstairs neighbor. Lady Q gave her some money to pick up some diapers and milk for her daughter. Hours went by and there was no sign of either woman. Finally, later that evening, the neighbor showed up alone and told her Vivian had decided to leave RJ that day without cluing Lady Q in on her plans.

Lady Q understood why Vivian wanted to leave RJ—she applauded it and thought Vivian should have done this years before. But to do it in this manner—not telling Lady Q and possibly leaving her and her daughter in harm's way because of RJ's explosive temper—left Lady Q furious. Staying with RJ was out of the question, so Vivian's actions essentially left Lady Q homeless again.

Lady Q worried, but at least the situation wasn't like Lancaster, where everyone had turned their backs on her. She had befriended a woman named Cuca while working at Rhythm of the Night. Cuca regularly invited the club's patrons back to her place to continue the party after the club closed. She had a little boy, age one and a half, and a little girl, age six. Each child had a different father, neither of whom was around. Despite being a single parent, somehow Cuca always found the time and means to party at the club. She was also a promiscuous welfare princess who lent out her home to gang members for anything and everything from the storage of guns to the distribution of drugs and the hiding of gang members after they'd committed hits on rivals. Gang members were always present, any time of the day or night, and they treated the place as if it were their own home. Cuca accepted this as long as they provided her with a steady supply of drugs, alcohol, and sex. Lady Q liked Cuca and had been over to her place to party on many nights. She chose this place to call her new home for herself and her daughter.

In the short time Lady Q had been back in the city she had gone from being scared for her life to being the most admired and envied of all Latin Queens. She was now draped in designer clothes, as was her daughter, had gold and precious gems around her neck and on her fingers, and had power beyond her wildest dreams in the form of the largest and most violent Latino gang in the United States. Lady Q had reached her pinnacle as the Queen of Kings.

10

BUSINESS IS PERSONAL

THE WINTER OF 1986 settled over Chicago, and Lady Q got more and more involved in the partying going on in her new residence. She went to work at the club and left her daughter in Cuca's care. Lady Q knew what was going on in the apartment, but she assumed that since the Latin Kings were coming in and out of the apartment, and since she was known as the Inca's woman, no harm would come to her daughter. In many ways she was correct.

Her relationship with Tino had grown—she visited him weekly and was the only woman in his life. She often took Lisette with her on her visits. Lady Q grew to love the man, not the Inca. She listened to him; he trusted her. She also spoke plainly and honestly to him about what was happening on the street. She told him what was wrong—all of it. He came to trust her opinion.

Many Kings vyed for her attention—getting in good with the Inca (or the Inca's woman) meant more control over the gang's drug trade and therefore more money. But Lady Q was very good at assessing people's motives, and she frustrated many street soldiers who were only in it for profit, denying them access to Tino. She could quickly tell when their sole purpose was to use him to increase their influence on the street.

While she was working hard and doing a good job at protecting Tino's interests, she did little to take care of the needs of her one-year-old daughter, often leaving her in dangerous situations where neglect was commonplace. Lady Q's life had become a nonstop locomotion of drugs, alcohol, and sex. She went to work at the Rhythm of the Night, hooked up with someone who had cocaine or marijuana, and came home to dive into more chemicals. She slept with many of the Latin Kings who partied at Cuca's and were looking for sex with any intoxicated woman present. No feelings were shared, no promises made, no futures considered—it was nothing but raw, uncensored, and unprotected sex. No thoughts about diseases or pregnancies—they lived in the high of the moment. Lady Q was lucky that everyone was too afraid to tell Tino about her activities. Being cut off from the drug supply line, whether for profit or for personal use, was too great a risk.

For gang members who had no rank in the gang hierarchy, having sex with the Inca's woman was a great accomplishment, something they could brag about among their own little circle yet never mention around their leaders. And that was more than enough for them, since Lady Q could get heads busted at any time. Her loyalty to the King above all Kings was unwavering in all areas but this one.

Lady Q spent that holiday season in an alcohol- and drug-filled stupor. Lost in all the madness was her now two-year-old daughter, as well as Cuca's kids. On New Year's eve, Lady Q got so drunk that she passed out before midnight. She completely forgot she was supposed to work that night. As it turned out this was a good thing, because Rhythm of the Night burned down shortly after midnight. She awoke without her clothes on but had been so drunk the night before she didn't even know if she'd had sex with anyone—a frequent occurrence at this time in her life. The girls living with her told her that the drugs had knocked her out, so they had thrown her in the shower and then put her to bed. Lady Q suspected there was more to it but in her state of mind, she didn't give a fuck one way or the other.

Lady Q started 1987 without a job and with a big addiction to cocaine and sex. The hellhole she lived in provided her with all the encouragement she needed to indulge in both. The only income Lady Q had to fall back on was money she earned selling quarter bags of cocaine, which Tino arranged for her to have, and a monthly welfare check.

Lady Q had all the means and connections to become a major player in the Humboldt Park drug scene, but she either didn't care for it or didn't know how to go about it, or else was too much of a street soldier at heart to want to be anything else. She had never forgotten the street soldiers who'd stood by her side until the wee hours of the night when she was desperate to find a place to belong, and she still surrounded herself with these people.

Hanging out with these gang members kept Lady Q in non-stop party mode and also prompted her to participate at a moment's notice in gang violence. In the still bitterly cold month of March, the Latin Kings of Whipple and Wabansia came to Lady Q to report the possibility of a Latin Disciple spy among their ranks, a fifteen-year-old girl named Marabel who'd met and became the girlfriend of one of the younger Latin Kings and started coming into the 'hood with him. When their relationship soured, the girl began to take interest in another Latin King from the same section in his twenties. Before anything could develop between them, the first King reported seeing drawings of Latin Disciple gang insignias on her notebook. And then more pieces began to fall into place and a slew of coincidences began to surface: the girl lived in an area dominated by the Latin Disciples; she went to Roberto Clemente High School, which was known as a haven for rivals of the Latin Kings; and finally a notebook was produced with her name on the cover and Latin Disciples gang signs on the back cover and on several pages. No one ever questioned why the young Latin King had brought her around in the first place if it was so obvious the girl might be a rival gang member.

Upon seeing the notebook and its drawings Lady Q sprang into action, calling out "Where the fuck is this little bitch?" While some gang members presented the evidence to Lady Q, others entertained the presumed-guilty party at a car wash on North Avenue and Albany, keeping her busy until her fate caught up with her. Lady Q put on her coat and told Cuca to come along. They got into a car with the Whipple and Wabansia Kings who'd brought the news and waited to escort her back. It had been almost three years since Lady Q had taken part in any street justice, and she was eager to get to the car wash and get started. Her body was pumped full of toxins that made her heart race, and the adrenaline rush from the thought of smashing a rival had Lady Q almost out of control. When they arrived at the car wash, Lady Q rushed out of the car with the girl's notebook in hand and instantly got in the girl's face. The Kings who had kept the girl occupied quickly stepped away to get out of the line of fire and to give Lady Q plenty of room to move.

"Is this your notebook?" Lady Q demanded.

"Yes, it is. How—?" began the girl, who could say no more before Lady Q cracked her on the right side of her face. Lady Q followed this with an uppercut that broke her nose and a straight shot that landed on the girl's right eye when her head lunged upward. For the next thirty seconds, Lady Q put on a clinic of blows to the girl's body and head that Muhammad Ali would have admired. Only this wasn't a boxing tournament— it was a Latin Queen almost in her twenties beating the shit out of a fifteen-year-old girl. The girl finally fell to the ground on one knee. Lady Q kicked her in the rib cage, sending her sprawling to the cold concrete. From that point on it was a matter of whether someone would show mercy and stop the brutal beating or Lady Q would get tired. Lady Q's punches and kicks rained down on the girl from every direction, and she almost hit Cuca when she made a feeble attempt to get in on the action. Finally Lady Q stopped and looked down at her victim, who lay on the hard, cold, wet cement, completely defenseless and now horribly beaten. Lady Q said nothing. She turned and calmly walked away, got back into the car, and was driven back to her apartment.

Lady Q never found out what happened to the girl after she left. She never gave her a second thought. It's likely that the Latin Kings left the young girl lying on the ground to be discovered by someone else. This was the way it always was.

As spring started to warm the Chicago air, someone told Lady Q that her mother was back in town after being with Juan in Puerto Rico for about a year. She was living on the South

Side with Vivian. Lady Q also heard that her mother and Vivian had been in the 'hood looking for her. This surprised her at first, but then she was happy to hear it.

The warm weather inspired Lady Q to become active in more lucrative areas of the cocaine business, such as being a courier between suppliers and buyers. She began making some pretty decent money. It was no secret around the neighborhood about Lady Q's upward mobility, and eventually this news made its way to Vivian and her mother. One day Lady Q sat in the kitchen of Cuca's apartment packaging cocaine into quarter bags to be distributed on the streets when Vivian and Marta showed up at the door. Lady Q didn't know how to react to their visit but asked them to come in without caring whether or not they witnessed her illegal activity—their opinion of her was the furthest thing from Lady Q's mind. Vivian explained that she was still estranged from RJ, and her mother seemed to be a calmer, gentler person. It didn't take long for them to ask Lady Q to come live with them. Without a single hesitation or asking any questions why, Lady Q agreed. She didn't know where on the South Side she was headed and didn't care. She was ready to make a change, and getting help with Lisette from her family would be welcome.

Relocating to the South Side of the city came at a good time for Lady Q in terms of the kind of business she was doing. Living in a Latin Kings' hangout and all-night party place was not wise for someone now being counted on to move large amounts of cocaine and money, and that is exactly what Lady Q was getting involved in. On the South Side the family lived in a second-floor apartment on Cermak and Whipple in the 'hood of a gang called the Stone Kents but in an area still dominated by the Latin

Kings. Ironically, just as it was on the North Side, rival gang 'hoods were divided by Sacramento Boulevard, with the Kings west of Sacramento and their rivals to the east. Another similarity to the North Side was that the vast majority of gang violence was committed by Latino gangs against other Latino gangs, only instead of Puerto Ricans killing Puerto Ricans it was Mexicans killing Mexicans.

Lady Q joined Vivian, her mother, and her three younger siblings at the beginning of the summer and found that Gigi had also been invited. But this no longer bothered Lady Q. Her feelings toward Gigi had changed, and she now accepted her as part of the family. For Lady Q this was a chance for her to spend time with her mother and sister without the interference of men who tried to manipulate them in one way or another. She was anxious about how this woman-led household would influence her relationship with them. Lady Q understood that Vivian was still considered the head of the household, despite Lady's Q's status as Queen of the Kings, so she went to Vivian for permission to sell quarter bags of cocaine from the apartment so that additional money could be brought into the household. Vivian granted her permission.

Lady Q's merchandise was of better quality and quantity than that distributed by the Stone Kents, and it didn't take long for tensions to develop over customers. One day Lady Q was sitting and looking out the front window of the apartment that overlooked Cermak Avenue. Gigi was at her side as she talked to Tino on the phone. Tino called Lady Q collect every day at this time. He knew the money she earned from the sale of cocaine was more than enough to pay the phone bill. As Lady Q chatted with Tino, a Stone Kent gang member exited a bar directly across the street from her apartment. He began yelling threats up to her in the window. The Kent called her a bitch and demanded she stop selling cocaine or face extreme consequences. As the Kent's voice rose and his threats grew bolder, Tino could clearly hear him and asked Lady Q who the man was and who he was addressing. Lady Q explained that the vulgarity and intimidation were directed at her.

Tino maintained his calm and soft-spoken demeanor, but his voice disclosed his irritation.

"Hang up the phone, babe, I'll call you right back," Tino told Lady Q, and before she could respond she heard a dial tone.

The Stone Kent went back into the bar. Lady Q walked away from the window wondering why Tino had cut their conversation short. She checked on four-year-old Lisette, who was taking a nap, and then returned to the window to be near the phone when Tino called back.

Within a half hour, three four-door sedans pulled up in front of the bar across the street. Her first thought was that detectives had come to bust someone. She thought about getting rid of the cocaine in her house, but then she saw J-Cool get out of one of the cars. She realized that the passengers in all three cars were Latin Kings and Queens, and they weren't the typical street-punk variety. One of the Kings walked across the street toward Lady Q's apartment along with two Queens. They knocked on the door, introduced themselves, and asked what had happened. Lady Q gave the trio details about what the member of the Stone Kents had said. Gigi, who had also seen the guy, walked over to the bar with them to point him out. Lady Q went back to the window and watched as Gigi led the posse of Kings and Queens into the bar. She saw people quickly scatter behind cars to avoid being victims but also to get a ringside view of the scene going down.

Moments after entering the bar, the Latin Kings came back out onto the street with the brother of the Kent who had insulted Lady Q. One of the Kings had him in a choke hold with a gun pointed to his head. They forced him to his knees, held him by his hair, and forced him to look up to Lady Q's apartment as they talked to him and slapped him across the face and head with the gun.

"You see that woman up there? Do you see her, mother-fucker?" The King continued to pistol-whip him into a bloody mess as he yelled at the Kent. "You tell your brother that if he ever even looks her way again, his shit is going to get rocked. You understand that, motherfucker?"

When the Kings finally released him, he fell to the sidewalk. It was clear he needed medical attention. Then the Kings and Queens got back in their cars and drove away just as quickly as they had arrived. From that day forward, Lady Q was the sole purveyor of cocaine to all customers at Cermak and Whipple. The Kings' message about her power was communicated so clearly that the Stone Kents began bringing her customers, and a few members of that gang became her dealers. Lady Q's supremacy was just beginning.

THE RELATIONSHIP THAT Lady Q had always dreamed of sharing with Vivian and her mother finally seemed to be coming true. It even appeared as if Lady Q was replacing Vivian as the head of the household. Lady Q was consulted on every decision and was counted on to solve any problem that arose within the family. To foster their growing sisterhood, Lady Q took

Vivian to visit Tino and hooked her up with another top player in the Latin King Nation who was also in jail called King Pops. They became a couple. The respect and attention paid to Lady Q by other gang members now included Vivian, too.

Soon Vivian developed a friendly relationship with J-Cool and began to get involved in the cocaine business, all the while maintaining her government job. She and her mother prepared the quarter bags they sold out of the apartment, and they shared in the profits. While Vivian and Marta bagged the cocaine, JC or a street soldier picked up Lady Q nearly every day and drove her out to an area near Maywood, Illinois, where she picked up either kilos of cocaine or large sums of cash. Then she'd bring them back into the city by bus. On any given day, Lady Q might carry between one and ten kilos of cocaine or thousands of dollars in cash in a duffel bag. She would ride public transportation into the city and drop off the merchandise at J-Cool's mother's house near Humboldt Park and then continue by bus to her own home off Cermak. She never felt nervous about what she was doing or afraid of getting caught. She focused completely on making money, and she made a lot of it. For every kilo of cocaine Lady Q transported, she received one thousand dollars as compensation. She was paid only several hundred to carry cash, so she preferred to deliver drugs.

One evening after a job, Lady Q called Vivian into her bedroom and spread five thousand dollars on the bed. Vivian's eyes bulged at the sight of so much money. Lady Q picked up the money, handed it to Vivian, and asked her to put it into a bank for her. Lady Q wanted to save the money in Vivian's name because she had a steady job and could account for where it came from.

Lady Q took care of everything in the household. When the refrigerator stopped working, she coughed up two thousand dollars for a brand-new one with modern features. As the school year approached, she took her three younger siblings shopping and bought them all the clothes and supplies they needed. In addition, she bought clothes for her daughter and Vivian's son and never once considered asking Vivian to pay her back.

Large quantities of money can corrupt souls and breed greed in all sectors of society, including within families, and perhaps more so in families with a history of dysfunction. Vivian started to turn her attention away from King Pops and began visiting Gigi's brother, Stone, who had been her boyfriend about five years earlier and was now doing time for drug possession. When Vivian started visiting Stone, he was only weeks away from being released. He moved in with her immediately after regaining his freedom. The romance between Vivian and Stone hadn't lasted very long the first time around, and this second time was no different. Lady Q had always gotten along well with Stone— he seemed to have an easier time communicating with her than with Vivian. At one point soon after Stone moved in, Vivian started looking for ways to pick fights with Lady Q, including accusing her of sleeping with Stone. Stone began leaving the house and coming back hours later wasted on heroin. Vivian had no tolerance for that, and after about two weeks she kicked Stone back out of her life just as easily as she had allowed him back in.

Lady Q and Vivian began having confrontations about selling cocaine out of the apartment. Vivian reminded Lady Q that it was her home and no one else's. Lady Q reminded Vivian that she was the one who'd been paying all the bills, including the rent, since she arrived. The arguments gave Lady Q the feeling that Vivian wanted to get rid of her so that she could keep the cocaine business for herself. But Lady Q had started this business and made it successful. Next, Vivian kicked her mother out over a fight they had when Vivian accused one of her younger siblings of stealing money from her. Her mother quickly found an apartment and prepared to move out with the younger kids, and that left only Lady Q. It didn't take Lady Q long to realize that RJ was back in Vivian's life, and she knew he was manipulating her. Since RJ and Lady Q had never gotten along, it was no surprise when Vivian wanted her out of the apartment. Vivian kicked out Lady Q, RJ moved back in, and Lady Q found herself again homeless for the moment.

The night Vivian kicked Lady Q out of the apartment, Lady Q reached out to her mother, who was already set up in her own apartment, to care for Lisette while she found somewhere to live. Marta declined, leaving Lady Q with no other choice but to lean on Tino. When Tino heard what Vivian had done to Lady Q, he sent J-Cool to pick up Lady Q and take her to his mother's house. Tino was usually very private when it came to sending people to his mother's, but for Lady Q he made an exception. Tino didn't want his business broadcast to his family, so while Lady Q stayed at his mother's house, it was all love and no business when they spoke on the phone. Yet there was one sore subject that they couldn't avoid discussing—Vivian.

Word from the South Side was that RJ had moved in with Vivian and together they were making the most out of the pharmaceutical shop Lady Q had established. Tino wanted to send Latin Kings over to the apartment to take away their drugs and money and teach Vivian a lesson in loyalty, but Lady Q asked him not to. She was pissed off at what Vivian had done to her but chose to show mercy to her sister. What Tino did instead was put the word out that no one in the Nation was to supply Vivian with the merchandise to keep the business going. Any Latin King found making deals with Vivian would be subject to a violation regardless of how much rank they held within the gang. It didn't take long for Vivian and RJ to feel the repercussions of that order.

A little less than two months after Lady Q moved in with Tino's mother, he got her an apartment across the street from Humboldt Park. Ironically it was the same first-floor apartment where her mother had lived when Lady Q fled Chicago for Lancaster, Pennsylvania, over three years ago. The apartment quickly became the new headquarters for most of the Latin Kings' drug transactions. Latin Kings from all over the city came there to talk to Tino (via Lady Q), pick up or drop off merchandise, and wait on Lady Q hand and foot. The apartment was lavishly furnished and was never calm and silent. Lady Q dressed herself and her daughter in the latest designer clothes, lavishly accessorized with gold and other precious baubles. Many of the Kings who frequented Cuca's came around looking for the Lady Q they had known back then but were tremendously disappointed because the Lady Q they now encountered was all business. Although she didn't deny any Latin King or Queen space in her world, she didn't have time for pettiness or phony friendships.

The cocaine business is lucrative, and it came to dominate every aspect of gang society. Now everyone Lady Q came in contact with came because they wanted a piece of the action. After getting burned by Vivian, Lady Q was very wary of anyone who demonstrated the slightest bit of greed, and she kept those people at arm's length not only from herself but from Tino as well. Lady Q fulfilled the role of the Queen of Kings, and she was smart enough to know that to survive in that role she had to maintain close relationships with the street soldiers. She was well aware of the mistake Tammy had made by offending the street soldiers and therefore becoming a target for them. Lady Q understood that as long as the street soldiers were on her side, there would always be someone ready to protect her and the honor of the gang.

Vivian and RJ visited Lady Q about two weeks after she moved into her new apartment. They came to tell her about how the Stone Kents were talking shit about Tino all over Cermak Avenue. Lady Q didn't believe a word they said. She had a feeling that their sudden interest in Tino's reputation had more to do with their own self-interest than anything else. It didn't matter to her what, if anything, the Stone Kents said as they were considered neither an asset nor a threat. But Lady Q's curiosity prompted her to inquire with the South Side Latin Kings to learn what was happening on Cermak and Whipple in her absence. They told her that the word was out that Vivian's apartment was no longer a dealing point for Latin King merchandise, so the Stone Kents had started to reclaim their former customers and territory. They saw it as a great opportunity to reestablish the control they had lost.

Around this same time, an acquaintance of Lady Q's named Queen Psycho went to the South Side and burned Vivian out of an eight ball (an eighth of an ounce, or 3.5 grams) of cocaine. Vivian contacted Lady Q and demanded that she collect money from Queen Psycho. Lady Q told her there was nothing she could do to help in this situation and reminded Vivian she shouldn't be dealing cocaine in the first place. Vivian became furious. This incident with Queen Psycho brought to light the discovery that J-Cool was in fact supplying Vivian cocaine in defiance of Tino's order. Lady Q communicated this to Tino. And while she never personally witnessed how Tino then disciplined one of his top generals, word on the street was that it wasn't pretty.

It didn't take long for Vivian to find out that being a drug dealer wasn't easy without the muscle required to protect the territory. The Chicago Police Department Narcotics Unit raided Vivian's apartment soon thereafter, supposedly because Vivian sold a quarter bag of cocaine to an undercover officer. They found only a small amount of cocaine in the apartment, and Gigi was the only one arrested. Gigi for some reason decided to take the fall for Vivian. She had to fight the case on her own since Vivian offered her no help acquiring a lawyer. Eventually Gigi was sentenced to probation, but she now had a felony record she'd have to live with for the rest of her life. As for Vivian, she was forced not only to close up shop but also to leave the neighborhood. She rented an apartment on the other side of the boulevard in the heart of the Satan Disciples' 'hood— the primary rival of the South Side Latin Kings.

Soon after Vivian moved, Lady Q reached her to ask about a huge unpaid light bill in her name for the apartment on Cermak. Vivian suggested that Lady Q get the money to pay for the light bill from Queen Psycho. That evening when Lady Q made her scheduled call to Tino, she was noticeably upset. After he learned why, Tino wanted to send the Latin Kings to Vivian's new place to collect the money from her. Lady Q knew it would be an ugly scene if the Latin Kings showed up at Vivian's place and so she talked Tino out of doing this. About two weeks later there was an electrical fire in Vivian's South Side apartment that damaged everything inside. Lady Q's mother immediately reached out to Lady Q and Tino asking for financial assistance. Lady Q told Vivian to use the light bill money as assistance or the five grand she'd asked her to store away for her in a bank account. Soon thereafter Vivian and Marta paid Lady Q a visit. After they knocked on the door and Lady Q opened it, they walked in her apartment through one door and out the other without saying a word. Lady Q couldn't care less about this show of defiance. She was happy in the knowledge that even though her man was in jail, she had a palace for an apartment without even working, while Vivian's man did nothing but leech off her as she struggled to survive.

After this defiant visit from Vivian and her mother, it would be a long time before Lady Q saw either of them again. She was in no mood to visit any of her family members and preferred that they stay away from her, too. She was completely consumed by doing right by Tino and helping his business flourish. Lady Q began to gain the respect and admiration of many of the elite members of the Latin Kings, most of whom were doing time. Soon many called her to just talk, to ask for advice, or to ask for her help with one of their family members.

The Inca of the Latin Kings of Whipple and Wabansia, a twenty-something career gang member called Bibi, was assigned the task of taking care of Lady Q's every financial need. In exchange he was provided with large quantities of cocaine to sell to cover Lady Q's expenses and then some. But greed is hard to resist on the streets, and Bibi was no exception. Through

Tino, Lady Q asked for a half ounce of cocaine for a friend of hers, and Tino asked Bibi to supply this. Bibi questioned the logic of giving Lady Q cocaine for free. Nevertheless he did as he was told. Lady Q passed the cocaine to her friend, who in turn sold it on the street. Since it was top quality, it sold quickly. Days after she'd gotten the first half ounce, Lady Q requested another half ounce from Tino for her friend—again from Bibi— only this time she paid for it. Bibi delivered the cocaine and Lady Q took out a small amount for her own personal use before giving the package to her friend. When Lady Q snorted the cocaine her nose began to bleed, and she instantly knew that something was being added to the cocaine to extend it. The next day Lady Q told Tino she suspected that Bibi was messing with the merchandise by cutting it with an additive. Tino was not surprised by this accusation because other people he'd sent to get cocaine from Bibi had also complained about the quality.

Tino summoned Bibi and a Latin King named Cuba to Lady Q's apartment at a time when he would call. Over the speakerphone, Tino asked Lady Q to tell Bibi what she suspected. Bibi denied that he'd added anything to the cocaine and instead suggested that the drug had already been manipulated in this way when he got it. Tino ordered Bibi to turn over all the drugs and money to Cuba immediately and warned him that everything needed to be accounted for.

Once Cuba received the merchandise, it became clear that Bibi was in fact cutting the cocaine with a product known on the street as Bolivian Rock, a substance sold at local drug paraphernalia shops and used as a powdered local anesthetic. It mimicked cocaine's numbing effect, making it a perfect additive. When the drug was cut with small amounts of Bolivian Rock, it allowed a dealer to make more profit while maintaining the quality of the original product. But Bibi had become so greedy that he was extending one kilo into three with Bolivian Rock, rendering the cocaine almost worthless. For those who purchased cocaine to cook into a freebase form and smoke it, the cut didn't make much difference, but it was torture for those who snorted it.

They recovered very little useable cocaine from Bibi, and a large amount of money was missing as well. Lady Q felt certain that Bibi's life would come to an abrupt end at the hands of the Latin Kings and that it was just a matter of time before it happened. She was surprised when Bibi wasn't touched and actually went back into business selling his own merchandise within a week.

Bibi was involved in another incident a couple of months later, when Queen Psycho supposedly shot herself while in the company of Bibi and another Latin King. No gunpowder was found on her hand or on the side of her head, and Lady Q and many others found it hard to believe that a woman with so much pride who had recently became a mother would suddenly decide to commit suicide. But the police asked few questions, and they quickly dismissed the incident as a suicide. But Lady Q couldn't dismiss it so easily. She had known Queen Psycho well and refused to believe that she would take such an extreme measure at a time when she had so much to live for. In her mind, Queen Psycho had been murdered, and Bibi had either done it or was directly involved in the crime.

Lady Q began to realize that the gangs who ruled the streets had become more divided against each other than ever and that loyalty was a folktale from ancient gang history. She witnessed gang members jumping from one gang to another without any fear of repercussions from the gang they'd joined or the gang they'd deserted. Suspicious hits began to occur where deaths were blamed on rival gangs yet expanded the drug-selling territory of a different leader in the same gang. It was becoming a world where every gang member was for him- or herself with no loyalties even while standing in the midst of thousands representing the same colors.

The Latin Kings were not the only gang guilty of such treachery, but because they were the most recognized they developed a reputation on the streets as backstabbers. Lady Q witnessed this growing stupidity and destruction occurring all around her, yet her loyalty to the black and gold remained. She was the Queen of Kings and the protector of Inca Tino's domain, even as his domain grew increasingly smaller and began spiraling out of control.

11

THE PRICE OF LOYALTY

As THE WINTER of 1988 approached, Lady Q, now twenty-one, was on top of the world and living large, but that was about to change. The Federal Bureau of Investigation started looking into the role Tino played in the Latin Kings. On paper, Tino was the model prisoner, and the date when he would be eligible for parole was fast approaching. The authorities knew that Tino headed the Almighty Latin King Nation and the criminal empire they controlled, but they had no concrete evidence to prove this. They suspected that Tino had the final word regarding murders on the street and in jail, including attacks on Illinois Department of Corrections guards. Word got out that the FBI was building a case to ensure that Tino would never leave prison or have the opportunity to oversee the Latin King Nation as a free man.

Lady Q believed the FBI feared that once Tino was out of prison he would help re-create the extremely disciplined and well-structured organization that had once made the King Nation such a fierce opponent, and that he would reestablish the Kings as a trusted part of the community. The Latin King Nation was now a nationwide organization with more than a hundred thousand members. With the kind of leadership Tino could provide if released from prison, Lady Q believed, the Kings could become a force to be reckoned with on both legal and illegal issues.

It was rumored that the FBI was looking for substantial information they could use against Tino. Targeting those closest to him would help them gather such evidence. That meant targeting Lady Q. As soon as such speculations were heard on the street, Tino called Lady Q and told her to prepare to move to Aurora until this story could be confirmed or dismissed. On the very same night as his call, three members of the Aurora Latin Kings showed up at Lady Q's apartment. They took her, her daughter, and a handful of clothes out of the city to an undisclosed location, where Lady Q quickly found herself in the company of strangers. In the middle of the night they packed the rest of her belongings, loaded them into a truck, and brought them to her new home; her old apartment was abandoned.

LADY Q NEVER once questioned Tino's decision, not because she was afraid of him but because she respected him and loved him dearly. Tino was the only man who ever took the time to talk to her, share secrets with her, and treat her with respect. Tino never asked her to do anything she didn't want to do and always maintained complete confidence in her every word.

Tino had put his trust in Lady Q very quickly. Soon after she'd started visiting him, at their fourth meeting in fact, he'd told her the story of how he was doing time for a crime he didn't commit—the murder of two Vice Lords. Tino had been at a family birthday party the night of the murders, but the next day the cops picked him up. His brother asked him to serve as his alibi. Tino trusted his brother and didn't want him to get in trouble with the army since his brother was a soldier who had gone AWOL. Unfortunately for Tino, his brother didn't care about him as much as he cared about his freedom, and he sold Tino out. After Tino's arrest, his brother made a deal with the cops to get the AWOL erased from his record if he testified that Tino wasn't at the family gathering so the cops could place him in the bar where the murders had occurred. Tino was charged with first-degree murder and was eventually convicted and sentenced to thirty to sixty years. Lady Q knew that many inmates claim innocence, but she believed Tino when he told her this story and continues to believe him to this day.

In prison Tino found solace among other Latinos who were members of the Latin Kings. He gained the rank of Inca by being quick to respond to anyone who even remotely disrespected the Latin Kings and for his bravado during an all-out gang fight that took place in the Pontiac Correctional Center on July 22, 1978. The fight left three prison guards dead and two others critically injured. Seventeen Pontiac Correctional Center inmates were eventually indicted on charges of murder, attempted murder, mob action, and conspiracy for this action.

IN AURORA, LADY Q and Lisette lived in the basement apartment of a woman named Glenda, who was like Cuca—a woman who remained loyal to the Latin Kings and the Insane Deuces in order to stay high. Glenda was a six-foot-tall white single mother on welfare with two boys from different fathers. Her older son had muscular dystrophy and was bedridden. He didn't have to be bedridden, but his mother was too busy getting high to do anything else for him. Glenda picked at her facial blemishes whenever she was desperate for cocaine, her drug of choice, and she was desperate often. Minutes after snorting enough cocaine to satisfy her, she went looking for more. The result was a face full of craters, scars, and old and fresh scabs along with bleeding wounds that made her difficult to look at. But as bad as she looked, she always found someone to have sex with. There were always plenty of young intoxicated men around her apartment to be willing partners. Glenda was the most desperate woman Lady Q had ever come across. She completely ignored personal hygiene and housework and allowed the Latin Kings and Insane Deuces to do whatever they pleased in her apartment so that she wouldn't have to pay for drugs—an impossibility with two kids and only a welfare check to cover their expenses. From the moment she arrived, Lady Q couldn't wait to get out of this apartment.

In Chicago there were ugly wars between the Kings and the Deuces. These gangs were bitter rivals, mostly around the Diversey Projects area, but in Aurora they had a good working relationship. Nevertheless Lady Q was surprised and initially cautious about the strength of this alliance.

As soon as Lady Q arrived, a security detail was assigned to her that required the designated Kings to never leave her side, especially when she left the house. If Lady Q needed diapers or milk for her daughter, the Latin Kings had to either pick them up for her or go with her to the store to purchase them. If any of these bodyguards were caught away from her side, fellow gang members would punish them with a violation.

Lady Q was used to her independence. She was accustomed to being on her own and taking a walk whenever she felt like it instead of waiting for someone to take her somewhere or walk with her whenever she wanted to go someplace. Sometimes she dressed herself and her daughter to go for a walk around the block or to the nearest store without thinking about alerting those serving as her bodyguards. Such occasions always ended up with the Latin Kings in hot water and upset with Lady Q because of it. Such an intensive bodyguard detail wasn't a problem at first since many of the Aurora Latin Kings were eager to know their Inca's woman, but most of them were teenage boys and it didn't take long for Lady Q to become a burden on their time.

About a month after Lady Q arrived in Aurora, the apartment upstairs became vacant, and Lady Q made a phone call to Tino. He then made a call that provided the funds for Lady Q to rent the apartment, with enough extra money to provide for the comfort of herself and Lisette and the bodyguards. But the bodyguard routine began to get old for both the Latin Kings and Lady Q. Whenever the chief of the Aurora Kings came by and found that one of the teenagers he'd ordered to watch over Lady Q wasn't there, he'd call a violation on that member. After several violations on a couple of different Latin Kings, they began to resent Lady Q and walked around her apartment with visible hostility. Lady Q became sick of it and asked to attend one of their meetings so she could let them all know how she felt.

At the meeting Lady Q stood before the Aurora Latin Kings and told them she didn't want them as her bodyguards, and that it was Tino's doing and they needed to talk to him about that. Lady Q didn't want to get a reputation like Tammy's. That ended the antagonism against Lady Q, and this also marked the end of the bodyguards always being around her. But the fact that the Latin Kings no longer had to wait on Lady Q didn't stop them from coming by daily to hang out and get high. Lady Q continued to sell coke during this relocation period, and the all-day-and-all-night drug party that used to take place in Glenda's apartment now occurred in Lady Q's. Glenda was not happy—in one night her cocaine, marijuana, and alcohol supply dried up. She came upstairs every so often in search of drugs, but now they weren't as readily available. Eventually Glenda stopped coming to Lady Q's apartment altogether, stopped talking to her, and avoided her at all costs. Lady Q noticed but couldn't care less.

THE HOLIDAY SEASON came and went without any visit from the FBI. Nothing in Lady Q's life changed—gang warfare and territorial wars usually declined during the cold winter months in the Chicago area, but the presence of gang members and drug deals in Lady Q's apartment continued unabated. Being in Aurora, Lady Q got to know Tiny, the chief of all Latin Kings on the South Side of Chicago and the city's southern suburbs. Like Tino, he ruled over his portion of the kingdom from the penitentiary. Tiny would call Lady Q to make sure his boys were taking care of all her needs and that she was well protected. Their conversations led them to become good friends, and Tiny began to count on Lady Q to relay messages to his street soldiers. This was the case when a section of Latin Kings consisting of a lot of white boys opened up in Elgin, Illinois. Tiny asked Lady Q to go there and meet with the leaders of that section to set up a subsequent meeting with the Elgin Latin Kings and other well-established brothers, who would supply them with the drugs necessary to maintain the new section.

Lady Q and several Aurora Latin Kings made the trek to Elgin, to a neighborhood where King Tiny had told them they would find members of this new gang section. When they arrived at the destination they found nothing but empty streets. They circled around several times before seeing a couple of white boys who displayed an inner-city-street-thug appearance. As they approached the white boys, one of the Kings opened the car window and flashed the Latin Kings hand sign. The salute was returned. So the Aurora Kings and Lady Q decided they had found their contacts and parked the car.

The white boys from Elgin were defensive and questioned their gang affiliation even after one of the Aurora Latin Kings lifted his shirt to reveal a large five-pointed crown tattooed on his torso. The Elgin guys were drunk and belligerent. Because of this mistrust, an argument ensued, and spit from one of the Elgin gang members' mouths landed on the face of an Aurora King. The Aurora King stopped yelling, wiped his face, and began throwing punches. The white boys were overpowered and badly beaten, and the crew from Aurora got into their car and drove off feeling indestructible—so much so that they decided to circle back around to the site of the fight and take one more look at their handiwork. Lady Q objected to this and asked to be taken home but to no avail. As their car approached the spot where the white boys had been beaten, local gang members of various nationalities were already gathering. It was like they were monkeys coming down out of the trees, Lady Q thought. The car was surrounded. Before Lady Q and the Aurora Kings could speed off, another car blocked their exit. The Aurora Kings jumped out of the car and a free-for-all gang fight immediately ensued, interrupted only by the Elgin police.

When the police arrived, the participants began running every which way, but not many got away. Once gathered, the two groups argued, accusing the other side of starting the melee. The Elgin police ignored all accounts and arrested everyone. At the station all the arrestees were placed in a single large room and lectured by the cops. Then the Elgin police took pictures of everyone and classified them as members of the Latin Kings. The detainees were told they'd be watched and would be immediately arrested if any gang activity was evident in their city. Lady Q and the Aurora Latin Kings were charged with Unlawful Use of a Weapon (UUW) due to a loaded gun found in their car. After spending the night in jail, they were each given an I-bond and released from jail on a signature and without a fine.

Soon thereafter, King Tiny paid for an attorney and they were all sentenced to three months of court supervision. Each conviction would be wiped off their record if they kept clean for that time period. Three months later Lady Q's criminal record was once again clean. At the initial court hearing the Elgin Latin Kings had shown up to apologize and extend their loyalty to the Queen of the Kings. The actions they had taken the day of the fight had earned them a visit from some high-ranking South Side Latin Kings who'd handed out severe punishment. This was the last time Lady Q ever visited Elgin.

A COUPLE OF months after the Elgin episode, Tino needed a couple of guys to make a run for him into Chicago, where they would deliver twenty-five thousand dollars to a Latin King named Radamous and return with two kilos of cocaine. It was the type of transaction that happens without incident on a daily basis in the world of street gangs. It's an especially risk-free transaction when the deal is between members of the same gang. The two guys chosen for the job were an Aurora Latin King named Twin and the chief of the Insane Deuces, nicknamed Lil Man. Lady Q had grown close to both of these gang members, and they were also good friends with each other. Lil Man and Twin went into the city with twenty-five thousand dollars in cash and peace of mind because they'd be dealing with allies.

While awaiting the meet-up, the Latin King who was to meet them in Chicago, Radamous, had worked himself into a frenzy of hate. He'd been told the deal was with the chief of the Insane Deuces from this far western suburb of Chicago, yet the Insane Deuces were sworn enemies of the Kings in the city. When the two young men walked through the doorway of the meet-up building they were immediately shot, their money was taken, and they were left for dead. Miraculously they survived but would never be the same—the chief of the Deuces was left paralyzed from the neck down, and the Latin King needed the help of a walker to get around. It's not clear if Radamous knew ahead of time that a Latin King would be accompanying the Deuce or if he'd ignored this information to justify his premeditated plan.

The consequences to Radamous for his actions reveal the mentality of gangs: there were no consequences. He was well known for bringing in a large cash flow to the gang. So his actions were excused with the claim that either he didn't know there was a King present or he didn't know the Aurora Deuces were allies to the Latin Kings of the city. The twenty-five grand was never recovered either. Gang life and alliances continued unchanged on the streets of Chicago, but the relationship between the Latin Kings and Insane Deuces of Aurora changed completely. Soon the sour stench and unpleasant taste of the inner city would spread to the small suburban town.

Lady Q was sickened by this news and by what had happened to her two friends. She didn't understand why Radamous was allowed to get away with it. And when she came to understand that it was even beyond her power or Tino's to bestow discipline on a gang member with Radamous's rank and money-making power, she understood that even Tino's reach had its limits. All she could do was apologize and share the grief of the Kings and the Deuces of Aurora. The Latin Kings were forced to accept the lack of consequences of these actions; the Deuces stopped coming around to hang out with Lady Q after the shooting.

Three days after the shooting, Lady Q sat in her living room with her daughter and a young woman she had befriended who wanted to become a Queen when there was a knock at the front door. Lady Q looked out the side window and saw Smurf and Yo-Yo, two Deuces she knew very well, so she let them in.

"Where the fuck have you guys been? I hope you don't think I had something to do with what happened to your chief," Lady Q said as she walked away from the door.

"Get some clothes and stuff for you and your daughter and come with us," Smurf instructed Lady Q.

"I ain't going no-fuckin'-where."

Smurf repeated his request two more times. Lady Q responded in the same way each time. Smurf made the request more forcefully the fourth time.

The television blared and Lisette banged a toy on the floor as she played, yet Lady Q could hear no sound. She stared at Smurf but didn't move.

"Lady Q, we don't want to hurt you but you're coming with us the easy way or the hard way," Smurf continued as he pulled a nine-millimeter semiautomatic gun from the waistband of his pants. Yo-Yo revealed an Uzi submachine gun, which he pointed at Lady Q. She slowly got up from the couch and walked to her bedroom with Smurf following right behind. She grabbed a duffel bag from the closet and began putting things in it for herself and her daughter while she wondered what Smurf and Yo-Yo were capable of.

The Deuces led Lady Q, Lisette, and the young would-be Queen to a car parked right in front of the house and drove them to a hotel. At the hotel Lady Q was assured that neither she nor her daughter would be hurt if the Chicago Latin Kings turned over Radamous in exchange—their demand for her safe release. The Deuces debated over what to do about the young woman with Lady Q. The Deuces knew her well and knew that she wasn't in a gang. Lady Q asked to be allowed to use the bathroom and while in there she quickly scribbled a telephone number in Chicago where she knew Tino would call once he wasn't able to locate Lady Q. She returned to the room, sat next to the girl, and secretly gave her the piece of paper. She waited a little while before asking the Deuces to let the girl go. She said the girl had nothing to do with what had happened to their chief so there was no reason to keep her. The Deuces decided to let her go, but before they did they searched her and found the phone number that Lady Q had passed to her. Yo-Yo held the Uzi to the girl's head, threatened to kill her and her family if she said anything about Lady Q's kidnapping, and then told her she could go. The Deuces waited about a half hour after the girl left and then moved Lady Q and her daughter to another hotel.

For the next three days the Deuces moved Lady Q from hotel to hotel. They didn't disrespect her in any way and made sure that she and her daughter were well fed and comfortable. The Deuces even shared their weed with Lady Q. By the second day it became apparent to Lady Q that the Deuces had no clue how to carry out their plan—they would have to go through Tino to get their demands met, and to go through Tino they would have to allow Lady Q to go someplace where Tino could contact her or allow her to call one of his top generals to relay the message to him. Neither of these seemed like good options since in each case they would need to face gang members they weren't prepared to deal with. The Deuces began to realize that even if the Kings agreed to exchange Radamous for Lady Q and her daughter, the Kings wouldn't just drive away and call it a day. They knew, too, it wouldn't be young street punks showing up for the exchange but older hard-core members of the Latin Kings, Kings who would kill them on sight.

On the morning of the third day, the Deuces put her and Lisette into their car and drove them home, dropping them off unharmed. They said nothing to Lady Q as they drove her back to her apartment; she said nothing to them as she and her daughter exited the car, but she turned and looked them both dead in the eye before they drove away, and with that they knew their ordeal was just beginning.

Lady Q immediately began calling people to inform them what had happened and asked that Tino be informed. No more than thirty minutes had elapsed when Aurora Latin Kings began showing up in droves and circling Lady Q's Aurora neighborhood looking for members of the Insane Deuces. The two gangs had been close allies, and both had had members who became

victims of a senseless act of violence, and now they were looking to destroy each other. Lady Q's safety was entrusted to four
Latin Kings sent to watch over her, but these Kings were
teenagers pretending to be gangsters, each with a handgun and
words of bravado, talking tough about the fate that would
befall any Deuce who showed up that day. But the day progressed quietly. By nightfall Lady Q and her four bodyguards
were convinced that nothing was going to happen. They smoked
weed and watched television late into the night until exhaus-
tion overcame them. Lady Q dozed off sitting on the sofa holding her daughter. Sleeping in front of the couch was a
sixteen-year-old, and on the floor on either side of the couch
was a fifteen-year-old bodyguard. The eldest bodyguard, age seventeen, slept on the floor in the living room.

Loud repetitive bangs woke up Lady Q at about three in
the morning. The sound came from the back door and stopped
almost as soon as it began. Before anyone could investigate, they
heard what sounded like a stampede from the downstairs apartment. Lady Q sat up and held her daughter as she woke up the
young guardian who slept before her. Two of the Kings walked
around, looking bewildered, trying to figure out what was happening. Suddenly the banging sound resumed, only this time it
was much louder, and as the bangs continued holes began to
appear in the living room floor. At once everyone scrambled to
get away from the living room as bullets flew up from below.

When there was a momentary pause in the bullet storm,
Lady Q ran into her bedroom, put Lisette in the corner of her
closet, and threw all the clothes she could find on top of her to
conceal her. She then ran back out of the bedroom, distancing
herself from her daughter. She was certain the Deuces would

come upstairs and kill her. At least, she reasoned, they wouldn't find her daughter, so her life would be spared. As Lady Q reached the door, the shooting stopped. She scanned the living room and saw her bodyguards pasted to the corners of the room. She realized she only saw three of them; the fourth, the one who had fallen asleep on the floor by the sofa, was still on the floor, bleeding and gasping for air. Again they heard running toward the back of the house. One of the Latin Kings ran out the front door, crossed the street, and banged on a neighbor's door, asking them to call the police. After this King had left, Lady Q went back into her bedroom, grabbed Lisette, and ran out of the front of the building to be hidden within the gathering crowd of people, waiting for the police to arrive, which was within minutes.

While the Aurora police responded quickly, they weren't fast enough to apprehend the perpetrators. The police called an ambulance for the fifteen-year-old bodyguard. He'd been hit twice in one leg and once in the back. He survived the incident. Lady Q realized that she never saw any of the other three bodyguards draw their weapons to defend her, but they did manage to gather their guns and their drugs and get them out of the apartment before the police arrived. Once the police declared the area safe, Lady Q went back into her apartment to answer their questions. All she offered was that bullets had been fired from the unit below, and she didn't know who the shooters were. The cops told Lady Q that she had a guardian angel that night because a dozen rounds had been emptied into the lock of the back door, but it hadn't budged. They told her that they had never seen a lock take so many direct hits and still remain secure. The police eventually left, frustrated that the five young people who had nearly been murdered couldn't give them any information to help them track down the shooters. Less than an hour after the cops left the apartment, Lady Q was in a car and on her way out of Aurora. She had lived there for a year.

Lady Q ended up in Joliet, another suburb outside Chicago, staying among the Latin Kings there. Again she was forced to live with people she didn't know and wasn't certain she could trust. Luckily for Lady Q the flow of cocaine followed her wherever she went, so she was always welcome. She didn't deal coke at this time, but it was always present.

Lady Q moved in with a woman who did her best to keep her life separate from the dealings of her boyfriend, the father of one of her children. He was a member of the Latin Kings and currently locked up with Tino. The woman, a petite Mexican who worked an office job, had no choice but to accept Lady Q into her home. Although she wasn't happy to be hosting Lady Q, or with the Latin King traffic that was part of the deal, she was delighted to receive the money she was paid for Lady Q and Lisette's room and board. Also, she had no objection to smoking weed with Lady Q on a daily basis, even in front of her own children.

While Lady Q was safe and relaxing in Joliet, all hell broke loose in Aurora. Other than her clothes and her daughter's clothes, Lady Q had abandoned all of her belongings. The day after she vacated the apartment, the Latin Kings of Aurora went to recover some of her possessions for their own use, and the Deuces fired into the apartment from the street. An intense gun battle took place over the next few minutes, which miraculously didn't leave any casualties. The outside of the building and the cars parked on the street in front of it were targeted.

Two days later the Insane Deuces returned and, although the apartment was now empty, riddled it with bullets once again. Lady Q learned of these events from the front-page news stories that appeared for five days straight.

Other news that reached Lady Q in Joliet from her time in Aurora was the death of Glenda's sick, neglected son. Glenda had gone to the penitentiary to visit her new boyfriend, whom she'd met through an acquaintance while he was already doing time. She left her kids with a woman who was just as desperate for drugs as she was. Neither Glenda nor the babysitter checked in on Glenda's son with muscular dystrophy until the next day, when he was found dead. Lady Q was saddened by the news but felt that death was a better option for him than the life he'd been dealt.

Lady Q didn't stay long in Joliet. It soon became clear that the FBI investigation of Tino's associates didn't involve her. In a matter of weeks she was on her way back to Chicago.

WHILE LADY Q was away from Chicago she had not only witnessed the changing alliances and allegiances within and between gangs based on money and power. She also had gained new insight into the lives of girls in gangs. She came into contact with many young women who'd become mothers too early in life, often parenting children fathered by gang members who either left them to fend for themselves or stuck around to make their lives even worse. Lady Q discovered time and again that many young women were ignorant, never imagining they'd get pregnant out of wedlock. Because of her status among the Queens, many of these young women waited on Lady Q hand and foot and did so willingly. Being around Lady Q brought them free and plentiful drugs and good-looking gang members to screw. Lady Q thought herself better than such young women because she kept Lisette clean and well dressed, and they always had a place to live and good food to eat because Tino provided for them. In this way Tino had pretty much adopted Lisette as his own, so there weren't a multitude of men in her life that Lisette confused with daddy. At the same time, however, Lisette was exposed to more drugs than many people see in a lifetime and probably witnessed a lot of alcohol-infused sexual behavior, too—situations that Lady Q never thought to conceal from her.

ONCE BACK IN Chicago, Lady Q found an apartment in an area surrounded by gangs but with little gang activity on her block itself. As soon as she settled in, she resumed her drug-trafficking business. Once again she headed out to the western suburbs to pick up cocaine and deliver the kilos to specified locations in Chicago for J-Cool. Lady Q made a lot of money and spent it just as fast as she made it. She continued to indulge in the merchandise she was dealing.

On one occasion Lady Q took part in the movement of twenty-one kilos of cocaine. There was no way she could carry so much by herself, so Tino's cousin Pablo traveled with her and J-Cool. She recalled once sitting at J-Cool's living room table with more money than she had ever seen in her life—more than one hundred thousand dollars—being counted out and rubber-banded into bundles of five thousand each. The money belonged to a group of Arabs who for some reason unknown to Lady Q had a good relationship with Tino. The twenty-one kilos were for them.

The Latin Kings' primary drug suppliers were Mexicans with connections to the Herrera drug cartel of Mexico. They always insisted on meeting in various locations in or around Maywood, Illinois, and routinely followed the same procedure for exchanging drugs for money—the Latin Kings would give the Mexicans a detailed description of the car they would be driving and would park in a place predetermined by the Mexicans. Normally the Mexicans were already waiting and had several cars parked at the meeting place. One driver would flash his headlights one time to signal to the Latin Kings which vehicle to go to and make the transaction. The exchange took place not in the signaling car but in the car parked directly in front of that one.

This particular deal involving the twenty-one kilos of pure cocaine was arranged to take place in nearby Melrose Park, in the parking lot of an amusement park known as KiddieLand. The transaction was scheduled to occur during the park's regular hours of operation so the parking lot would be full and reduce any suspicion raised by isolated cars. Both the Latin Kings and the Mexicans always followed the rules of their arranged transaction to the letter, so it seemed extremely odd when the Mexicans altered these arrangements.

J-Cool entered the KiddieLand parking lot and found a spot to park where it was easy to scan a large area of the lot for flashing headlights. Lady Q sat on the passenger seat next to J-Cool with Pablo sitting on the rear passenger-side seat. All three of them peered into the darkness looking around for the signal. J-Cool had turned off his car's headlights but kept the motor running, prepared to drive off at the first sign of police or anything that didn't seem normal. As the three concentrated on locating the signal, a car pulled up next to them on the passenger side. The driver-side window rolled down to reveal one of the Mexicans they were waiting for. In Spanish, the Mexican driver instructed Pablo to get in the backseat of his car and bring the money. This was a complete deviation from the standard transaction, but these people had done business with the Latin Kings for decades, so there was no reason to mistrust them. J-Cool activated a button in the glove compartment of his car that unlocked the trunk as Pablo exited the car. Pablo opened the trunk and retrieved the duffel bag containing the cash and got into the backseat of the car driven by the Mexican. As Pablo opened the rear door, Lady Q noticed there was another man sitting in the backseat and a second man in the passenger side of the front seat. As soon as Pablo got into the car, the Mexican drove off and parked a short distance away in an area visible to J-Cool and Lady Q. No one worried. After about five minutes, Pablo exited the Mexican's car and began walking toward J-Cool and Lady Q, empty-handed.

"What the fuck?" Lady Q said softly.

Pablo got into the car and told J-Cool that the Mexicans didn't want to count so much money out in the open and had requested that they be allowed to go count it elsewhere and return within a half hour. They said that J-Cool should flash his headlights once to signal that it was OK for them to proceed. J-Cool was not at all amused by the lack of trust being displayed by the Latin Kings' longtime drug-trafficking partners, but he had no reason to doubt them. He flashed his lights once and the Mexicans drove away.

J-Cool, Lady Q, and Pablo didn't move from their original location for six hours, waiting and praying for the Mexicans to return. J-Cool was infuriated at first, but as time passed his anger turned to panic. Unbeknownst to Lady Q or Pablo, J-Cool had been making cocaine deals with the Mexicans that didn't involve the Latin Kings. He was expanding his business to include all street gangs, be they friend or foe to the Latin Kings, supplying anyone who wanted to set up shop as a drug dealer. Recently J-Cool had gotten greedy. He had received a large amount of cocaine from the Mexicans but was having a hard time repaying the debt. The amount of money J-Cool owed the Mexicans was only a quarter of the one hundred thousand–plus dollars they drove away with, but his bill was long overdue. Apparently the Mexicans decided that a lot of interest was due, too.

Lady Q watched J-Cool's hands tremble as he held on to the steering wheel during the drive back into the city. The air conditioner was on and yet she saw perspiration forming on his forehead. He had fucked up royally and he knew it. His only hope was to convince Tino to use his leverage with the Mexican business partners to retrieve either the cocaine or the money that belonged to the Arabs. In any case, J-Cool understood that an unpleasant future awaited him. While J-Cool didn't come clean, Lady Q started to put the pieces together.

That night J-Cool ignored all phone calls and pages, most of which came from the Arabs. Lady Q witnessed this. The next day he answered only one call—a call from Tino, who demanded to know why J-Cool was ignoring the Arabs. When J-Cool told Tino what had taken place, the normally calm and collected Inca of the Latin Kings reached a breaking point. Lady Q sat about ten feet away from J-Cool but could hear every curse being uttered by Tino loud and clear. Then there was silence. J-Cool didn't say a word. He just hung up the phone and sat on the love seat in his living room. He didn't move until the phone rang again about an hour later. Lady Q answered the phone and exchanged pleasantries with a Latin King general called Dead Eye before handing the phone to J-Cool. Dead Eye and J-Cool spoke on the phone for about ten minutes. It was mostly a one-way conversation, with Dead Eye talking and J-Cool listening. About two hours after that phone call, a silver Mercedes Benz pulled up in front of J-Cool's house and two Arab men and a woman got out and came toward the house. Before the trio had gotten halfway up the steps, J-Cool instructed Lady Q to open the door and let them in. The Arabs were polite but all business. They hadn't come to socialize; they'd come to collect items belonging to J-Cool as payment for the money he'd lost. These items included a brand-new customized Corvette and all of his jewelry. J-Cool's taste in jewelry would make even the flashiest rapper drool. Altogether, the Arabs walked away with much more than they had lost, and J-Cool was allowed to keep his life.

During a subsequent conversation with Tino, Lady Q realized how difficult it had been for Tino not only to salvage his relationship with the Arabs and the Mexicans but also to convince them to spare J-Cool's life. Tino was loyal to a fault to all his generals, especially ones he had grown up with such as J-Cool. But J-Cool's betrayal didn't occur without a cost—he was cut off from major dealings and was supposed to get a violation because of his actions. But Lady Q never found out if this violation took place—after that she was permanently separated from J-Cool.

Tino's cousin George became the main drug runner for Tino and the Latin Kings on the North Side. Lady Q and George quickly became inseparable to the point where there were rumors about the two being romantically involved. (She denies ever having sex with George.) At this time, George's son ran with the Imperial Gangsters. George gave him a kilo to sell. To cover for this missing kilo, George stepped on his merchandise with enough Bolivian Rock to make two or three kilos from the one. When he was caught, he was cut off from the Latin Kings drug pipeline and was shot in the knee as discipline and a reminder to others. Lady Q's business relationship with George came to an end.

It was now 1990. First Lady Nancy Reagan's Just Say No to Drugs campaign was in full swing, and people got locked up left and right for possession of narcotics. Anyone unlucky enough to get caught with cocaine during this period was treated worse than a rapist or murderer. Consequently cocaine became more scarce, the price rose, and the number of users declined. Lady Q had originally begun dealing because of the high demand for the drug. When the demand declined, she got out of the business.

12

THY KINGDOM GONE

LADY Q BECAME the landlord of the Humboldt Park drug-dealing scene on the Latin King side of the park. She no longer dealt herself, but she was now the overseer of the dealers who remained in the business. At least twenty to twenty-five different dealers sold a plethora of illegal drugs along an inner park road named Luis Munoz Marin Drive, named after Puerto Rico's first elected governor and the man responsible for the island becoming a Commonwealth of the United States. The Latin Kings ruled a portion of this drive, where people from all over the city could come to feed their addictions. Although most of the dealers were Latin Kings or in some way related to them, many were in business for themselves but purchased their supply from the Latin Kings.

As landlord, Lady Q collected fifty dollars a week from each dealer, including Latin Kings who wanted to open up shop in an area west of Sacramento Avenue in Humboldt Park. In return for their rent each week, the dealers could come to Lady Q with any complaints about misconduct by street soldiers or other dealers invading their territory, and Lady Q would respond by sending a group of Latin Kings to take care of the problem.

Those who tried to deal without permission or decided not to pay dues to Lady Q were brutally beaten in public to teach them and other potential rebels a lesson. This task made the Queen of Kings both loved and feared.

By the early 1990s, the upper echelon of the Latin Kings hierarchy had grown tired of all the mismanagement and greed infesting the Nation. They once again turned to the strong-arm tactics that had built their reputation as a fierce and ruthless gang a decade earlier. Because of Lady Q's love and loyalty to Tino, she turned in any King who played games that fed his own greed. Lady Q informed Tino about the misdeeds and then bluntly repeated the facts in the face of the accused when the high-ranking members were ready to extract their punishment. Staying true to Tino in this manner made it very hard suddenly for Lady Q to find rides to visit Tino in Menard. Consequently her visits to him diminished dramatically, but they continued to talk regularly during this period.

Lady Q also started realizing that some of the high-ranking members of the Latin Kings—the ones Tino counted on to be his eyes, ears, and muscle—were also burning the Nation for their personal gain. She witnessed the Latin Kings proclaiming themselves a united organization, but it was in name only. This became crystal clear to her one day when she was standing at the window of her apartment. As she turned away from the window she heard gunshots ring out. She turned back to the window, quickly scanned the park, and saw a car speed off out onto North Avenue, heading west and almost crashing into oncoming traffic. A crowd quickly gathered around a bench in the park, almost directly across from her apartment. Lady Q didn't bother going outside to find out what had happened. She knew the news would reach her soon enough. Later that day she was informed that one of the generals of the Latin Kings, an original member of the gang, had been murdered execution-style by another King. The murdered general had long ago begun to use his position for his own personal gain, repeatedly burning the gang out of drugs, weapons, and money without any repercussions due to his rank within the organization. He was even accused of killing a Latin Queen who refused his sexual advances. But on this day, his luck ran out. This murder, however, was more about sending a message to others in the gang that betrayal of the Latin King Nation would not be tolerated than it was a payback for his past misdeeds against the Nation.

Lady Q finally decided to make drastic changes in her life after seeing gang members turn against and kill each other, seeing high-ranking officials in the gang make decisions based on greed, and especially after realizing that some people in the Nation, some of those she'd trusted the most, were telling Tino lies about her behavior. She no longer felt there was any way one Latin King or Queen could trust another. She had been on the streets long enough to know when it was time to move on.

She began to make arrangements to separate herself from all but a handful of Latin Kings and Queens. She needed to do this for herself—to stay alive—and she needed to make certain her daughter was safe from anyone who might seek revenge against her. She quit her landlord duties, but she stayed in contact with Tino over the phone.

One of the only other people who Lady Q had remained in contact with over the years and still trusted was a woman named Sol, the wife of Tito, a Beach and Spaulding King who was in prison with Tino. Sol (her nickname means "sun" in Spanish) was a tall, fair-skinned, attractive Italian woman. Like Lady Q, Sol garnered a lot of respect from the Latin Kings and Queens on the street not just because of her husband but also because of her solidarity with the street soldiers. When Lady Q finally decided it was time to break away from the Latin Kings, she reached out to Sol, who was making her own exit from the old ways. Lady Q and Lisette moved in with Sol in another area of Chicago known as K-Town, located on and around Division just west of Pulaski and extending all the way to Cicero.

The name of this area comes from the street names, which all begin with the letter K. The building where Lady Q and Sol lived was located on Keeler and Division deep in the heart of the K-Town Insane Unknowns' 'hood. The building had twelve apartments, six in front and six in the rear. A member of the Unknowns managed it. A haven for criminal activity, you could find all the drugs you could find on the street within the confines of this building—marijuana, cocaine, various forms of LSD. With Lady Q's arrival a new drug was added to the list: China White heroin.

Lady Q needed to find a new way to make money to finance her departure from the Latin Kings and make it stick. A couple of Kings had started a booming business selling heroin on the far North Side of the city. She maintained contact with these two Kings even as she made moves to extract herself from the gang. They supplied Lady Q with a small amount of heroin to see how it would sell in K-Town. It sold quickly, and word spread within the junkie community that quality China White was available in her building at Division and Keeler. The small amount she started with quickly turned into ounces, and overnight Lady Q had a booming heroin shop raking in thousands of dollars a day, allowing her to finance her own apartment. Almost two months after Lady Q moved in with Sol, a second-floor rear apartment became vacant and Lady Q became its new tenant.

Her business grew so quickly and was so profitable that she hired members of the Unknowns to sell the drug for her on the streets in shifts that ran from ten to ten. She didn't want to deal 24/7 out of fear she'd get hot too quickly. Lady Q made sure to pay her dealers well, thereby earning their unconditional loyalty and respect. Unlike many of the Latin Kings she had dealt with in the past, the Unknowns treated her like a mother figure. They would shy away from using offensive language in her presence. Lady Q noticed this change and appreciated it enough to return the favor.

Sol and Lady Q remained friends, but Sol began a new romance and stopped going to visit Tito. Sol had driven both herself and Lady Q to the prison, so now Lady Q could rarely visit Tino. But that didn't mean her communication or connection to Tino ceased. In fact, it increased. The Unknowns had a scam going in the building where they'd have a phone hooked up using a bogus name, would run up the bill into the thousands, and when the line was finally disconnected, they'd repeat the same process in a different apartment. Lady Q didn't have a clue whose name the phone was installed under, or where it would be connected next, and she didn't care as long as she could talk to Tino daily.

Even without the responsibility for Tino's cocaine business or having his loyal members hanging around her, Lady Q's relationship with Tino continued to grow. Because Lady Q no longer counted on Tino to supply her with merchandise or money, she felt a lot more comfortable calling herself his woman and was elated by his continuing trust in her. Without Latin Kings street business to discuss, Lady Q and Tino's conversations instead turned to issues of family, their future, and even the possibility of marriage. Tino's divorce from Tammy had been finalized a few years before, so he was a free man and ready to build a future with the woman he trusted the most. Lady Q was speechless whenever Tino brought up the subject of marriage. She knew she could never go through with a wedding as long as he was in jail. She was sensitive to Tino's feelings and discussed the subject with him but was careful not to promise anything or lead him to believe that she wanted a wedding to happen between them.

Lisette was now five years old and attending school. She was a very cute, quick-witted child with good street smarts and a sense of humor. She was also a very bright little girl, and complimentary letters about her excellent schoolwork were sent home to her mother. Lady Q was very proud of her daughter but didn't even think about making changes in her lifestyle that would encourage Lisette's educational growth. Not a day went by that Lady Q's apartment wasn't completely polluted with marijuana smoke, which her little girl was breathing and had been for the majority of her life. Along with continuously exposing her daughter to drug use and drug packaging for street sale, guns were always present, as was promiscuous sexual behavior. This was not a safe environment to raise a child in, and it's not an unusual way for kids in the 'hood to grow up. Lisette was always nicely dressed in the latest styles and was always polite, and whenever Lady Q dropped her daughter off in the morning or picked her up from school at night she seemed a model of responsibility. No one in the outside world would know that Lisette's mother was one of the top drug dealers in the neighborhood or that she could pick up the phone and have someone killed. Sadly, Lisette was not the only child who lived this double life.

Lady Q's China White business became a fifteen-thousand-dollar-a-week operation. The Kings who had helped her start the business were extremely pleased with the profits they made from Lady Q's shop, but they also felt the stress of her high demand for the drug. On the first of the month when government checks were handed out, a line of junkies waiting to purchase their fix formed outside her building. More often than not, Lady Q's stash ran out on these days no matter how well prepared she thought she was. She could make as much as fifteen or twenty thousand dollars on those days. The junkies who couldn't get their fix from the first batch would hang around the building until another batch was delivered. It got to the point where the Unknowns had to chase junkies from the building to keep away unwanted attention from the cops. But the entrance to the building faced a high-traffic street, and there was no way to keep this bevy of activity from being noticed. With all the drugs being sold out of Lady Q's apartment and with the building being a known gang hangout, a visit from the Chicago Police Department was inevitable.

When Lady Q lived with Sol, she had become acquainted with a single mother named Alee who lived in the rear apartment right across from them. She was in her midtwenties, with three kids from different fathers who she supported with a welfare check. Oftentimes, however, she used this money for drugs rather than food or rent. Alee's mismanagement of the little money she received got her evicted after she failed to pay her rent for three months in a row. The rumor going around the building was that she got away with skipping out on the rent for three months because she was fucking the building manager, who was married and lived in the same building. But when the building manager's wife grew suspicious, he was forced to evict her. Alee had nowhere to go and was on the verge of becoming homeless with winter fast approaching. Lady Q heard about Alee's fate and remembered how much she herself had suffered as a homeless mother walking the streets of Lancaster, so she offered Alee and her children shelter in her apartment. Lady Q and Alee became good friends. They shared a love of smoking marijuana and snorting cocaine.

Alee became Lady Q's gofer, but she embraced the responsibility. The women in the building and outside the building stopped bothering Alee because now she was living with Tino's woman, and that commanded respect that covered her as well. She started carrying herself in a more confident way and was even able to meet a guy who didn't think badly of her. Her new boyfriend, a member of the Insane Unknowns named Joey, visited her often. During one visit he gave her a western-style collector's gun to hold for him. It was an old gun, but it was in perfect working order and loaded.

When the summer of 1991 came around, the streets filled with people in search of drugs, and the gangbangers went out in full force ready to supply the goods, willing to cut each other's life short—or any innocent bystander unlucky enough to be at the wrong place at the wrong time—for the opportunity to make the sale. During the warm weather in Chicago, gang members often lost what little self-control they had and committed senseless acts of violence without any thought to the consequences of their actions. Gang members opened fire on cars they believed contained rivals and then ran for cover in places where they routinely hung out or sold drugs.

On a Tuesday morning shortly after Lady Q took Lisette to school, the Kings who supplied her with heroin dropped off a delivery of 129 quarter bags of China White heroin. Business was so good that the supply accounted for only one day's worth of sales. About a half hour afterward, Lady Q had just finished recounting the bags of heroin and was carrying them in a plastic bag into her bedroom to get a joint when there was a loud knock at the door. Alee went to see who it was. As she approached the door there was another loud knock and a man's voice yelled "Police!" followed by a loud bang as the door was kicked completely off its hinges. Six or seven plainclothes police officers charged into the apartment, guns drawn, and screamed at Alee to sit down. Lady Q heard footsteps approaching her so quickly that she had no time to do anything with the bags of heroin in her hands except to throw them toward the open window in her bedroom and hope for the best. No sooner did Lady Q let fly the drugs than her bedroom door swung open and a gun was pressed against the back of her head.

"Get your ass out here slowly," the cop yelled at Lady Q as he backed out of the room with his gun still pointed directly at her head. She came face-to-face with Detective O'Quinn of the Grand and Central Gang Crime Unit. Detective O'Quinn, a large Irish man and veteran of the unit, was well known by most gang members. The detective recognized Lady Q from her days on Homer and Albany. They sat down at the kitchen table, and O'Quinn asked Lady Q if her mother still lived in that same neighborhood. It was an odd juxtaposition of niceties with the violence going down at the same time. He placed his warrant in her hands and asked if there were any guns in the house. O'Quinn told Lady Q that it had been the Unknowns running inside the building after shooting at rivals that led them to her because, after all, she was the Queen of Kings. Lady Q told the detective that the only weapon in her apartment was an old western pistol that probably didn't even work. As she told him this she heard one cop say "Oh, man, look at this," and another began to laugh. Two detectives walked out of Lady Q's bedroom, one of them carrying the loaded gun, the other carrying the plastic bag of heroin.

"You know where she hid this shit?" the detective carrying the drugs asked Detective O'Quinn. "In her kid's fuckin' toy box," he finished before O'Quinn had a chance to say a word. Alee had hidden her boyfriend's gun at the bottom of a toy box that neither her kids nor Lisette paid much attention to, and when Lady Q had thrown the bag of heroin toward the window it landed instead in the same toy box. It didn't look good from any perspective.

Lady Q was taken into custody and charged with possession of a controlled substance with the intent to deliver and unlawful use of a weapon. At the police station Detective O'Quinn took Lady Q into a room and sat her down at a table where a white guy in a suit sat with dozens of photographs before him. Lady Q's chair was directly in front of the photographs. The man pushed the pictures toward her. She was shocked to see pictures of herself, Sol and her husband Tito, Tino, J-Cool, and many more of the high-ranking Latin Kings and Queens. The man identified himself as an FBI agent and told Lady Q that he'd rather talk to her at another location where they could be open and frank with each other if she was interested in having the charges against her dropped. Lady Q sat back in her chair and chuckled sarcastically.

"This is about Tino, isn't it?" she said. "You want me to help fuck up Tino. There is nothing to say. That man should be free and you know it."

The agent started picking up the pictures as he told Lady Q this was a onetime offer and that she should take advantage of it. She said she wasn't interested and yelled for Detective O'Quinn at the top of her lungs, demanding she be removed from the room.

Lady Q was taken into the Narcotics division for processing and was given the opportunity to make a phone call. She called Sol and asked her if she could pick up Lisette from school and take care of her in her absence. Lady Q told Sol that at some point her mother or sister would probably come around to claim Lisette and that Sol shouldn't, under any circumstances, let them take her. Lady Q knew she was screwed and prepared for the worst. After the arrest paperwork was completed, she was taken to a small jail cell to share with two African American women who had been picked up for prostituting themselves to make money to buy heroin. One of the women lay sleeping on the single metal bench in the cell; the other lay on the floor. Neither batted an eye when the cell door clanged open or when it slammed shut. Lady Q's two roommates woke up the next time the cell door was opened, about five in the evening, when a guard came to tell Lady Q she had a visitor.

For all the street smarts and experience Lady Q had in the criminal world, she had no experience behind bars, other than as a visitor. (Her overnight stay after the Elgin incident had been a misdemeanor, with no worries about serious jail time.) Now that tables had turned, even though she was just in a precinct lockup, it felt like a maximum-security prison to her. Visitors were not usually permitted in local police stations except when the visitor is an attorney, and that was who Lady Q's visitor was. The Kings who supplied Lady Q with China White had sent a lawyer to represent her. He told her that things didn't look good for getting her out that day. She was more than likely going to spend the night in jail and would have to appear before a judge in the morning. Lady Q told the lawyer to tell his boys who'd hired him that she had made a hell of a lot of money for them and that she would spend the night in jail, but she wanted out the next day. The attorney left and Lady Q was led back to her cell, now with a glimmer of hope that she might get out without doing jail time after all. That feeling wouldn't last long, however, as she had a long night behind bars to think about her situation.

Lady Q had been taken into custody just before noon and hadn't had anything to eat or drink since then. As night set in, the guards came around the cells handing out cold bologna sandwiches and eight-ounce boxes of grape juice. Although Lady Q was starving, she couldn't stomach the sandwich, which consisted of a half-inch-thick piece of baloney between two stale, squashed pieces of white bread. She drank the juice but gave the sandwich to one of her junkie cell mates, who split it with the other.

In the cell block where Lady Q sat in a corner against metal walls, it was as cold as an icebox. Her body shivered and trembled uncontrollably, so she hugged herself as tightly as she possibly could to try to keep warm. She was exhausted, but the cold coupled with thoughts racing through her head didn't allow her to sleep. As she sat there looking at her cell mates sleeping soundly as if they were accustomed to the accommodations, reality suddenly hit Lady Q, and she no longer felt confident she would ever again see the outside world. Up until then she had all but dismissed that she had been arrested for possession of a significant amount of heroin and a loaded gun. Her cockiness and streetwise ways had carried her through this day so far, but sitting in that cold cell, reality finally kicked her in the ass and woke her up to the seriousness of the situation. There was not much she could do. Her life was in the hands of others.

The next morning the loud clanking noise of cell doors startled her. A guard walked around telling everyone to prepare for court. Lady Q was taken into a holding cell behind the courthouse at the twenty-fifth district court located inside the Grand and Central Police Department to wait for her turn in front of the judge. As she waited, two attorneys came in to speak to her and let her know they would be representing her—one was the lawyer she'd spoken with the previous day; Tino had sent the other. The attorneys told Lady Q that because of the loaded weapon and the fact that it was found in a toy box along with the narcotics, the judge would likely deny an I-bond request and set a high bail. They advised her that they would do everything in their power to get her an I-bond or at the least the lowest bail possible. The attorneys reiterated several times that in their opinion there was no possible way an I-bond would be granted because Lady Q was charged with a Class X felony—the most severe felony in the Illinois penal code.

Lady Q was not pleased with the news and worried that she might not see her daughter for a long time. She knew of too many people who had been arrested and ended up serving additional time for crimes they were forced to commit while in custody. Behind prison walls she would be recognized as Inca Tino's woman, the Almighty Queen of Kings, and more than likely her toughness would be tested even among women from her own ranks.

Lady Q sat on a steel bench with her back against the wall, deliberately not making eye contact with those who stared at her but not turning away either. A momentary glare to let a possible instigator know that she wasn't going to put up with any shit was a mandatory survival tool she needed to utilize that day and possibly for a long time to come. Lady Q let her savage instincts overtake her as she prepared to cope with whatever her prison reality would become. Finally her name was called, and she walked into the courtroom in handcuffs. She saw her attorneys standing before the judge, and her heroin suppliers sitting as observers to the procedures. She felt like millions of eyes were staring her way, judging her very being. She felt humiliated. She stood before the judge and remained silent as her attorneys had advised. The attorneys entered a plea of "not guilty" and requested an I-bond on her behalf for countless reasons that Lady Q didn't quite hear as she was lost in this moment of shame. She lifted her head in attention and waited for the negotiating between the attorneys and the judge on her bail to begin, but it never happened. The judge granted Lady Q a fifteen-thousand-dollar I-bond without elaborating on his decision. Lady Q was free to go home pending a court date when she would face the charges against her.

Lady Q walked out of the Grand and Central station with a new outlook on life. She appreciated the attorney the Kings had sent, but she didn't want to do business with them any longer. This single night in jail woke up Lady Q to the reality that she could lose her daughter if she was sentenced to a long stint in jail. Until now Lisette had always been an afterthought, someone she took care of and had pride in, but now the thought of losing her made Lady Q realize how valuable her daughter was, and it scared her straight.

Lady Q cut herself off from any drug dealing and contacted her family. Vivian began coming around from time to time to visit but never stayed long. Her mother never came by. In the absence of money and drugs, many of the people who had appeared regularly in Lady Q's life disappeared, and she found herself in the company of only her daughter and her roommate Alee and her kids. The two women supported themselves and their kids with government assistance and the money that Tino occasionally provided Lady Q. She went to court every month to fight the charges against her. The attorney her heroin connections had sent was no longer on the case, but Lady Q still had Tino in her life, and his lawyer continued to represent her. For seven months she went to every court appearance as her case went through one continuance after another. During this time Lady Q stayed on her best behavior and always showed up at court respectably dressed. Finally she was granted a bench trial.

On the day of her trial, Lady Q dressed especially nicely in order to make a good impression. She sat at the defendant's table next to her lawyer and listened attentively as people who had no clue about the circumstances that had led to her arrest passed judgment on her. During Lady Q's trial no one wanted to hear how she had been raped by her uncle and cousin and beaten

senseless by her mother. There was no room or time to hear
about a mother living in the streets with a newborn child in the
dead cold of winter. According to the court, Lady Q was a casu-
alty in the battle between good and evil, and only people who
had never experienced this world could save her. It all felt very
hypocritical to her—hypocrisy disguised as justice. She stood
before the judge during the trial only to hear arguments of how
the evil drugs that were damning an entire nation had claimed
yet another victim.

Lady Q was found guilty, and the judge offered her a deal:
three years probation, with the first year being intensive probation where she would meet with her probation officer three
times a week and have a curfew from seven P.M. to seven A.M.
Her probation officer could drop in on her at any time, and she
had to appear before the judge every three months along with
the probation officer, who would testify about her behavior and
compliance with these strict rules. The final two years of probation would be less intensive. With all her ill will aside, Lady
Q was grateful that she wouldn't serve any prison time.

Lady Q's rise and fall in the world of drugs was quite common in inner-city neighborhoods. It never occurred to her that
her heroin connections might have given her up to save their
own skins, as drug dealers often do. That Lady Q ended up practically alone once she separated herself from all dealing didn't
surprise her—it was the way of the streets. It did surprise her that
Tino maintained his loyalty to her, even as her visits to him
diminished. She felt a love from him that she had never felt from
anyone else in her life, and that love, combined with the love of
her daughter, sustained her.

13

CHANGE BUT STILL THE SAME

A couple of days after the judgment against Lady Q was passed, Vivian surprised her by asking her to leave the drug-infested building where she lived in K-Town and move in with her. The move took Lady Q out of the Latin Kings' domain for the first time in her life in Chicago. Her new residence was northwest of Humboldt Park, around Fullerton and Cicero. No gangs hung around the immediate area, but there was Spanish Cobra graffiti indicating a possible spread of their territory.

During Lady Q's stay at Vivian's, her sister reminded her several times to go get a biopsy as the doctor had requested when she'd returned from Lancaster. But Lady Q took a fuck-it attitude toward her health. The doctor had suspected she had cancer, and his suspicion was now more than four years old; still Lady Q did nothing. As much as she loved her daughter, her decision to ignore this potentially life-threatening illness reflected her own selfishness and not wanting what was best for her child.

Vivian's nagging about this was just part of the tension that was present from the very beginning of Lady Q's stay. The road leading to her current living arrangement was a rocky one. The presence of RJ, who still didn't get along with Lady Q, and their son, who was older than Lisette, created additional obstacles. Two months after moving in, Lady Q complained about something Vivian's son was doing to bother Lisette. Between this, Lady Q's court-imposed curfew, and her daily phone calls from Tino, Vivian had had enough, and she started to make it difficult for Lady Q to remain there. Luckily Lady Q had taken a job at a local video-rental store, so she was able to rent a basement apartment nearby. Once she moved out, although they lived in the same neighborhood, the two sisters rarely saw each other. It seemed as if Lady Q was well on her way to a responsible life. She remained in touch with Tino but stayed out of the drug business.

Lady Q had a job and independence from the gangs, but this independence looked pretty destitute. Her basement apartment was practically empty. She had no table, only a used love seat to sit on, where she watched her thirteen-inch black-and-white television, with a queen-size mattress placed on the bare floor of the bedroom she shared with her daughter. The glamour that had colored her life since she began her relationship with Tino was gone. Her fancy clothes were replaced with older and out-of-style rags. She sold the gold and precious gems that had once adorned her body to pay for day-to-day necessities. Lady Q had no phone, so her conversations with Tino became few and far between. Every so often, Tino would find a way to arrange a three-way conversation where Lady Q would wait at a pay phone near her home for someone to connect his call through to her, otherwise there was no other way for the couple to communicate. They no longer discussed the possibility of marriage. Their conversations were mostly about how Lisette and she were doing and how Tino was faring. No matter how dire her circumstances, Lady Q stayed free from the drugs that had poisoned her thoughts, and in this way she felt successful.

Lady Q may have been a poster child for extreme poverty, but she and her daughter were happy. For the first time since Lady Q had walked the streets as a homeless mother, she was alone with Lisette. There were no Latin Kings or Queens walking in and out of her home, no junkies or drug dealers competing for Lady Q's attention, and she didn't feel like she ruled the world. Now her life was that of a mother and daughter alone in the world struggling to live life on its simplest terms.

According to the terms of her sentence, Lady Q reported to a probation officer once a month. The center where she reported offered GED classes not only to people who were under supervision by the Illinois Department of Corrections but also to the general public. Lady Q enrolled in the program. After a while Gigi heard about the program and wanted to join, too, and Lady Q obtained special permission from the teacher and made it possible for Gigi to attend. Gigi was now a single mother of a son and was also struggling to survive after years of roaming the streets with gangs and without an adequate education. She and Lady Q provided motivational support for each other. They took the bus to the center every day regardless of whether it was raining, snowing, or bitterly cold. Their GED instructor admired their will to succeed and even went out of his way to drive the two women downtown so they could sign up to take the test at the end of their course.

Both women failed portions of the test the first time around. Gigi scored below standards on two subjects, and Lady Q failed in the social studies part of the exam. But neither of them accepted this failure as a defeat. Rather, it emboldened them to continue to study so they'd do better on their next attempt.

The day of the second exam was cold and rainy, so Lady Q and Gigi scraped together enough money for a cab ride to the testing center. During the days following the test Lady Q anxiously awaited the results. Because she had already passed all segments of the test except for social studies, the second test covered only that subject for her; Gigi's covered only the two sections that she had failed. A few days after the test, Gigi came over to Lady Q's apartment and told her about a toll-free number she could call to get her test results. Gigi had called the number and found out that she'd failed again. After consoling Gigi, Lady Q rushed to a pay phone, eager to learn how she had done but worried that she, too, may have fallen short of her goal. She felt incredibly anxious as she struggled to correctly dial the number and follow the prompts of the automated system. She started yelling and cussing at the automated voice, which couldn't recognize the numbers she was punching in on the overused and abused pay phone buttons. Finally the system transferred her to the correct prompt, and an automated voice pronounced her an official General Equivalency Diploma graduate. Lady Q took a deep breath and then let out a joyful scream. She was full of pride, having accomplished something significant on her own.

She danced her way home with her head held high, wearing a big ear-to-ear smile. Gigi waited for her back at her apartment. Lady Q shared her great news. Gigi, still fresh from her own defeat this second time, took it in, expressing no joy for Lady Q's accomplishment, and left soon thereafter. Lady Q celebrated her moment of victory with her daughter. In 1994 Lady Q received her diploma following a cap-and-gown ceremony held for the GED center graduates. Three of her friends attended the ceremony along with Lisette, who presented her mother with a bouquet of flowers. This was a very good day in Lady Q's life.

But her celebration and joy were short-lived. Soon after receiving her diploma, events began to take place that left her wondering why God hated her so much that he would continue to punish her even as she tried her best to straighten out her life. Lady Q's job, which provided minimal financial assistance but did keep her busy and gave her something to look forward to, came to an end. The owners of the video-rental store decided to close down their business, and Lady Q suddenly found herself unemployed and unable to pay her rent. In less than two months she was asked to move out of her basement apartment. She had nowhere to go other than into the home of a fifteen-year-old neighbor named Michele whom she'd befriended. Michele was a short, pretty white girl with green eyes who didn't know much about the way the world worked. Michele lived in an extreme situation of her own—her mother had walked out on her father for another man, and her father had left soon after this. Her mother disappeared with her new boyfriend for weeks at a time, leaving her daughter completely unattended. The girl would sit on the front steps of her house, heavy with depression. That's how Lady Q had met her.

Lady Q and Lisette lived with Michele for two and half months. During this time, Michele's mother showed up only to get the bills, gather some belongings, and then quickly return to the arms of her boyfriend. Her mother didn't inquire about the strange woman living in her house or talk to Michele about anything, including why she was never home or when she planned to return. Eventually Michele's father showed up and became enraged over how his estranged wife had abandoned their daughter. He left, taking Michele with him. Lady Q had to leave, too. Again she was about to be homeless. She reached out to her mother for help this time.

Marta lived with a female friend in a third-floor apartment around Grand Avenue and Ashland. Lady Q went there to ask for shelter until she could find another job and get her own place. She expected rejection and was extremely surprised when her mother's friend agreed to the proposition, prompting her mother to agree to it as well.

It was a blessing for Lady Q to find somewhere for her and Lisette to live, especially with the winter months fast approaching, but it was also a curse because the neighbors were so friendly. Across the hall from Lady Q's new home lived a young couple whose daily routine included getting high on crack cocaine. Once they met Lady Q, they invited her right over to join them. Still on probation, it had been a little over a year since Lady Q had done drugs of any kind; up to this point she'd been successful at avoiding the temptation. But several things filled Lady Q with anxiety—she was having a tough time finding a job, the welcome mat at her mother's place was already wearing thin, and Lisette had problems in school.

Lisette had been a star pupil when she was younger, but she began to have issues about the time that Lady Q had her own legal problems. Lisette, now in third grade, couldn't understand any of the work she was given to do in school or to take home. School officials contacted Lady Q and asked her to meet with them so they could discuss Lisette's problems. At the meeting, teachers pointed out that Lisette was failing badly and asked for Lady Q's consent to test Lisette for learning disabilities. Lady Q readily agreed. The tests showed that Lisette was reading at kindergarten level. They told Lady Q that Lisette shouldn't have left first grade until her reading improved and that they didn't know how Lisette had passed the second grade. They concluded that Lisette had a learning disability that would require special educational attention that could not be provided at a public school. Lady Q was advised that, in conjunction with Lisette's normal school schedule, she should be enrolled in a separate after-school special education program. The news made Lady Q's heart drop. She didn't know what to say or do. She was mad because her daughter had been passed from grade to grade without learning a thing, and she was certain that the final passing grades Lisette had received in first and second grades were smoke screens hiding the incompetence of the teachers entrusted with her daughter's education. But none of this finger-pointing did anything to resolve Lisette's learning disability.

Lady Q handled this new stress in the only way she knew how—avoidance. She started smoking crack with her neighbors, either forgetting that she was still being drug tested as part of her probation or just not caring anymore. She was dropped (tested) three or four days after the first time she got high and several more times before she went in front of the judge for a report on her progress. She was not given the results of her drug tests by her probation officer and assumed she'd gotten away with smoking crack, so she continued and had no plans to quit. She quickly developed a serious habit—she craved crack even as she made fun of the crackheads who roamed the street performing any and all desperate acts to get money for their next fix. When she appeared before the judge, her probation officer announced that she'd tested positive on three occasions.

Lady Q's heart stopped momentarily as she heard the judge scold her for not taking her probation seriously. He ordered the court bailiff to arrest her on the spot. She looked around the courtroom like a lost child, not knowing what to do as she was led away to the lockup area behind the courtroom. She was placed in a cell with other residents of Cook County Jail who had been brought in to face the judge that day. She found a place on the floor, sat down, and tried to come to terms with her new reality, this one of her own making. She had violated her probation with more than a year and a half remaining. Now the state would seek to put her behind bars for the remainder of her time, away from the temptations of crack but also away from her daughter.

Lady Q had to wait in lockup until all the other women had made their court appearances. There were about twenty women of all ages and races but mostly African American and Latino. One by one their names were called, and they were taken into the courtroom to see the judge. All but two or three were given continuances, where nothing was decided other than that they would have to go through the same procedure all over again. Of all the women in lockup, only a handful had private attorneys representing them; the rest had public defenders and believed that spending time in the penitentiary was inevitable. Lady Q was too busy condemning herself for her actions, trying to maintain a cool and calm exterior to show no weakness, to stop and think about who would stand up in her defense.

Around six o'clock that night Lady Q lined up with the rest of the women and marched down a long hallway leading to what looked like a long tunnel. As the women were led down one side of the hall, a group of men marched on the other side in the opposite direction. These men were being released from custody and were walking toward their freedom. Lady Q recognized one of them as a Latin King from Beach and Spaulding. She was able to tell him her mother's phone number so he could call her and inform her of Lady Q's predicament. It was a long shot that the King would remember the phone number or even care enough to do her the favor, but hope was all Lady Q had as she walked to her uncertain future.

Lady Q's group was led into the Cook County Jail's Female Inmate Housing Unit, where the inmates who were making court appearances from inside the jail were separated from those, such as Lady Q, who had been taken into custody that same day. Lady Q was fingerprinted and then placed into a holding cell with other women awaiting processing. After another two-hour wait, Lady Q and all the women who accompanied her were led into yet another long hallway and asked to strip as they stood side by side. There were only female guards present along with members of the jail's medical staff. Lady Q was embarrassed but disrobed as she was instructed and tossed her clothing in a bundle in front of her. A couple of guards stood watch at each end of the line of naked bodies as another guard walked from woman to woman accompanied by the medical staff. One by one they checked each woman's hair, ears, eyes, and mouth and looked for signs of intravenous drug use. The women were also asked to crouch and cough so that any object they may have inserted into their vagina would fall out.

After every woman was examined, they were ordered to pick up their belongings and walk single file into a processing area. Lady Q waited in line patiently and tried as best she could to shield herself from the stares of women she identified as possible lesbians. She reached a counter where she was asked to place her belongings. Her items were then searched and bagged, and Lady Q signed a release saying she had witnessed all her items being stored away. A guard and a couple of inmates with the job of collecting and securing others' possessions as they were introduced into the prison population received the items behind the counter. Lady Q was then handed a new pair of underwear and a standard-issue beige two-piece outfit—a baggy pair of beige pants and a matching oversized shirt with the ironed-on letters IDOC. After acquiring their uniforms, the women were led to a shower area where they bathed, dressed, and were taken for further examination by the medical staff, which included drawing blood. By the time Lady Q arrived at the place she would call home for the next long while, it was almost midnight.

Although Lady Q had been inside the most infamous penitentiaries in Illinois, she'd always been a visitor and had never seen what the prisoners' living quarters looked like. She wasn't happy about seeing it firsthand now. Cook County Jail was far from Statesville, Pontiac, or Menard, but it was Lady Q's first experience being locked up for more than one night, and her initial reaction was fear. As she walked across the floor of the quiet cell block, she looked around to see eyes peering down at her from cells on the top tier and eyes looking up from the bottom tier. She was led into a cell on the top tier where a brown-skinned Puerto Rican girl of medium build woke up when Lady Q was brought inside the cell and the door slammed closed behind her. The girl lifted her head momentarily to see who her new cell mate was, then curled up and went back to sleep. Lady Q fixed the top bunk with the sheets they had issued her during processing and then climbed up to stare at the ceiling and deal with her new reality.

A million thoughts raced through Lady Q's mind as soon as she rested her head on the thin state-issued pillow. She had never imagined she'd do time behind bars. She thought of her daughter and wondered about her fate in the care of her mother, who had been so brutal to her when she was Lisette's age. Lady Q's mind raced on. She began seeing images of her Uncle Jose and Cousin Nito who had molested her, her stepfather Juan who humiliated her in public, all the family members who had beaten her—her mother Marta and her sister Vivian. But as all these faces raced by, Lady Q clearly saw Lisette, not herself, being the victim of their abuse, and as she realized that she could no longer provide protection for her daughter, Lady Q began to sob uncontrollably.

Finally through her sobs she heard a voice in the distance. It was her cell mate speaking. "Hey, are you OK?"

"My daughter," Lady Q responded. "I'm afraid for my daughter."

"Don't think anything other than she'll be fine. Otherwise you'll go fuckin' crazy in here," the Puerto Rican girl advised. And then silence.

Lady Q stayed wide awake and lost in her thoughts all night. By morning she had mentally prepared herself to do time behind bars. In one way or another she had always been involved in crime. She knew she could be strong, would be strong, because that's what she needed to survive. If she showed any fear she knew she risked being taken advantage of. Lady Q was far from a novice when it came to dealing with people who presented a threat to her well-being. She was, in fact, at her best when she was in a position where violence was the only language.

Just as Lady Q closed her eyes to rest, the clanking sound of cell doors being unlocked echoed throughout the cavernous cell block. Inmates were being let out for breakfast. Lady Q's initial thought was to put the pillow over her face and sleep, but she hadn't eaten for almost twenty-four hours and she was starving. She crawled to the end of her bunk, jumped down, steadied herself, and headed out through her cell door to join the line of female inmates waiting to be led down to the open area in the middle of the cell block, where metal tables with metal benches were bolted to the concrete floor along the edges. As the women filed into what was known as the day room, the door leading into the cell block opened to allow a couple of guards who escorted two inmate kitchen workers to come in and place three stacks of beige plastic trays on one of the tables. The trays carried that day's breakfast of bland powdered scrambled eggs, dry oatmeal, stale toasted bread, and a pint of milk. It was the nastiest food Lady Q had ever tasted, but her hunger forced her to devour every last crumb. She was so hungry that she paid attention only to her food and made no eye contact with any of the other inmates. After breakfast all the inmates went back into their cells and the doors were again locked; they would be reopened more than an hour later after all the food trays were picked up and taken away.

Lady Q went into her cell, brushed her teeth with the toothbrush and paste issued by the prison, and then sat down to talk to her cell mate. Lucy was only eighteen years old and facing time for drugs that belonged to a guy she was dating. She told Lady Q that as the police approached the car she sat in with her boyfriend, he handed her a plastic bag and asked her to hold it. The fact that her boyfriend was a known drug dealer and a member of the Latin Disciples didn't cross her mind when she took the drugs from him and placed them in her purse. She counted on the cops' usual practice of not paying much attention to women when seeking out criminals, but unfortunately for her the police did a thorough search of her boyfriend, his car, and her that day. They found almost an ounce of cocaine inside her bag, divided into quarter- and eighth-of-an-ounce bags ready for sale. Her boyfriend immediately denied knowing anything about the drugs. Even though the police knew the cocaine didn't belong to her, they had to arrest her because it was in her possession. That was the last time she's seen or heard from her so-called boyfriend. Now she faced two to fifteen years in the penitentiary for doing nothing other than being in the company of an asshole.

Lady Q listened to Lucy's story and was overwhelmed by her regretful tone of voice. Lucy was not a gang member but was riding with them because of where she lived, the people she knew, and for her own protection. Lady Q shared her incarceration story with Lucy and watched her facial expression change as Lucy realized she was sharing a cell with the Queen of all Kings. Their conversation was interrupted by the unlocking of cell doors and inmates being herded out into the day room to watch television or play cards while others headed to the showers. Lady Q was exhausted and refused her cell mate's invitation to go out into the general population with her. She climbed up onto her bunk to take a nap instead.

Lady Q slept for about four hours and was awakened by the cell doors being slammed shut for the midday lockdown, which lasted until the lunch trays were brought into the cell block. She remained in her bed until the doors were reopened. Then she got up and walked straight into the bathroom area to wash her face. When she walked out of the bathroom she didn't see any more lunch trays available. She thought she'd have to get into a confrontation to get a meal, but before Lady Q could approach anyone about it an African American woman walked up to her and led her to a table where a lunch tray and a place on a bench was reserved for her. Fifteen to twenty women sat at two tables joined together. All of them except two were African American, and they represented the Peoples' faction of Illinois prison gangs, which included the Latin Kings and all of their gang allies. Most of the women were members of the Lady Vice Lords. Every single person at the table already knew who Lady Q was.

IT'S COMMON KNOWLEDGE that it's easier for a gang member to do jail time than a prisoner with no gang affiliations. Once in the Illinois correctional system, many inmates without a gang affiliation will join one to have a more peaceful stay while imprisoned. For the black and Latino inmates who make up the majority of the Illinois prison population, there are four major gangs to choose alliances with: the Latin Kings or the Vice Lords—both of the Peoples' organization of gangs—or the Black Gangster Disciples or Latin Disciples, of the Folks' gang alliance. White inmates without a gang affiliation could align themselves with Peoples or Folks but usually chose to ride with the North Siders, a White Supremacist group connected with the Aryan Nation and the Ku Klux Klan. Many people who joined gangs while in prison disagreed with everything that gangs stood for and would not be caught dead in one on the outside, but behind bars it was a matter of survival. Gang members who followed the unwritten rules of their posse lived a comfortable life behind bars, and for those with the reputation and rank that Lady Q possessed, comfort was guaranteed.

DURING LUNCH, LADY Q became aware that her cell mate had told enough people that everyone in her cell block now knew she was the King of all King's woman. After lunch, she was given cigarettes, bath soap, shampoo, and other items that can only be obtained via commissary purchases by those lucky enough to have money sent from the outside. Lady Q was conscious that she was given special treatment because of her connections and her ability to possibly get illegal items, mainly drugs, brought into Cook County Jail by guards who worked for the Latin Kings. It was a game she was well versed in and knew how to control. Lady Q made certain not to offer or promise anything in return for the items she received other than the pleasure that her fellow cell block members received for considering themselves associates of the mighty Queen of all Kings. She treated everyone with respect and as her equal even though she was perceived to wield extreme amounts of power.

Lady Q's charisma made her well liked throughout the cell block, which would translate into an easy time behind bars. But no matter how easy, Lady Q was still in jail and still unable to be with her daughter or have her freedom. And unless there was some kind of divine intervention, she would be there for almost two years because of her probation violation. Lady Q knew how to survive behind bars, but she felt lost and alone even while surrounded by those who paid her respect.

On the second day of her incarceration, Lady Q was surprised when her name was called out. She had a visitor. It wasn't a regular visitation day for her cell block, and only attorneys were allowed to see their clients on such days. To Lady Q's surprise, the Latin King she had passed in the hallway when she was being processed remembered the phone number she'd told him and had called to notify her family of her whereabouts. When Tino called her mother's house to speak with Lady Q, Marta told him about her arrest and he sent a lawyer. The attorney he sent was her visitor that day and every day thereafter while he tried to get her probation reinstated. He brought her cigarettes each day and gave her the chance to get out of the cell block and relax. In the meantime he advised her to be a model prisoner and not make herself known as a gang leader during her imprisonment for fear that it would be used by the state to keep her behind bars.

Lady Q had no problem with this request because she was completely separated from the Latin King/Queen Nation except for her relationship with Tino. Because of Lucy, everyone knew that Lady Q was the Queen of all Kings, but she didn't use her title to demand anything from anyone, so there was no trouble. There was no way she would jeopardize her chance for freedom because of some jailhouse bullshit. Lady Q was very fortunate that all the women she was incarcerated with shared her desire to do whatever it took to get out of jail. Therefore they all helped maintain a peaceful environment. Days passed without incident, and Lady Q was grateful. During her incarceration her lawyer called Lisette every day and assured her that he'd bring her mother home.

Lady Q noticed that there were many lesbians in her cell block and wondered if these inmates had been lesbians before their incarceration or whether their desire for sex while imprisoned converted them. She wondered if any of them found her attractive but concluded that the knowledge of her relationship with Tino kept her from getting hit on.

There were several lesbian couples within her cell block, each consisting of one masculine-looking woman with a feminine-looking partner. Displays of affection between female inmates were constant and public and for the most part accepted. Once even a wedding took place between two cell mates. The couple consisted of a large African American butch lesbian and her small, feminine, light-skinned and very attractive African American girlfriend, who was also her cell mate. Both women were members of the Lady Vice Lords, and an inmate considered a senior member of that gang performed a ceremony to unite them. Toilet paper was folded to create decorative banners and hung in their cell for adornment. Some inmates attended the ceremony while others kept watch for the guards. Then the newly married couple enjoyed a five-day honeymoon period during which they spent the vast majority of their time in their cell, counting on other inmates to alert them if guards entered the cell block so that they wouldn't be caught in a compromising position. Lady Q didn't agree with these actions, but she welcomed the diversion to pass the time. Time, after all, was the only thing Lady Q and every other woman in her cell block had.

The other major event that occurred in Lady Q's cell block was an all-out search for drugs. A woman who was released during Lady Q's incarceration had told her cell mate that she had drugs in her coat at the time of her arrest, and the coat was being kept in her box of possessions. The woman's cell mate passed this information along to inmates who worked in the area where their possessions were kept. When the woman's items were returned, her coat was badly ripped and the drugs were gone. She informed someone, and the entire women's division was put under lockdown. No one was permitted out of the cells until a thorough search was completed. When the guards came to inspect Lady Q's cell block, they unlocked the cell doors and asked everyone to step out of their cells and then demanded that any extra sheets or pillows be thrown into the middle of the day room area. Anyone caught with these items would be taken to the hole (solitary confinement). Lady Q marveled at the cascade of laundry that showered the floor and realized why she was offered cigarettes and food but never extra blankets—there were none to be had. No illegal contraband was found in the entire women's division, and the day after the search the lockdown was terminated.

On the third week of Lady Q's incarceration she was summoned to appear before a judge. Unlike inmates who were waiting for their criminal case to be decided and were granted continuance after continuance for whatever reason, Lady Q did not have to wait for a decision. She had already had her day before a judge and was returning because of her failure to obey the court's original ruling. Only one of two things could happen that day: her probation would be reinstated and she could go home, or her attorney's request would be denied and she would be ordered to serve the remainder of her time in the penitentiary.

From the minute she woke up that morning, as she dressed and struggled to choke down a few bites of food, fear gripped Lady Q's insides as she awaited her fate. A guard came and led her down the same long, cavernous hallways. She walked in handcuffs along with dozens of other women going before the judge that day. When they reached the holding cell behind the court, Lady Q took her familiar place on the floor with her back against the wall and became lost in her thoughts, struggling to keep a positive attitude. Two or three hours after she arrived her name was called and she was led inside the courtroom. As she entered, everyone turned to her and stared. Shame engulfed her. She didn't make eye contact with anyone but her attorney, who stood about three feet in front of the judge waiting for her. As in the past, Lady Q remained quiet and respectful while her lawyer did all the talking and pled her case. Her lawyer asked for a sidebar conference with the judge. It was granted, and Lady Q was sent back to a holding cell. After about twenty minutes her lawyer came and spoke to her.

"How'd you feel if you went home today?" he asked.

"For real?!"

"Yes."

"Hell, yeah."

The bailiff collected Lady Q and took her before the judge. The judge asked her some procedural questions and then warned Lady Q that if she violated her probation again, she would serve out the remainder of her probation behind bars.

It was still early in the day, and after the sentence was handed down Lady Q still had to wait until the day's court proceedings ended before she would be set free. Back in the holding cell, Lady Q concealed her good fortune as the precious thing that it was, being careful not to boast since there were many other women who weren't as lucky. She was taken back to her cell block where her new friends congratulated her but otherwise didn't make a big deal of her news. Everyone within Cook County Jail dreamed of going home one day, and hearing about someone else's release was no cause for celebration.

Lady Q was anxious to get home and rejoin her daughter. She waited for the Department of Corrections to process her, and it felt like an eternity. The cell block was locked down and the lights shut off for the night and Lady Q was still there. She began to think that the decision she'd heard the judge hand down was a cruel joke and that she wasn't actually being released. Why was she still behind bars? Then at two o'clock in the morning a guard came and unlocked her cell, and she was asked to exit. She was given back her street clothes. After changing into them she was led down the long, cold hallways for the last time and released to the streets of Chicago at three in the morning, with only a bus token to get herself home. It was bone-chilling cold outside, and the train that would leave Lady Q near her destination was a mile away. She saw an African American woman who had also been set free in the wee hours of the night getting into a car and called out to her. Lady Q offered the woman forty dollars for a ride home. Thankfully, the driver agreed to the proposition.

About forty-five minutes after being released from Cook County Jail, Lady Q was reunited with Lisette with a new outlook on life. She made a pledge never to leave her daughter's side again.

14

MOVING ON, PAINFULLY

LADY Q'S RETURN to society was not a cause for celebration for her or those around her. Instead, it was an opportunity for people, in particular her family, to point out how stupid she was and that she'd gotten what she deserved for disobeying the law. There was no doubt in Lady Q's mind that she had made a grave mistake and therefore deserved every bit of criticism. However, it would have been easier to stomach if those doing the criticizing weren't also using illegal drugs. They were "innocent" only because they hadn't been caught and therefore felt above the law.

Some people always need drama in their lives. Somehow, soon after Lady Q's release, word got back to Vivian that Lady Q had said she wanted to kick her ass. Lady Q was staying with her mother, and Vivian showed up at Marta's apartment with Jazmin and Gigi in tow to confront Lady Q. An argument ensued. True to form, Marta sided with Vivian and kicked Lady Q and Lisette out of the apartment. Lady Q had known it would happen sooner or later—it always did. She contacted Tino and told him what was going on and he provided money for her to get her own apartment. Tino's acts of kindness toward Lady Q had become habitual and expected.

It was the middle of winter when Lady Q got her new third-floor apartment two blocks from where her mother lived. She had no furniture and it was extremely cold. Shortly before she moved, she applied for a job at a nearby hamburger joint and was hired on the spot. Still, she had little money for luxuries. A couple of comforters on the carpeted floor served as a bed, and she used a couple more as covers. She had heat but no stove, so she used a hot plate as her stove and the windowsill as a refrigerator. Both Lady Q and her daughter, now age eight, slept fully clothed and huddled together to stay warm. She held Lisette tightly to ensure the chill she was feeling did not affect her little girl. That winter in Chicago was like every other—bitterly cold, to the point where Lady Q would get up in the morning and find the liquids she'd placed by the window frozen solid. It was a desperate, humbling situation, but Lady Q was happy to be on her own, with her daughter, and out of jail. This was a time in her life when she and her daughter grew closer—the best time in their relationship—and their love for each other helped them forget the realties of their living conditions.

Lisette still suffered in school due to her learning disability. Lady Q applied for Social Security disability benefits (SSI) on her behalf to help pay for Lisette's clothing, shelter, and food. With the documentation Lisette's teachers provided to prove her condition, the benefits were approved, and Lady Q received a check for twenty-five hundred dollars. With that money she was able to buy furniture, beds, a stove, and a refrigerator. Most everything she bought was used but a great improvement over the nothing they replaced. A monthly stipend of a little over four hundred dollars was also sent for Lisette, which helped supplement the money Lady Q earned at her job. Lady Q's existence was nowhere near the high-society lifestyle she'd enjoyed as the Queen above all Queens and the surrogate mother of all Latin Kings, but for once she was comfortable in her own skin and in being just Sonia again. She saw the error of her past ways and knew that it would be a long, hard struggle to recover the years she had lost to the ignorance of the streets. Now Tino was the only connection she maintained to that time in her life.

As the warm weather approached, Sonia began to get noticed by the youth of the neighborhood because of her hair, which was dyed blonde and had black roots coming in. She had been out of the 'hood too long to know it, but this hairstyle had become a way for Latin Queens to represent their colors—black and gold. The only thing that kept Sonia from being approached by others in the 'hood was that she was obviously, now at age twenty-six, older than the typical gangbanger. Otherwise she would have been asked about her gang affiliation. The neighborhood where Sonia now lived was relatively quiet, but it was Cobra and Milwaukee Kings turf—both bitter rivals of the Latin Kings—and it just so happened that some of them hung out on the corner right in front of her building.

Sonia became good friends with the landlord of the building, a middle-aged Mexican woman who lived on the first floor. During the spring and into the summer, Sonia sat out in front of the building with her landlord, and she began to meet the gang members who roamed the area. Soon Sonia was part of the 'hood. No one disrespected her or questioned her hair color except once—a Spanish Cobra made a comment about her being from "the other side." Sonia responded by pointing out that the only side she belonged to was the side of her eight-year-old daughter. Not another word was ever said about her past or present affiliation.

Shortly after that episode, Sonia celebrated Lisette's ninth birthday with a party in her apartment. Tino sent a couple of his generals over, including a confidant named Cito, to deliver some cash and a photograph as a gift to Lisette. Although the Kings came and went unnoticed by others in the 'hood, Sonia was bothered by the photograph they gave Lisette—a picture of Tino surrounded by a group of Kings Sonia knew were back-stabbing him. A while back Sonia had asked for and received a copy of the transcript of Cito's cousin's trial, where it was clear that Cito had turned state's evidence against his own cousin. She knew in her heart that he would do the same to Tino. Sonia had warned Tino repeatedly to discuss no business over the phone and to make his generals visit him in jail if they had busi-ness. But he never listened, and when Sonia saw Cito in her apartment she knew it would just be a matter of time before he'd help bring Tino down, too. She also knew that Tino knew those pictured with him didn't give a fuck about him or any other Latin King. Tino's reasoning was to keep his friends close and his enemies closer, so he felt he'd be safe with this arrange-ment. Seeing this photo, realizing that Tino would never change his attitude and never break his ties with the Nation as she had begged him to do on so many occasions—times when they'd talk about creating a life as husband and wife when he was released—Sonia decided to cut off all ties with Tino and elimi-nate this final thread connecting her to the Latin King/Queen Nation.

Sonia was well on her way to eliminating the demons that haunted her past. She continued to smoke marijuana but only just after visiting her probation officer; then she'd stay clean as her next appointment approached to allow her body time to cleanse. She never tested positive for drug use again and eventually finished serving her probation. In the meantime, Sonia's landlord introduced her to a cousin named Miguel who came around to visit a friend who lived in a neighboring building. Miguel and Sonia hit it off right away, and he began to stop by every day to see her. At first they'd just smoke weed together and hang out, but as time went on they began dating. Sonia had finally met a man who wasn't locked up and who cared for her.

Miguel was a Mexican American the same age as Sonia and just a couple of inches taller. He wore glasses, was polite and soft-spoken, and held a steady job. This was the first time Sonia had met a man she was interested in romantically who was not and never had been in a gang. It was a heady feeling. Miguel took Sonia out on real dates—out to eat, to the movies, and out dancing. Not since Baldi had she been pursued with such niceties. With Baldi, everything had turned out all wrong after he took Sonia's virginity. In contrast, Miguel was a total gentleman in every sense of the word, but what impressed Sonia the most was how he treated Lisette. Miguel was never bothered by Lisette's presence. Whenever he came around he'd bring something for her, even the smallest of toys. Miguel always wanted to make Lisette smile, and this made Sonia happy.

A loving relationship developed between Sonia and Miguel unlike any she'd ever experienced. The connection she had established with Tino was special and one she would always cherish, but unfortunately they could never walk down the street hand in hand or hold each other all night. Miguel offered all the kindness and sensitivity she had always received from

Tino, but he was also there next to her to touch her, kiss her, make her laugh, and regularly show her how much he appreciated her. Throughout that summer Sonia, Miguel, and Lisette became inseparable, and after six months of dating the three became a family under one roof.

Sonia was well into her midtwenties, and for the first time she experienced the responsibilities of living with a man. The only other time she'd briefly undergone this was with Lisette's father, Pedro, but that had been fleeting and focused mostly on survival before drugs and responsibilities tore them apart. This time was very different—Sonia felt loved, respected, and valued. She felt there wasn't a thing in the world she could do wrong that Miguel would not understand and laugh about with her. Miguel gave that same attention and understanding to Lisette, who adored him. Even Sonia's mother, who Sonia saw infrequently now, approved of Miguel, telling Sonia that she thought she'd made a wise decision for once.

Because Sonia didn't have any role models when it came to a healthy relationship, she relied on her fantasies of how a couple should behave. Initially it seemed that Sonia's interpretation of how a family unit should function, especially in terms of how a man and woman should be with each other, was right on the money. They settled every difference through dialogue followed by adjustments in behavior to avoid repetition. In her wildest dreams Sonia couldn't conjure up a better situation for her and her daughter.

But all was not well in this family-focused environment. Sonia and Miguel shared a love of marijuana, and, now that Sonia's probation period was over, they smoked it regularly and even in Lisette's presence, without regard to the message it gave her or the effects on her health. Additionally, Miguel drank excessively, which he explained away as a man-being-a-man habit. Miguel's drink of choice was beer. He drank it with meals, he drank it to relax, he drank it with friends. Without beer he was discontented and didn't find any pleasure in life. There were obvious signs that he was an alcoholic and needed help, but the signs were explained away or Sonia adjusted her behavior yet again to avoid any confrontation.

A year into their relationship, Sonia learned that she was pregnant. This was unexpected, but the news brought great joy to the couple and fed their love for one another as everyone they knew came by to congratulate them and wish them well.

By this time Sonia had forgotten about her irregular Pap smear and the doctor who'd wanted to do a biopsy eight years before. When she finally went to the OB to confirm that she was pregnant, she was almost two months along and oblivious to any possible difficulties. The doctor looked at her records, saw the irregular Pap smear results, and said that he wouldn't be able to treat her because this was now a high-risk pregnancy. He referred her to a specialist, who confirmed that Sonia had advanced cervical cancer, which would have to wait to be treated until after the baby was born.

Sonia's pregnancy would be risky, but she was ready to do whatever it took to give birth to Miguel's child. There was a good chance that she could miscarry, so she needed to be examined weekly rather than monthly. Every Wednesday she faithfully went to her appointment at Norwegian Hospital. Throughout her pregnancy Miguel attended to Sonia's needs and made certain she didn't create any further risk to the baby's health by smoking cigarettes or marijuana.

Miguel hoped for a daughter, and his joy and hope were destroyed when it was determined that the child would be male. Sonia was happy to have a boy to go with the little girl she already had, but Miguel was noticeably disappointed. He continued to make certain Sonia was comfortable, but he started to smoke marijuana around her again. He also didn't curb his drinking. Having a baby on the way gave him all the more reason to indulge. At least Sonia found one blessing to count—he continued to be kind to Lisette.

Even with her cancer, Sonia's pregnancy continued without complications, and the doctor continued to say that the baby was growing at a normal rate. She was religious about keeping her appointments whether she had a ride to the hospital or not. From time to time Miguel wasn't able to take off from work, so Sonia would either get a ride from a friend or take the bus.

Sonia did feel a bit guilty that she hadn't followed through taking care of her own illness and now she was putting the life of her unborn child at risk. In the seventh month of her pregnancy, she went to her regularly scheduled appointment and relaxed as the nurse did an ultrasound exam. Sonia looked at the monitor with excitement as she waited to catch a glimpse of her unborn child and get a printout from the machine so she could show the world. The nurse scanned Sonia's belly back and forth and over and over and became worried when there was no movement. The nurse left the room. Sonia didn't know what was going on and waited anxiously for the nurse to return. Minutes later the nurse came back with the doctor in tow, and they immediately started doing the ultrasound again and listening inside Sonia's belly with a stethoscope. The good news was that the baby's heart was beating normally; the bad news was that the lack of movement was a sign that the cervical cancer could be affecting the child. The doctor told Sonia that he didn't want her to take any chances on further endangering the baby's health. They needed to induce labor. She called Miguel, and he drove straight to the hospital while arranging for Lisette to be watched by a relative.

Sonia was admitted to the hospital and taken to a delivery room where she was given drugs that helped start her contractions. When she started feeling labor pains, she prayed that if one of them had to die it would be her. God had different plans, though, and both Sonia and her child made it through the delivery. In the spring of 1995 Sonia gave birth to a beautiful baby boy who was christened Tony.

Tony, born prematurely, had infant jaundice. Since this was not a life-threatening condition, Sonia was permitted to take him home the day after he was born, but she was told to bring him back the next day so they could both be checked for improvement. The next day Tony's skin color had not changed, so the doctor told Sonia he would have to stay in the hospital in an incubator under an orange light. He urged Sonia to prepare for treatments for her cervical cancer. She spent two days in the hospital next to her son and promised herself that this time she would be more diligent about ridding herself of this life-threatening illness that was eating her from within. Now she had two little lives to care for. They were her motivation to defeat her cancer.

After a couple of days in the incubator, Tony's skin color normalized, and he finally went home for good. The first few weeks at home with their new son were very peaceful. This was a time filled with joy. Miguel took care of everything around the apartment so she could rest. He was totally enamored with his newborn son. He did scream a few times at Lisette, insisting she be quiet while Tony slept, but other than that their home was a peaceful and loving place. Sonia didn't think much of this screaming, dismissing it as Miguel asserting his fatherly authority and a result of the additional responsibilities with two children in the household. But as time went by, Miguel's yelling at Lisette became constant and was soon combined with curse words and senseless anger.

It became evident Miguel no longer desired to share his love and understanding with Lisette, and her mere presence antagonized him. Soon Sonia began to see the same pattern of abuse in Miguel that she had endured from her stepfather Juan when she became a hand-me-down child. Unlike her own mother, Sonia quickly came to Lisette's defense, but like her mother she did nothing to alter or get away from the situation. Arguments between Sonia and Miguel over his treatment of Lisette could be heard on the street almost daily. Sonia's concern for her own health again disappeared.

Sonia had become a stay-at-home mother during her pregnancy because the owners of the restaurant where she worked sold the business and Miguel asked her to stay home. Now, however, being unemployed became a weapon that Miguel started to use against her. During their arguments he tried to hurt her with the fact that he was the only one earning money. To make matters worse, Miguel began to go out drinking with his friends after work instead of coming home. He sometimes spent his entire paycheck on booze, neglecting his responsibilities to his family. With Miguel's support and physical presence gone, Sonia fell back into the old patterns of her childhood when she was just Sonia, alone and afraid. She started hating herself and wishing she were dead. While she loved Tony and Lisette dearly, her self-loathing kept her once again from taking care of her illness. If Miguel didn't love her enough to take care of her, then there was no reason for her to live.

One day during this dark period, Sonia called Miguel to tell him that there was nothing to eat in the house. She asked him if he could either come home early enough so that she could get to the store to shop or else bring home food himself for his family. Time went by and Miguel didn't show up. That night Sonia and Lisette ate only because their neighbor across the hall was kind enough to share dinner with them. Tony was still taking formula, and there was a good stock of that so he didn't go without. Throughout the night Sonia called Miguel on his cell phone but he never picked up. At about three o'clock in the morning Miguel finally showed up. He was drunk, belligerent, and loud, slamming doors and yelling at the top of his lungs, waking up everyone in the apartment and throughout the building.

"What the fuck do you want to eat?" Miguel screamed as he threw open the bedroom door where Sonia lay. Tony slept in a crib in that bedroom and started crying when the door hit the wall.

"Shut the hell up!" she said. "You woke up the baby!"

Miguel was barely able to stand. He turned around, walked into the living room, slumped over the sofa, and fell asleep.

It was quiet for the rest of the night, but the psychological damage was done. From that point on the fights between the couple escalated. Sonia was completely dependent on Miguel— she had no job, very little education or work experience, and she still couldn't drive. Aside from the little bit of money she received from SSI on Lisette's behalf, Miguel was her sole means of support. Even though she never let Miguel touch Lisette, Sonia had become little more than a literate version of her own mother.

As Sonia's relationship with Miguel continued to deteriorate, she discovered that Miguel had inherited his problem with alcohol from his father, who was not only an alcoholic but when he was completely and utterly out of control from drinking would brutally beat his wife. Sonia could see that it was just a matter of time before Miguel would start victimizing her as his father did to his mother. But still she didn't leave. She feared she'd be on the street with two kids and couldn't see how she could make things work without Miguel's financial support, so she stayed and waited for the next shoe to drop.

Sonia began to understand the circumstances that had made her own mother remain in horrible, abusive relationships. She could have easily done as her mother did and start taking out her frustrations on her own daughter. This would at least satisfy Miguel, who saw Lisette as the main problem in the household. To her credit Sonia did not take this route, but neither did she stop the arguing or confront Miguel. It was just a matter of time before he began beating Sonia.

The argument that gave birth to this new physical level of violence in Sonia's home life started like all the others. Miguel was bothered by Lisette's existence, so he began to scream at her and call out her name.

"You fuckin' stupid little bitch," Miguel said.

"I told you, motherfucker, don't you be calling her a bitch," Sonia jumped in Miguel's face.

Normally Miguel and Sonia would exchange insults and then one of them would go into a separate room, or Miguel would leave the house to get even more drunk than he already was, but this time it was different. Miguel stepped forward and bumped Sonia as he threatened to kick her ass. She was holding Tony at the time. She had never in her life backed down from a fight, but she couldn't fight while holding her son. So when she yelled at Miguel to go ahead and try to kick her ass if he could and he punched her in the face, she immediately became defenseless. Miguel's fist hit Sonia on the left side of her face near her eye and sent her falling backward and down to the floor. Sonia hit the floor but still protectively cradled Tony. Miguel rushed over to her and slapped her several times on both sides of her head. Lisette screamed for him to leave her mother alone and baby Tony cried from the commotion.

Finally Miguel stopped hitting Sonia. She got up, took Tony over to her neighbors, and came back to continue the fight. She told Lisette to go to the neighbor's apartment, but Lisette wouldn't leave her mother. Sonia and Miguel continued to curse at each other and argue. Sonia finally told him she was going to call the police, and Miguel stormed out of the apartment. She went and held Lisette and they cried together. When Sonia finally went to the bathroom and looked in the mirror she was horrified to see how swollen her eye was. She was devastated. Miguel's love was surely gone, and she would again be a victim of physical abuse. Completely spent and depressed, she put ice on her face to help take down the swelling and began to think of ways to make sure nobody saw her in this condition. The next day Miguel apologized and promised that it would never happen again. Sonia knew these were empty words; she knew he didn't mean them.

Beatings followed by empty promises were the next phase in the life of the Queen of all Kings. It seemed there was no way for her to stop it. At least once a week Miguel would take out his alcohol-infused frustrations on her. He no longer needed to attack Lisette and have Sonia come to her defense for the violence to start. Miguel began to beat Sonia whenever he felt like it. Sonia spent her days and nights fearing the next attack. Before a black eye could heal, she'd be nursing a busted lip, painful shoulder, bruised legs, or sore ribs. Sonia had essentially become Miguel's punching bag, and her primary activity became hiding so no one could see her condition. She avoided everyone and tried never to leave the house. She wasn't strong enough to leave him; she didn't think anyone would help her, and she couldn't bear the thought of her kids being hungry and homeless.

Miguel's parents came by from time to time. They'd never liked Sonia; they were there to visit their grandson. They saw the obvious signs of domestic violence but said nothing and took no action. One day Vivian came over when Miguel's mother was visiting. Miguel had beaten Sonia so badly that her face was blackened from the bruising.

"How could your son do something like this?" Vivian demanded to know.

"I've put up with it for a lot longer than she has," was Miguel's mother's only response.

Sonia knew that if Tino found out about her living conditions that he would have Miguel killed. But she didn't want Tony to grow up without a father or for Tino to get another charge leveled against him. Tino's sentence was nearing its end, and the FBI held him under a microscope as they tried to gather evidence against him. After twenty-five years in prison, a record of good behavior, and countless parole denials by the state of Illinois, they would no longer be able to hold Tino behind bars and he would soon be set free. At least Sonia hoped this would be the case, and she didn't want to do anything to jeopardize this possibility. She continued to put up with Miguel's brutality and hoped prayer would make him stop.

15

IF I SHOULD DIE
BEFORE I WAKE

WHILE SONIA STRUGGLED with her own family issues, others in her immediate family were getting their shit together, especially Vivian. Vivian had grown out of the drug scene and had not only stopped selling them but stopped doing all narcotics. She became a great success at her job with the Social Security department, earning multiple promotions and making enough money to purchase a three-story building in Logan Square. Vivian began reaching out to Sonia. Regardless of the turmoil likely to occur with Sonia and RJ living in the same building, Vivian didn't hesitate to rent the second floor of her building to Sonia when Miguel's cousin sold the apartment building where Sonia and her family lived. Following the move, some peace and tranquility returned to Sonia's home. Miguel stopped being an asshole, probably because he knew Sonia's family would defend her. The beatings ceased, but still there was little happiness in Sonia's life.

Although the arguments between Sonia and Miguel decreased dramatically, tension between them continued to build and, like a volcano, could explode at any minute. Sonia was no fool; she was well aware of her situation and prayed that it would change, but she felt helpless to make things better. She remained completely dependent on a man she feared would act out violently at any time. But she continued to believe that it was best for her children for the family to stay together.

Sonia became a shell of her former proud self. No longer did she hold her head up high and walk with pride or a sense of self-respect. She sat in her apartment and wept as she prayed that her mother, who lived on the floor below her, would sense her need and come and counsel her. Sonia began to contemplate suicide again, but this time the thoughts were unceasing—they were vivid visions, calculated, and absent of any fear that had kept her from following through before. Going through the motions of life, which included lying on a bed staring up at the ceiling while a drunk reeking of alcohol humped her for his own pleasure, was more than she could bear. It got to the point where even breathing made Sonia break out into tears because she wanted it all to stop. She felt she had nothing to live for except her children, and she began to feel they'd be better off without her. A bit of joy finally did enter her life, however, when she discovered she was pregnant again.

Miguel was excited by the prospect of getting the daughter he desired, but this pregnancy didn't have the calming effect on his behavior that her first pregnancy had. He remained bossy and aggressive as if he was being forced to be somewhere he didn't want to be. Still, Sonia's mood lightened with this news. But her happiness was short-lived. Soon after finding out she was pregnant, her mother stood at the bottom of the stairwell and called up to her. There was a story on the news.

"*¡Sonia, Tino esta en la television!*" ("Sonia, Tino is on the television!"), Marta yelled.

Sonia rushed to turn on the television and tuned in to the local news channel just in time to see what her mother was so excited about. It was mid-September 1997, and Tino was being taken from Menard Correctional Center in downstate Illinois and brought to Chicago, where he faced a twenty-five-count indictment on federal drug conspiracy charges along with thirteen other members or associates of the Latin Kings. Like a cruel joke, the charges against Tino were being levied one day before he was to be set free for the first time since the age of seventeen. The charges allowed the authorities to hold Tino without bail, claiming he was a flight risk, and instead of going home he was given a ride to the Metropolitan Correctional Center in downtown Chicago.

It had been a couple of years since Sonia had heard from or spoken with Tino—he'd called for the last time just after Tony was born—but she still felt a connection to him and was floored by the news. All the memories of the times she went to visit him, their long telephone conversations, and the two times they came together as man and woman in the Menard prison yard replayed before her. She thought of how Tino must be feeling to have his freedom stripped away just as he was beginning to taste it. She was certain that the FBI had planned it that way—whatever evidence they had against Tino had been gathered long ago, and charges were intentionally filed the day before his release both to break his spirit and to send a message to the Latin Kings and other street gangs and their leaders. But because of all the years she'd spent as Tino's confidant, the one he shared his innermost thoughts with, Sonia was convinced that if he were set free, killings between Latino youths in Chicago would in fact decline and eventually end. That was the kind of power and respect Tino wielded.

Sonia's eyes welled with tears when she heard this news. She realized, too, how much she still loved him. She also believed that only divine intervention had prevented her from being one of the people indicted that day. She felt certain that her name had come up during the investigation, and there was no doubt in her mind that the majority of the evidence against Tino had come from Latin Kings who continued to walk the streets selling drugs and exploiting vulnerable Latino kids for their own gain.

Sonia's sadness over Tino couldn't have come at a worse time. She was already deeply depressed about her life and the prospect of bringing another child into her cruel world. But her mothering instincts had a tranquilizing effect on her mood, and this helped stop her suicidal thoughts. She went to see a doctor at Norwegian Hospital to begin the inevitable checkups and began to prepare herself mentally and emotionally just as she had done when she carried Tony.

Sonia hadn't thought about her cervical cancer in a long time. She assumed that when she went to see her doctor for this pregnancy, nothing would have changed since the last time she gave birth. But Sonia was wrong, terribly wrong. Upon her first examination at Norwegian Hospital Sonia was informed that her cervical cancer had progressed and that she would have to go to a facility better suited to handle both her cancer and her pregnancy. She was given contact information for Northwestern Memorial Hospital and was urged to immediately call and make an appointment.

Sonia worried about the well-being of her unborn child and was prepared to do whatever was necessary to ensure a healthy birth. She wasted no time in setting up an appointment at Northwestern Memorial. Miguel accompanied her to the appointment and remained there for the examination and the diagnosis. His presence felt like a sign of support, but Sonia thought that he was simply going through the motions, again hoping for a much-wanted daughter. She was given a pelvic exam and a Pap smear, along with another diagnostic test to determine her ability to carry a child to full term. Sonia and Miguel were asked to wait for the results and to meet with the doctors and a specialist to review the results and go over their options.

At this meeting Sonia was informed that the cervical cancer had worsened. Carrying a baby would not be as simple as being closely monitored each week. This time there was a much greater risk of miscarriage. There was a risk, too, that neither she nor the baby would survive the delivery and that if the child did survive, he or she would likely have disabilities. There was also a chance that they would both be fine, but if she wanted to continue the pregnancy, she'd have to accept these risks. If she decided to proceed, then she could be treated for her cancer after the baby was born by having a hysterectomy or by undergoing sessions of chemotherapy and radiology. The other option was that she could have an abortion followed by a hysterectomy.

After all the options were presented, Sonia and Miguel sat there silently. Their eyes met momentarily, and Sonia saw no desperation in Miguel's expression, no sadness or remorse. Her thoughts turned to assessing the world that this newborn would enter. She thought about the fights between her and Miguel and the beatings she had suffered at his hands. She thought about the unhappiness that Lisette and Tony endured because of the loveless relationship that bound the family together. Sonia could clearly see herself sitting at home staring at nothing with tear-swelled eyes, not being able to function for hours on end. This was her world—a world without love and understanding or an ounce of hope for a better future. There wasn't enough attention or consideration for the children already present, so thinking that everything would transform with the introduction of a new life wasn't realistic. Then there was the possibility that the new child would be handicapped and require special attention. Her thoughts were interrupted by the words of one of the doctors.

"You can go home and think about it, but a decision has to be made rather quickly."

"No," Sonia said. "An abortion. I want an abortion." She spoke without hesitation and without consulting with or even looking at Miguel.

"Are you sure?" the doctor asked.

"Yes, I want to get it over with." Sonia grew more assertive. "When can it be done?"

Miguel didn't say a word for or against Sonia's decision. This was her body and life; she made the decision. The doctor began explaining the preparations for the abortion and hysterectomy.

Sonia was already in her fourth month of pregnancy; her personal problems and depression had caused her to get so far along without proper prenatal care. Because of the size of the fetus and the cervical cancer, an apparatus would have to be inserted inside her to open up her cervix so the abortion could be performed. Just after this meeting with the doctors, she was taken to a room where this was done. The apparatus would remain in her overnight. She was to return early the next morning to have the abortion.

Miguel and Sonia didn't speak during the drive back to their apartment. Miguel kept his eyes on the road, and Sonia stared

out the car window trying hard to keep from breaking down
and crying. She didn't believe in abortion—the decision she'd
made was tearing her up inside—but the more she thought
about her choice, the more rational it seemed. She knew very
well that what she was about to do would create an unpleasant memory that would be with her for the rest of her life, but
she was prepared to live with it. She couldn't deal with the pain
and regret that would come from bringing a sick child into an
environment where the basic elements that give a family a foundation were missing. The only thing she hoped for was understanding and forgiveness from God.

At home Sonia broke the news to her mother and sister. Although they exhibited some concern for her predicament, the strong support she'd hoped for was not there.
Vivian was busy with her job and plans for an upcoming
visit to RJ's family in Florida. Marta had never shown Sonia
much affection or support in the past, and this didn't change
even though her daughter desperately needed to be held and
comforted.

Early the next morning, Miguel dropped Sonia off at the
hospital and headed to work without going inside with her or
wishing her good luck. Sonia checked herself in, took a seat in
the waiting room, and tried to mentally prepare herself for
what was to come. She scanned the hospital waiting room and
saw other people there for various surgical procedures; family
members surrounded everyone else. Hands were being held
and words of encouragement were exchanged as Sonia looked
on, feeling both sad and embarrassed that she couldn't stop
herself from staring at the outward signs of warmth that she
wanted and needed. Waiting alone felt like further justifica-

tion that she had made the right choice and that she shouldn't feel guilty about it. By the time her name was called she had no regrets.

The hospital staff were surprised that Sonia was going through the abortion without anyone there to support her. When they asked why the father was absent, Sonia made up an excuse, saying his employer wouldn't give him the time off. The abortion occurred without any complications. Afterward Sonia was taken to a room where she could rest and wait for Miguel to pick her up and take her home. She was scheduled to return in about a month for a hysterectomy. In the mid-afternoon Miguel arrived and drove Sonia home, dropped her off, returned to work, and then went out drinking at the end of his workday. Neither that day nor on any days to follow did Miguel ask Sonia how she felt. Her feeling of isolation was further compounded by the lack of attention her immediate family continued to demonstrate. Apparently Vivian's trip to Florida was more worthy of everyone's attention than her abortion and impending surgery. Only Sonia's children comforted her.

The days leading up to Sonia's hysterectomy a month later were uneventful. She was left alone to ponder what it would be like; no one offered their time or attention to hear about her anxiety. Again, on the day of the surgery Miguel dropped Sonia off at the hospital and continued on his way to work; again, he offered no words of support or concern. Once again Sonia went through the awkward situation of sitting alone in a room filled with clusters of families accompanying their loved ones. Sonia thought her overwhelming feelings of hopelessness would be absent this time, but she was wrong; these feelings increased.

To keep herself from weeping uncontrollably Sonia laid her head back, closed her eyes, and pretended to sleep until her name was called.

About four hours after she was put under sedation, Sonia woke up in a hospital room with only a nurse by her side checking on her progress. Her uterus, ovaries, and fallopian tubes had been removed, and with them the cancer that threatened her life. She would no longer have to worry about getting pregnant and would not have to worry about the illness that eroded her from within. Sonia went home that same day with stern warnings from the doctor that she had to return in a month for a follow-up biopsy. She would need to have one at least every six months to ensure the cancer did not reoccur. She respectfully nodded in agreement to everything, knowing full well she had no intention of returning.

Miguel picked Sonia up from the hospital that evening and drove her home. Once again he showed no concern for her well-being and asked no questions on the drive home about how the procedure went or how she was feeling. He informed her that he was returning to work to put in some overtime, then dropped her off and didn't return home until the early hours of the morning, stone drunk.

Sonia was happy the medical procedures were over and she could go on with her life. But her negative thoughts returned and again prevented her from feeling able to change her life in a positive way. She blamed others for her misery, especially her family, who ignored her desperation. She remembered how they had sought her out for money and advice when she was Lady Q, the drug queen of the streets, but now that she had real need they deserted her, and she questioned their loyalty. These negative feelings took complete control over Sonia and made a bad situation worse.

Vivian was offered a promotion. She took it and decided to sell the building and move out of Chicago to be closer to her new job. This decision added to Sonia's seething anger. She and Miguel needed to find somewhere else to live since the new building owners would no doubt require lease agreements, security deposits, and more rent. The couple ended up back where they'd started—in the Ashland and Grand Avenue area where Miguel felt most comfortable. Sonia feared that Miguel would quickly revert to his old violent ways once she was isolated again from her family. Miguel had not curbed his attitude toward her or Lisette—he'd merely suppressed his rage due to their proximity to her family members, but now, again on their own, Sonia awaited its return. But she had reached a breaking point—she would no longer be a victim; she would fight back. It was a firestorm awaiting only a spark to ignite. Lisette was now nearly a teenager and more vocal about her disapproval of Miguel. She had developed the fiery temper and quick-to-attack mouth of her mother and wasn't afraid of confrontation.

Their new residence was a third-floor apartment on Ohio Street about a block and a half from where they had previously lived. Once they returned, old neighborhood friends began to visit, hang out, and get high. Miguel and Sonia never fought when they shared a joint, but that was the only time. And Miguel had always preferred drinking over any other activity, which again led to verbal attacks on Lisette and caused huge arguments with Sonia that eventually brought back the violence.

The first time Miguel hit Sonia in their new apartment, he caught her unaware and beat her black and blue. It happened after a night of drinking. He walked into the apartment and immediately punched Sonia in the face without warning or provocation. This time, she retaliated. Even though she was badly beaten, Sonia got up, swung her fist, and threw a few things at Miguel as she worked her way toward the front door. Then she ran out and asked a neighbor to call the police. This was the first time Sonia took the initiative to press charges against Miguel for domestic violence. Miguel panicked when he realized what Sonia was doing and left the house before the police arrived. When the police arrived, she needed to explain little; her fat lip, the blood on her blouse, and the bruises on her arms told the story. Within the hour Miguel was picked up and arrested for domestic violence.

Miguel's father bailed him out of jail. Miguel returned home, not to pursue another fight but to apologize and make promises to change his behavior. Regretful alcoholic tales came out of his mouth and Sonia fell for them, just as millions of other victims of domestic violence do. She forgave him without agreements or ultimatums and dropped the charges.

After the sweetness ended, Miguel reverted to his abusive ways, and Sonia exchanged blows with him as best she could. All the while Lisette and Tony witnessed the constant violence between their parents, and their screams of terror could be heard throughout the building.

The battles wore Sonia out emotionally and mentally. She wanted out of the relationship but didn't know how to achieve that goal. A little over a year after Sonia had Miguel arrested, he again caught her unaware and beat her senseless. He walked up behind her, grabbed her by her hair, and pulled her backward with so much force that she stumbled and fell. On her way down Miguel stepped back to let her fall, kicked her, then pinned her to the floor and began whaling on her. Lisette was not home and Tony was with his grandparents, so Miguel was undeterred in his attack. There was nothing Sonia could do to fight back with Miguel sitting on top of her raining blows down upon her from every direction. When it was over Sonia lay on the floor a bloody mess. Miguel left the apartment as if nothing had happened.

Sonia's neighbor heard her crying and came to her aid. Her upper arms and shoulders were badly bruised and her face was swollen up like a water balloon. She was bleeding from her nose and mouth and could hardly breathe. Her neighbor immediately called the police and paramedics without asking Sonia's permission. It didn't take long for the ambulance and cops to arrive. They administered first aid, but Sonia refused to go to the hospital or press charges against Miguel. She didn't think it would make a difference whether or not she had him arrested, as he would quickly make bail. One of the responding police officers became sick to his stomach at her condition. Then he got angry. Furious that Sonia refused to press charges, he vowed to seek Miguel out and arrest him for domestic violence regardless of what Sonia said. Miguel was once again taken to jail that night, but just as before, nothing came of it. The beating Sonia endured left visible marks that lasted for several months. These marks deterred Miguel from further attacks, but it was just a matter of time before it happened again.

Sonia followed in her mother's footsteps by ignoring the abuse around her in order to provide for her children. Marta, however, was never manhandled the way Sonia allowed herself to be. As Sonia healed, she found that she no longer worried about Miguel beating her again. She began to pull a knife on him whenever he raised his voice. Sick and tired of living this way, she finally asked Miguel to pack up his belongings and leave. Miguel's answer to her repeated request was always the same—he'd go out drinking and come back belligerent. Only now Sonia met him with the pointed end of a knife. Miguel had no doubt that Sonia would stab him and so he'd back off whenever she pulled the weapon.

On one occasion Miguel caught Sonia where he could block her path to the kitchen and began arguing with her. Sonia sensed that an attack was coming and warned Miguel not to hit her or he'd regret it. He was drunk as always, and instead of walking away he took Sonia's words as an invitation to approach her in a hostile manner. Miguel's actions were predictable, and Sonia waited for him to come toward her. She didn't scream, didn't try to run for cover, and didn't prepare herself to take an ass-whipping. As Miguel got within arm's reach of her, Sonia hauled back and punched him on the right side of his face, breaking his glasses and sending him sprawling backward. A cut opened up on Miguel's cheek just below his eye as a result of the shattered glasses. Sonia expected him to get up and charge her violently, but he didn't do anything. He just looked at Sonia in bewilderment. Then he turned around, went into their bedroom, and went to sleep. Sonia slept on the sofa that night, cautiously because she assumed Miguel would try to extract his revenge. But that didn't happen.

The next day Miguel got up and went to work without saying a word to Sonia. This left her to think and worry about what would happen when he returned later that evening in his usual drunken state. This combination of anxiety, fear, and frustration forced Sonia to arrive at a final decision: Miguel had to go. She had enough trouble in her life with two kids to raise— two kids who constantly squabbled, with Lisette now a teenager and on the verge of getting out of control. Sonia had had enough of life as a victim and was prepared to force her way into a peaceful place if not one of respectability. While Miguel was at work, she gathered all of his belongings and set them by the door where he would find them when he arrived that night. As always, Miguel stopped into a bar for a few drinks after work, but surprisingly he wasn't as drunk as usual when he got home. He didn't have the opportunity to take more than three steps into the apartment before Sonia confronted him and asked him to take his things and leave. She held Tony away from Miguel and advised him that he would have plenty of opportunities to be with his son, but presently he'd better leave or she'd call the police. Miguel didn't become angry.

"Are you sure this is what you want?" he asked.

"It doesn't matter what I want; it's how it has to be," she responded.

These words marked the end of their relationship, which had started out with Miguel the best man who'd ever entered Sonia's life. Instead, he ended up being the most traumatic experience she would ever endure.

Sonia knew she would struggle without Miguel's financial support, but her decision was final.

16

RESULTS OF A DISCARDED LIFE

WITH MIGUEL GONE, Sonia tried to pick up the pieces of a life that had been challenging since the time she could walk. She collected Social Security and did pickup jobs around the neighborhood. A couple of months after kicking Miguel out, she took a step in the right direction—she started working at the Cheesecake Factory restaurant in the DisneyQuest store. It didn't pay much, but it was better than not working and sitting around moping, waiting for a man to come into her life for financial support. As for Miguel, he came around to see Tony, but Sonia refused to allow him to spend time with his son. She was still hurt and angry with Miguel, and seeing him show up with his new girlfriend made her even angrier. Miguel had moved on to another woman very quickly and tried to make her part of Tony's life just weeks after leaving Sonia. The idea of a woman she didn't know and Miguel had just met being put in a position to play stepmother to Tony infuriated Sonia.

Miguel's parents—Tony's grandparents—had been very involved in Tony's life since he was born. The fact that Sonia and Miguel were no longer together didn't deter them from continuing their relationship with their grandson. Sonia knew that while Tony was with his grandparents Miguel had full access to him, but at least she didn't have to see him. After a few months Sonia began to realize that in the long run her attitude would only be detrimental to her son, and so she began allowing Tony to spend more time with his father.

Sonia's employment at the Cheesecake Factory lasted a little over a month before that location closed. She suddenly found herself with only the money she received from Lisette's SSI and state-issued food stamps to support her family. She got a little help from Tony's grandparents in the form of clothes and shoes for Tony but didn't receive any support from Miguel. The family of three struggled, but at least their home was more peaceful, no longer filled with constant fighting and cursing.

To make ends meet, Sonia soon resorted to the only business she knew very well—selling drugs. Crack cocaine had overtaken powder cocaine as the street drug of choice. Cheap and highly addictive, it crippled the inner city like no other drug had done. But desperation drove Sonia to dismiss her memory of what had happened the last time. She bought some crack from the Cobras to resell. This time around, she was very strict about who she sold to and would routinely turn down business with anyone she didn't know. She had learned her lesson about trusting individuals or relying on street loyalties where people threw around words like *brother* and *sister* but rarely meant them.

Living through the trauma with Miguel had made Sonia stronger and harder, but it didn't prepare her for the rebellion of her teenage daughter. Lisette, now thirteen, and Sonia had a pretty good mother-daughter relationship with plenty of communication between them and a feeling that each was the only one the other had. But a life full of turmoil had planted seeds of anger and despair in Lisette that made the confusion and drama of being a teenager significantly more extreme. There wasn't room for Sonia to lecture her daughter about the dangers of drugs after having raised her in the midst of drug use, including her own, which hadn't ceased. When Sonia demanded that Lisette stay out of trouble by obeying the law, Lisette dismissed it. Why should she listen to her mother, who had been involved in some form of illegal activity for the majority of her life and was currently selling crack? On top of this, Lisette had to deal with her own learning disability, which put her in special education classes, where she would remain until she could improve enough to become an A- or B-level student, and she was far from achieving this. Sonia also demanded that Lisette not date gang members even though Sonia had been involved with the leader of one of the largest and most violent Latino gangs in the United States.

Lisette's not having the material possessions other girls her age had left her feeling constantly deprived. This agitated her. She was well aware of her mother's financial constraints, but that didn't stop her from demanding things and getting angry when she didn't get them. Maybe Lisette wasn't any different from any other teenager in this respect, but deeper issues underlay her demands. She also began staying out late at night and then arguing with her mother when she returned home. Next she started dating Andre, a member of the Satan Disciples, a rival gang to the Kings. He hung around the area where they lived. They saw each other against Sonia's wishes. The young man was African American, which Sonia didn't have a problem with, but she did have a problem with the fact that he belonged to a gang, and she thought he had no future based on the many times she saw him loitering in the neighborhood during school hours. But Sonia's disapproval of this relationship and the steps she took to try and prevent it had an even greater negative impact—Lisette started to see her boyfriend behind her mother's back.

Sonia began second-guessing herself daily about what she would and would not permit Lisette to do. But one thing she always permitted Lisette to do was hang out with a teenage girl who lived down the street; this girl was Lisette's best friend. Sonia had no problem whenever Lisette wanted to stay over at her friend's house or have her friend come spend the night in their home. She even encouraged it. One night during the summer, Lisette asked to sleep over at her best friend's house. Sonia agreed, but later that night she had an overwhelming feeling that she should see if her daughter was OK. She decided to take a walk and check on her. She soon discovered that neither Lisette nor her best friend were anywhere to be found. The girl's parents, unaware that the two of them had snuck out, quickly joined Sonia as she hit the streets looking for her daughter.

They asked everyone who lived in the neighborhood if they had seen the girls and asked them to be alert for any signs of them. Within a half hour, the news reached Sonia that the girls had been spotted in a station wagon with Lisette's boyfriend and some other guy. That bit of information infuriated Sonia, and she threatened to beat the shit out of Lisette as soon as she laid eyes on her. She waited outside her building where she could clearly see the front of Lisette's friend's house. She knew that sooner or later they'd show up. Midnight came and went and still there was no sign of the girls. Sonia got angrier as it grew later and later.

At a little after three in the morning, Lisette and her friend came walking around the corner. They weren't surprised to see Sonia waiting; others in the neighborhood had warned them. While the girls were only thirteen, they had somehow managed to get into a club. What bothered Sonia the most, even more than the late hour, was that, even though Lisette knew her mother was waiting for her, she came around the corner laughing and joking as if she were proud of herself. "Where the fuck have you been? Who the fuck do you think you are, coming home at three in the fucking morning?" Sonia screamed at Lisette.

Lisette didn't get a chance to answer as Sonia slapped her across the face. Lisette tried to protect herself as her mother continued to hit her, but she was overwhelmed by the number of punches Sonia threw. Although it was three in the morning, plenty of people were present to witness Sonia discipline her teenage daughter so violently. Someone told some of the Satan Disciples that Lisette was being attacked, and they immediately came to her aid. A half dozen or so guys came running down the street from Ashland Avenue toward Sonia at full speed. Fortunately for Sonia, a neighbor who knew the guys witnessed this exchange and let them know she was Lisette's mother before they reached her.

Lisette received the beating of her life that night in public. Not once did Sonia stop and think about the psychological damage she was inflicting on her daughter. She failed to remember how it felt when she had been beaten in public as a child, or how she had wanted to kill herself because of how embarrassed she felt afterward. Sonia beat Lisette in public once more during this summer. Lisette just became more rebellious after each occurrence.

In the new year that was now 2000, when Lisette was about to turn fourteen and Sonia continued to try to keep her from seeing her gangbanger boyfriend, news came from Lancaster, Pennsylvania, that an uncle of Sonia's had passed away. Vivian, RJ, and Marta decided to drive from Chicago to Lancaster for the funeral, and they invited Sonia along at the last minute. They said there was no room for Lisette. Sonia agreed to go and made arrangements with Tony's grandparents to care for him. Lisette stayed with Sonia's sister-in-law.

The ride to Lancaster was long, boring, and uneventful, and little was said. They arrived late at night and settled into the homes of various family members. The next day, everyone gathered together to mourn the dearly departed and to share stories of remembrance. For Sonia it was a reunion with the relatives who had turned their backs on her while she lived on the streets with her newborn child, and with Pedro, Lisette's father, who had beaten her and didn't care that she and her daughter were sleeping out in the cold.

Initially Sonia had no good words to say to Pedro and didn't care to answer questions regarding Lisette's whereabouts and welfare. But more than a decade of separation helped her forgive and forget. In no time at all she allowed Pedro to sweet-talk his way into her good graces with drugs and romance. He even talked her into letting him go back to Chicago with her. Pedro claimed that he wanted to be with Sonia and his daughter and planned to find work in Chicago. He was going to change his life once he had a solid foundation to build upon.

With the wake and funeral behind them, Sonia and her family began the long trek back to Chicago, now with Pedro and new tensions and animosity. Neither Vivian nor her mother was happy with Sonia's decision to bring Pedro home with her. They'd tried to talk her out of it before they left. Their opinion was plain and simple—Sonia was yet again making a stupid mistake that would keep her from living a peaceful life.

As it turned out, Pedro did not stay in Chicago long. For two weeks he stayed with the kids while Sonia went to work, which allowed Lisette to get to know her father. The two seemed to get along very well and quickly formed a bond. When Pedro left, he asked Sonia if Lisette could travel back to Lancaster with him to meet the rest of her family. Sonia hesitated but noticed Lisette's desire to go and didn't want to cheat her out of the opportunity to make up for lost time with her father. School was out, and Lisette was bound to find ways to hang out with her boyfriend and the Satan Disciples, so reluctantly Sonia let her go.

In Lisette's absence, Sonia continued her drug dealing but began to work day labor jobs hoping to land something more permanent. She was very lucky that Tony's grandparents absolutely adored him and had no issues with caring for him while she worked. Lisette was gone for a month. She returned with an attitude even bigger and more obnoxious than before. Sonia wasn't clear exactly what happened to her daughter while she was gone, and Lisette wouldn't share any details, but whatever had happened, it had a negative affect on her. Now it wasn't just the lack of material things that prompted Lisette to make smart remarks toward her mother, and the two began arguing constantly. Then Sonia found a letter that Lisette had written to her father. It detailed how much she missed him and how tired she was of living with her mother. She said she couldn't take the bullshit at home anymore and begged him to send for her and rescue her from the hellhole she was living in. Sonia was devastated but said nothing about the letter. She watched, heartbroken, as Lisette mailed it. She struggled with the idea of her daughter leaving home forever but decided that she wouldn't stand in her way if Lisette hated her that much. Ultimately Sonia ended up having to pick up the pieces of Lisette's broken heart when her father didn't even bother to answer her letter or any other that she sent. He disappeared from her life just as suddenly as he had appeared. Again mother and daughter struggled to survive under one roof, with a little brother tagging along.

While the drama with her daughter raged on, Sonia suffered another blow to her heart—Tino, the only man she had ever felt truly loved her, was found guilty of drug conspiracy charges and sentenced to life in the federal penitentiary. Sonia cried when she heard the news. She could not control her tears for a long time whenever Tino entered her mind. She was certain that his spirit would be shattered by the sentence. Tino was taken out of Illinois and incarcerated in a federal prison somewhere in Colorado, far away from his family, Sonia, and the Latin Kings in Chicago.

Sonia continued to seek employment and to battle Lisette's romance with the Satan Disciple. She won the battle against unemployment, but her daughter proved to be more of a challenge. A catering company that staffed private cafeterias in downtown Chicago hired Sonia as a cashier. The job paid enough to make ends meet with help from Lisette's SSI, and finally she didn't have to sell crack anymore. She loved her job and picked up responsibilities quickly and with great enthusiasm. Her hard work and dedication earned her a promotion to head cashier in less than a year. Sonia was happier, but still she waited for some big disappointment to throw her off balance as it had every other time things seemed to be going smoothly in her life. She prayed for her destiny to be different this time around; she took nothing for granted.

Just when she was convinced that the bullshit phase of her life was over, Sonia was pushed back into its core. She had finally given up trying to keep Lisette from dating Andre and just accepted that Lisette was going to see him with or without her approval. He was about the same age as Lisette, and his only aspiration in life seemed to revolve around being a gangster. Of course it was hypocritical of Sonia to judge Andre negatively because of his gang affiliation when in many ways she had been instrumental in the recruitment of prospective gangsters, but she felt differently now that it was her own daughter getting involved in the gang scene. She worried that Lisette's life would be wasted. One day Sonia was sitting in her bedroom with a friend and Lisette discussing a rumor going around that a Satan Disciple they all knew had been murdered when Sonia decided to call Andre for confirmation. Andre's mother answered the phone and informed Sonia that Andre wasn't home. When Sonia asked Andre's mother if she could give him a message to call her, Andre's mother surprised the hell out of Sonia.

"Oh, so they finally told you."

"Told me what?"

As soon as Sonia asked that question, Lisette quickly got up and left the room. That's when Sonia realized her worst nightmare had become a reality—at the age of fifteen and a half, Lisette was pregnant with Andre's child. Sonia was devastated by the news. Her relationship with Lisette had gotten a little better since Pedro's carelessness with Lisette's heart, but a lot of tension still separated mother and daughter. Sonia sat Lisette and Andre down and talked to them about giving abortion some serious thought, since neither one of them was in a position to take on the responsibility of raising a child. Andre was a high-school dropout, and Lisette, not the best student, was on her way to becoming a dropout as well. Sonia explained that they would be better off concentrating on school without a child to care for. It would make their life simpler and help them get financially stable before beginning a family. Sonia pleaded with Lisette to give this option some serious thought so that she, too, wouldn't end up a teenage mother barely getting by. She didn't want her daughter's life to turn out like her own had; she wanted a better life for Lisette.

But Sonia's words of advice fell on deaf ears. Lisette and Andre decided to have the baby they could ill afford to support. Their decision made Sonia unhappy, but she remembered how it felt to have no one to turn to for love and encouragement when she was pregnant with Lisette, and she vowed not to let her daughter suffer as she had. Sonia got Andre a job with her and demanded that Lisette continue going to school during her pregnancy and to continue after the baby was born.

Everything seemed to be going well, but then Sonia ran into trouble at her job. As head cashier for the company, Sonia had access to items that only managerial personnel were allowed to handle, including admission tickets to various sports events around the city. Management discovered that someone had been stealing some of these tickets, and the company pointed the finger at Sonia. She denied taking the tickets and adamantly stated that she loved her job too much to do anything that would jeop-

ardize it, but no one listened. She was sent home while the investigation took place. The company's decision angered Sonia. She
knew she was innocent but had no way to prove it. She felt targeted because she was the only person on the management staff
who wasn't white. She wrote letters to the company's top manager proclaiming her innocence but never received a reply to any
of them. She received a response to her letter to the corporate
office, but it only informed Sonia that the matter would be
looked into further. There was no mention of her returning to
work.

Sonia never heard from the company again, and soon she
once again returned to dealing drugs. For a little while she sup-
plemented this with a job at a local food market, but the job
paid so little that she found it a waste of time and eventually
quit. She struggled to make ends meet and began to look to her
family for help.

Lisette had her baby, a boy, and moved to the South Side
to live with Andre and his family. Neither of the teenagers
worked or went to school, and they counted on Lisette's SSI
check, which Sonia also depended on, for items for the baby.
Sonia and Lisette fought over this, which intensified the bad feelings they already had for each other. Lisette had let Sonia down
by getting pregnant with a guy who couldn't support himself,
much less a family. Their arguments caused the emotional distance to grow rapidly and dramatically. In the meantime, Sonia
borrowed money from one family member or another to pay
her utility bills and put food on the table, as her drug business
wasn't as lucrative as it had been in the past. When she wasn't
asking for money to get her lights or gas turned back on, she
pleaded for cash to help pay her rent. Miguel continued to offer

no financial support for Tony, and his grandparents gave only emotional support. The situation was bleak for Sonia and her son, especially when her family began to see her as a hole in their pockets and began to avoid her. With no one else to turn to, Sonia tried to make peace with Lisette and asked if she and Andre would share the apartment with her and Tony so they could help each other out and also help them get away from the turmoil that had begun with Andre's family. Lisette accepted.

When Sonia, Tony, Lisette, Andre, and their child moved in together, it lifted the burden for everyone involved. But each person had a unique personality and a strong will, and this led to conflicts compounded by the fact that no one was employed. Reality meant deciding between eating and paying the bills, and it didn't help that marijuana and cigarettes more often than not took precedence over practical needs. The financial strains couldn't be overcome.

This extended family experiment lasted a mere six months, until Lisette concluded that putting up with Andre's family was less stressful than her mother's bullshit. With Lisette gone, Sonia had no way to maintain the apartment she lived in. She became homeless again. For two months Tony lived with his grandparents while Sonia walked the streets in search of food and shelter. She desperately tried to find a permanent job while working as a temporary laborer during the night. Sonia spent these two months filled with desperation and regret about all the bad choices she had made in her life that had led her to this point. She looked up at the sky and made peace with God. She prayed for help but took few steps to help those prayers get answered. Sonia vowed this would be the last time she would find herself depending on anyone else, and now that included her daughter. Finally she found a job as a cashier at a store, got an apartment, and reclaimed her son.

Sonia remained true to her word and never again let herself be in a position where she was on the verge of falling off the edge of the world. She realized she had never completely eliminated the seed of deception that being a gang member had planted in her mind—the idea that the streets and those who embrace them can be your saviors. But when everything that she loved and valued in her life was stripped away, including her kids and the shelter she needed to survive, she finally starved this seed enough so that it withered and died. She had survived abuse by many, some of which made her strong and some of which nearly destroyed her. She had lost her daughter to the gang life. Sonia needed to shed the ghost of Lady Q and move on to survive. She needed to save herself, and she needed to save her son from the streets.

EPILOGUE

by Sonia Rodriguez

"LISTEN, LISETTE, I know I haven't been the best mother, and I'm so sorry for not thinking about you when I was running around in a gang and exposing you to all that shit. You know how I feel, that my mother doesn't love me, and I don't want you to feel the same. I love you, Lisette, and I'm so sorry for not telling you how much I love you. I know I fucked up with you and I'm so sorry."

This is how I began reestablishing communication with my daughter. I have Reymundo to thank for this. He listened to the story of my life and he saw the parallels between me and my mother and me and Lisette. He heard the truth and he spoke it. He showed me that I was doing the same thing that my mother did to me, and if I didn't get my shit together, and soon, I'd lose my baby girl forever. And I couldn't afford to lose her.

It hasn't been easy. We still fight. But now I have her two children, my first grandbabies, in my life, and I have higher hopes for their futures. I know Lisette tries. I know she struggles to get along with Andre and to survive when she feels the world's weight pressing down on her, but I don't want my grandbabies to feel that way, so I do what I can to help them out and keep the lines of communication open. Even when we fight it's OK, 'cause at least we're talking, even if we're talking *at* each other; I know it'll come around 'cause I make sure it does.

My son Tony is a blessing in my life. His father is a son of a bitch but at least he did one thing right, one beautiful thing right. I got the courts to force Miguel to help pay child support for Tony. And he sees his dad from time to time, but I made sure he sees his money regularly. And his grandparents are still a part of his life. Tony's a bright kid—a straight-A student. Reminds me of me before my life crashed onto the streets and into gangs. I know I have to protect my baby boy from the gangs. I fear the day he comes home and tells me he's made a new friend and it's clear to me by the colors his friend wears that he ain't no friend. To help me keep Tony straight, I got him involved in the Boys and Girls Club. And I make sure that I meet and get to know every kid he calls friend. I may not have done many things in my life right, but I know I'm raising my son right. He's respectful, he has a quick mind, and he's good at handling new situations and keeping things in perspective. I talk to other parents and try and get them to get their kids involved in the Boys and Girls Club, too.

Every year I hold a barbecue where the neighborhood kids come and enjoy themselves. I don't expect anyone to pay for the food. The smiles on the kids' faces make it all worthwhile. I also help out at a local shelter for abused women and children to make a good Christmas meal and try and provide presents, too. I know my kids Tony and Lisette are proud of me when they see me doing for others. This makes it worthwhile, too. These kids need help just as Tony and Lisette need help. They've done without a lot. I have, too.

When I got pregnant the third time and found out that my untreated cervical cancer was now threatening my life and the life of my unborn child, I decided to end this pregnancy and get a hysterectomy. I still think it was the right choice. I don't need to bring any more kids into this world to suffer.

I still don't talk to my mother much; my sister neither. To this day I wonder what my life would be like if my mother told me she loved me, held me, took my side once or twice in an argument. She made me think the whole world's against me so I had to fight for everything. I've learned that's not the way things have to be. I hold out hope that someday we'll be closer, but that day's not here yet.

I want Tino to understand that I will always have him in my heart for he is a good man who deserves a second chance. The last time I talked to Tino was in 1996 after my son was born. He called to check up on me. I told him that now I had a son and I told him I was doing OK. I lied—I wasn't doing OK at that time. He and my daughter still write to each other, and he uses one of the two calls he's permitted each month to speak with her. To this day he believes she is his daughter—no one could tell him differently. While I don't speak to him now, he asks my daughter how I'm doing.

Tino no longer has any contact with anyone on the street, but now it's too late. I wish he would've listened to me earlier— not done any business on the phone, made his generals visit him if they had anything to say to him, but he didn't listen to me. I begged him to give up his crown when he was in prison, so he and I could make a life together when he got out, before the FBI indictments. He refused. I would have loved to make a life for him and me outside the Nation. I still love Tino—I'll always love him. He was real good to my daughter and me—there was nothing we couldn't ask for. I think about going to Colorado to visit him, sitting down and talking to him one last time.

Tino has one final appeal. If they deny his appeal this time, I think he'll just give up. I wish I could see him before this book comes out; maybe he would finally agree to tell his story.

I'm grateful Reymundo Sanchez came around to ask for my story, that somebody cares enough to share it. We still talk from time to time. He cares about all the people of the streets. He'd like to save them all, I know. I know that's why he wanted me to share my story with you. I'm raising a good little man, and I've got a good man looking out for me from far away. It's not much of a safety net but it's a hell of a lot more than I've had sometimes. And I survived those days. So I'll survive these days, too. I need to for my son, my daughter, and my grandbabies.

I didn't tell my story to hurt anyone or put anybody down. I just want people to understand how a person with big dreams can lose everything to the streets without the proper love and support. So don't let a day go by without you telling your kids you love them. If they don't feel your support at home, they'll seek it elsewhere and from people who only *say* they love them.

What people think about me is irrelevant, 'cause if I can save one life by telling my story, nothing else matters.

I've always tried to figure out why our people fight against each other over different colors, 'cause now that I'm older I realize how ignorant I was. I want to apologize to everybody I hurt one way or another when I was out there acting ignorant. If I could go back and change everything, I would.

Gangs look cool from the outside. But the only way to survive in a gang is on the backs of the weak. You're constantly fighting to hold your ground and sometimes that means ripping it out from under another kid, and it doesn't matter if he's in another gang or your own. Believe me, I know. I survived. And I still struggle every day of my life to stay straight. But I'd rather struggle than deal drugs.

I want people to understand that I'm living proof that you can walk away. When I walked away I lived in 'hoods where at one time I couldn't even safely walk. Now I've met a lot of the same individuals who used to chase me. I got to know them and learned that in a lot of ways they are just like me—kids with dreams and no one to support them.

Please understand that a lot of these kids you see on the corner acting hard-core, ones people see as bad kids, they're not bad kids. They're just misguided and misunderstood and they're looking for acceptance and love anywhere and any way they can find it.

I've met a lot of kids, some come from good families, some from no family at all, and they all won my heart in one way or another. The funny thing is they all belonged to different gangs and they all lost their lives to the streets:

Popeye, Latin King
PJ, Spanish Cobras
Rice, Latin King
Indio, Spanish Cobras
Lisa
Nutron

Junebug, Milwaukee King
Crazy, Latin Queen
Gottie, Spanish Cobras
Brenda (Lisa's best friend)
Special remembrance to Louie "LouBone" Hernandez
We can make a change and still survive in the 'hood.

Bear, you are a good man deep down inside and if there is anybody in my life who I wish I could change and save before it is too late, it would be you. Just remember no matter where I go, I will always have you in my mind and heart 'cause I truly love you.

AFTERWORD

by Reymundo Sanchez

MY DISCUSSIONS WITH Sonia in Chicago were emotionally draining and did nothing to prepare me for what was to come. I left Chicago with a good feeling about where her life was headed as she seemed to be taking all the right steps—she was beginning a new job, moving into a better apartment, and talking about separating herself from all forms of negativity, but that proved to be a hard task for her to accomplish. As we continued to work on this project on the phone, she became hard to reach because of her inability to pay her phone bill. Sonia's back-up plan for all her financial problems was to reach out to her family, who had pretty much made themselves unavailable to her for that same reason. It seems to me that although Sonia's days as Lady Q, the Queen of the streets of Chicago, are long behind her, she still lives life as if large amounts of cash will continue to fall into her lap without the necessity of earning it. Although I scolded her on several occasions about her dependency on others, she failed to understand that people, even family, have their own problems and agendas to worry about; they don't want to be dealing with a forty-year-old woman who refuses to get her shit together.

Sonia still has that magnetic personality that drove her popularity among the street soldiers of the Latin Kings and Queens. It has helped her gain opportunities to better herself, but she's squandered them all. Unfortunately, regardless of her perils, Sonia still smokes weed and keeps company with like-minded 'hood rats who do nothing but bring her down. But this is where she feels she belongs.

On more than one occasion during my work with Sonia, I became upset with her over her refusal to understand the damage she was doing to her son. I tried to get through her head that she needed to think about leaving the 'hood and try to give her son, who is an honor roll student, a better life. I reminded her that she herself had been an honor roll student whose mother's carelessness allowed her to get lost. Sonia agreed and promised, and promised and agreed, but did nothing. Chances to become independent came and went one after another, and she continues to live her life in fear of being thrown out onto the streets at any moment because of her inability to pay rent.

This is what has become of the great Lady Q. It is what becomes of most young women who give the best years of their lives to being 'hood rats. In some cases during their youth, family and friends help them get by, but eventually everyone gets tired of the same old shit and they move on, while women like Lady Q stay behind looking for answers in all the wrong places. They consider it the badge of honor to "not forget where I came from," but it's detrimental to their future to stay. As a result, they continue to carry burdens they are ill prepared to handle. For many of these young women, doing drugs and/or having kids feels like the answer for escaping their miseries, which sadly just puts another child in the 'hood to suffer the consequences of their parent or parents' stupidity.

As I concluded this book, Lady Q was worried about being evicted from her apartment and was once again looking to family members to help her out. Lady Q—Sonia—has yet to learn how to survive outside the 'hood. Young women who read this story need to realize that this is where they are headed regardless of how hard their "not me" attitude allows them to deny it. They need to look at all the dropout teenage mothers around them and understand that at one point they also said "not me." Without an education and the desire to stand strong on your own two feet, young women who choose gangs as their means of survival will end up 'hood rats with their dreams unrealized. I pray they learn that "not forgetting where they came from" makes them fight for a better future for themselves and their children since "where they came from" is a much too cold and dangerous place for a child to live.

AUGUST 2007

Also available by Reymundo Sanchez

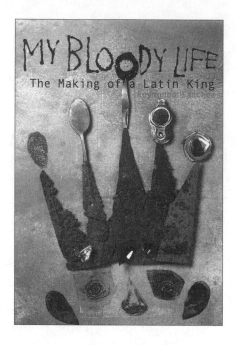

"A slow-motion riot of drugs, sex and gunplay."
—*Publishers Weekly*

"Sanchez writes plainly and powerfully."
—*Booklist*

"A viciously candid, self-deprecating memoir."
—*Chicago* magazine

My Bloody Life
The Making of a Latin King

Looking for an escape from childhood abuse, Reymundo Sanchez turned away from school and baseball to drugs, alcohol, and then sex, and was left to fend for himself before age fourteen. The Latin Kings, one of the largest and most notorious street gangs in America, became his refuge and his world, but its violence cost him friends, freedom, self-respect, and nearly his life.

320 pages, 6 × 9
Paper, $16.95 (CAN $18.95)
978-1-55652-427-1

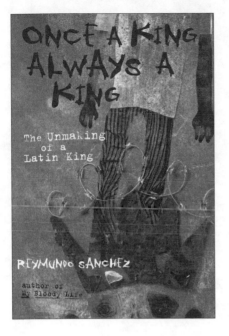

"A sorrowful memoir . . . whose power lies in the naked honesty with which [Sanchez] chronicles his ultimate deliverance from the past."

—Jeff Evans, author,
Undoing Time: American Prisoners in Their Own Words

"Courageously honest."
—*Washington Post Book World*

"Sanchez's story of survival in the face of great odds rings true." —*Publishers Weekly*

Once a King, Always a King
The Unmaking of a Latin King

This riveting sequel to *My Bloody Life* traces Reymundo Sanchez's struggle to create a normal life outside the Latin Kings and to move beyond his past. Sanchez illustrates how the Latin King motto "once a king, always a king" rings true and details the difficulty and danger of leaving that life behind.

304 pages, 6 × 9
Paper, $16.95 (CAN $25.95)
978-1-55652-553-7

CHICAGO REVIEW PRESS

Distributed by
Independent Publishers Group
www.ipgbook.com

www.chicagoreviewpress.com

Available at your favorite bookstore or by calling (800) 888-4741